THE LIFE OF TRAINING

Praise for *The Life of Training*

Boldly and constructively provocative. The broader notion, drawn ultimately from Arendt, of training as a scalpel for the refiguring of Kant's 'undifferentiated manifold' into the 'body temporal', surely offers a range of telling possibilities in calibrating and situating embodied practice in relation to these broader ontological and epistemological concerns.

Colin Ellwood,
Rose Bruford College of Theatre and Performance, UK

A very timely book to re-assert the value of training at a time when training institutions are finding it harder to attract funding at a conservatoire level of training (by Government or students) and persuade students to allocate time to train.

Highly engaging…a great counterpoint to the dominant discourse I encounter in sites of actor training.

Mark Cariston Seton,
University of Sydney, Australia

Matthews' perspective synthesises the pedagogic, existential and methodological questions at the heart of contemporary actor training. Moreover, the form of the text models the case study and practice-as-research method that we champion as best practice.

This book brings together the often neglected ideological, pedagogic and methodological questions at stake in a practice that demands that the student exposes the 'self'.

Jessica Hartley,
The Royal Central School of Speech and Drama, UK

The significance and originality of this research lies in its overturning of the existing narrative of the relationship between performance and training. It provides a rich thesis that shines an entirely new lens on the vital importance and nature of training systems. The book is rich and detailed in its historical reference points from philosophy and theatre history in particular, and deeply knowledgeable about a wide range of training practices. Each chapter offers its own treatise that is clearly presented and articulated, and the conclusion draws together the thesis of the book as a whole to underline its most significant insights to discourses of performance and training, particularly, but not limited to, the field of theatre and performance.

Liz Tomlin, Professor of Theatre and Performance,
University of Glasgow, UK

Praise for *Anatomy of Performance Training*

At a time in actor training institutions when the pressure is on to make vocational training more efficient/economical/expedient, it is refreshing and challenging to encounter a work of deep philosophical reflection and critical examination about what it is we think we are doing to, or for, those who want to become professional actors. This is not yet another book on acting techniques or systems – rather, more importantly, Matthews calls upon teachers and students alike to look 'beneath the skin' as it were and 'make strange' our valuing of, approaches to and experiences of, training. His lyrical meditations on various anatomical 'parts' of the embodied, human experience stretch us to consider afresh what is natural and 'un-natural' such that this polarity is no longer what it seems. One comes away from reading this book with many new insights and questions that hopefully will evoke new conversations for healthily sustainable training practices.

Mark Seton, Honorary Research Associate, Department
of Performance Studies, University of Sydney, Australia

Shamelessly eclectic and enduringly thought provoking, John Matthews' latest intervention into performance training criticism is a highly engaging study. Using an innovative structure of training-as-anatomy – HAND, FOOT, MOUTH, HEART, EAR – Matthews treats us to a delicately layered discussion of the 'nascent ideology of training', navigating confidently between evocative vignettes of training experiences to an applied critique of western philosophical thought. Throughout, it is simply and beautifully illustrated, interwoven with a discussion

*of the craft of woodcutting and printing, prompting us to think produc-
tively about the parallel tracks of competence, expertise and mastery.*

Jonathan Pitches, Professor of Theatre and Performance,
School of Performance and Cultural Industries,
University of Leeds, UK

*John Matthews returns to ground he would never call 'his own', but a
terroir marked 'training' that has provided the fertile soil for his recent
work. On this occasion, in collaboration with woodcut artist Andy Park, an
uncertain kind of 'know how' begins to emerge from meditations that allow
him to make neighbours of Tom Daley and John the Baptist. While eminent
philosophical figureheads such as Peter Sloterdijk are just getting around
to relations between personal training and the self-help generation,* Anatomy of Performance Training *insists such historical processes of preparation
for work are ontological and critical to the evolution of human being.*

Alan Read, Professor of Theatre and Director of
Performance Foundation, King's College London, UK

*A thoughtful, stimulating and wide-ranging text that moves seamlessly
across disparate fields of performance and reflects both on their spe-
cificities and their similarities.*

Franc Chamberlain, Professor of Drama,
Department of Drama, University of Huddersfield, UK

Anatomy of Performance Training *provides the student of performance
with a wonderful opportunity to delve into the profound physical
and philosophical world of the body. Filled with exciting insights and
stimulating provocations and challenges, it deepens their theoretical
understanding as well as their practice.*

Anatomy of Performance Training *proposes original innovative insights
on the link between theory and practice in performance training;
contributes new experiential perspectives to a growing body of writing about practice; provides detailed analysis of the use of the hand,
foot, ear, mouth and heart in performance training; and discusses the
symbolic and practical significance of that body part in training and in
a wider artistic and commercial context.*

Niamh Dowling, Head of School of Performance, Rose Bruford
College of Theatre and Performance, UK

A key contribution of the work is its unwillingness to take the value of training for granted, but instead to take training's claims for value 'seriously', and to look closely at the terms upon which such value is constructed.

Joe Kelleher, Professor of Theatre and Performance,
Roehampton University, London, UK

THE LIFE OF TRAINING

JOHN MATTHEWS

ILLUSTRATIONS BY ANDY PARK

methuen | drama

LONDON • NEW YORK • OXFORD • NEW DELHI • SYDNEY

METHUEN DRAMA
Bloomsbury Publishing Plc
50 Bedford Square, London, WC1B 3DP, UK
1385 Broadway, New York, NY 10018, USA

BLOOMSBURY, METHUEN DRAMA and the Methuen Drama logo are
trademarks of Bloomsbury Publishing Plc

First published in Great Britain 2019
Paperback edition published 2021

A catalogue record for this book is available from the British Library.

A catalog record for this book is available from the Library of Congress.

ISBN: HB: 978-1-3500-4640-5
           PB: 978-1-3502-1252-7
         ePDF: 978-1-3500-4642-9
        eBook: 978-1-3500-4641-2

Typeset by Integra Software Services Pvt. Ltd.

To find out more about our authors and books visit www.bloomsbury.com
and sign up for our newsletters.

For our beloved daughter, Efa

CONTENTS

Acknowledgements xii

Introduction: The seven characteristics of life 1

1 Homeostasis 15

2 Growth 37

3 Stimulation 55

4 Organization 77

5 Adaptation 101

6 Reproduction 121

7 Heritability 143

Notes 163
Bibliography 194
Index 201

ACKNOWLEDGEMENTS

In this, as ever, thank you, Faith, for everything. I love you.

Special thanks also to my mother and father and to Jef and Jan. The help and support that you have given us has made time and space for me to think and to write. Thanks also to Dave and Alexa, Max and Lorna and the cousins and great-grandparents who have enriched our lives with your kindness and good company during the writing of this book.

Thanks to my friends at the Plymouth Conservatoire, Lee, Victor, Ruth, Alex, Josh, Bob, Charlotte and Roberta for all your advice and guidance, and also to Adam, David, Russell, Heather and everyone who gave their time so generously to me while I was working on this book.

Thank you to Andy, for working with me again, and to Lucy, Anna and John at Methuen Drama for your editorial input and guidance.

INTRODUCTION: THE SEVEN CHARACTERISTICS OF LIFE

The Life of Training is my second book in collaboration with the illustrator Andy Park. The eerily human character of the marionette that adorns the cover and that appears in some form in each chapter illustration has emerged from many conversations and exchanges of words and drawings between me and Andy. The most obvious point of reference for this character for any reader coming from 'within the field' will probably be Heinrich von Kleist's famous essay *Über das Marionettentheater* (1810) and his provocative suggestions about performing and human nature. Kleist's essay has become something of an historical nodal point for performance theory and has given itself as the basis of a kind of triumvirate juxtaposition of nature, human beings and human things.

If Andy Park were to illustrate Kleist's essay, he might draw three images from it – the bear, the human and the rapier, perhaps, from the infamous set piece of the essay where a man fences with a brown bear chained up in a wood shed. Each image might stand in for these three related but differentiated categories of *Being*, *beings* and *things*, which are all imbricated in performance and which preoccupy this book.

Or perhaps Andy might draw a broken jug, a bird and a river, each representing in turn Heinrich von Kleist (whose first play was called *Der zerbrochne Krug*, or 'The Broken Jug'), his lover Henriette Vogel (*vogel* being German for bird) and the Little Wannsee lake on the River Havel, next to which the pair fulfilled their murder-suicide pact in 1811. That Heinrich von Kleist should euthanize his terminally ill lover and commit suicide alongside her would seem to be an event prefigured in his letters to perhaps the second most important woman in his life: his sister, Ulrike. In one missive to her twelve years before he would end his own life and the life of his lover, he wrote:

> A traveler who knows his destination and the route to that destination has a travel plan. What a travel plan is for a traveler, a life plan is for the person in general. To undertake a journey without a travel plan would mean to expect Chance to lead us to a goal we ourselves would not foreknow. To live without a life plan would mean leaving to chance whether we should arrive at a happiness, of which we ourselves have no prior conception. It is really incomprehensible to me how a person can live without a life plan, and in the secure way I make use of the present I feel with such inwardness the calm with which I look to the future, the priceless happiness that my life plan affords me; while the condition of being without a life plan, without a firm vocation, forever hesitant between uncertain desire, even in contradiction to my sense of duty, a play thing of chance, a puppet on the string of fate – such an ignoble condition would seem to me contemptible, would render me so unhappy that I would by far prefer death.[1]

Perhaps seeing this letter as somehow foreshadowing Kleist's death is an unhistorical invention of Kleist, overwriting the details of his life with significance that was never actually present therein. This would certainly be in keeping with the posthumous narrative of Kleist: a mostly unnoticed literary figure in life who achieved fame and celebration posthumously. This is a fact rather grotesquely inscribed by the Nazis who renovated his waterside grave in preparation for the 1936 Olympic Games, adorning his new and grand headstone mistakenly with a quote from the Jewish poet Max Ring: 'He lived, sang and suffered / in gloomy and difficult times / he sought death here / and found immortality.'[2] Perhaps Andy could, in art more gracefully than I could in words, connect the little jug, the bird and the flowing river without ever suggesting, as Kleist does in his letter, the string of fate.

I came across Kleist's 1799 letter to Ulrike late in the process of drafting this book and was taken aback by how many themes from within the book were seemingly portended by his writing: the life plan (*Lebensplan* in German), chance, the future, vocation, happiness, unhappiness and death. Each of these seven themes is relevant to the enterprise of training as it is explored in the seven chapters that follow this Introduction, and each chapter unfolds under one of Andy's illustrations of the character of the marionette.

In Andy's artworks this character unifies the three categories of Being, beings and things. The wood of which this puppet is made is inseparable from the Being which produced the tree out of which it was excised, just as the strings connect this Being to the human hands of the beings that animate it. In triangular exchange with these two interdependent ontic states is the almost counter-ontological status of the thing itself – the object, the puppet – which, in Kleist's essay, may dance and trill with such beauty in a 'completely mechanized' way, such that the 'last vestige of the human spirit' of the puppeteer is 'eliminated' from it. Whether as wood, as object or as amanuensistic extension of human performer, Andy's marionette accompanies each endeavour in this book to consider the ontological status of training.

Accounting for the ontological status of training entails considering this alongside the ontic nature of humans and of the things that they make, including the ephemeral ones that they call performances. Setting these concerns to the parameters of ephemeral events is less to do with the opening and closing of theatre curtains and more to do with the birthing and dying of human beings, and the temporal torsion in human Being achieved between creation and extinction. Training most certainly corresponds to the life plan that Kleist wrote about in his letters to his sister, as well as to the activity of thought that he practised and which he has posthumously inspired in Theatre and Performance Studies. Indeed, Kleist's triangulation of nature, man and objects, and especially the opposition he establishes between human and non-human actors, has given much impetus to the subfield of training.

This book follows the approach of my previous book, also illustrated by Andy Park, *Anatomy of Performance Training* (2014), and sits outside the more familiar methodological templates of this subfield of actor and performer training research. These two books, *Anatomy of Performance Training* and *The Life of Training*, bookend a six-year period of research

(2012–2018) that has coincided with a shift in emphasis in my own professional practice. The coincidence between this phase of my ongoing research into training and my increasing institutional responsibility for the training of others has stimulated, for me, many useful thoughts about training.

In 2013 I began work on a new honours degree programme, which would be for the training of actors. Uniquely, the degree would be co-delivered by the University of Plymouth and Theatre Royal Plymouth, and it would drive the development of a new drama school, The Plymouth Conservatoire, which was formally established in 2017. In 2015, we recruited our first intake of fifteen talented individuals to the Acting programme, and in 2018 this first cohort of actors graduated from our new Acting degree. The publication of these two books encloses a period of writing, planning and delivering this new degree programme through its first 'cycle', and they represent my intensified interest in the experience of *other people* in training and specifically other people whose training I am responsible for.

A primary research methodology of my first book, written while I was teaching at the already well-established drama school, Rose Bruford (the first institution to offer an Acting degree in the UK), was participant-observation; I was, at this stage, very self-consciously a trainee myself and keenly seeking new participatory experiences in diverse training practices motivated by my research imperatives and also a personally felt vocation towards performing and getting better at doing it. Although I have participated in the varied training practices described and discussed in this book, I have long since been cautioned by Alan Read's argument about the 'specious presenteeism' of accounts of practice that tacitly assert that 'being there', and being there 'for longer', is 'inherently "better"'.[3] Accordingly, I don't undertake to describe at any length my participation in training but scepticism of that 'worthy rhetorical tactic',[4] as Read has it, is less the issue: my research and writing has never been about *this* training or *that* training but is about training itself, which, as I argued in *Training for Performance* (2011), should be understood as its own philosophical category. The broad field of Theatre and Performance Studies ruminates on performances of all genres and styles as well as on performance itself, and the subfield of actor and performer training, especially since the launch of the *Theatre, Dance and Performance Training* journal, has been able to do the same.

Unlike several successful books in the field making use of the well-established research templates of historiography and epistemology, my research for *Anatomy of Performance Training* and *The Life of Training* is not, methodologically speaking, historical or epistemological. This is because my object of study – training – although emergent within time and comprehensible as and in episteme, is not reducible to a product of them; in fact, my contention in this book is rather the opposite. My research, and specifically this book, might be described as 'training theory' in the sense that this may be equivalent to what we commonly call 'performance theory'. However, my key point of reference here is Arendt's meta-theoretical approach to her own discipline, of philosophy, in *The Life of the Mind* (1978) and her classical systematic-philosophical methodology of reasoning.

Against the established research-norm of scientific evidence or proof, 'reason' may sound rather inconclusive. Reason, of course, works with evidence and proof but, in the philosophical sense, should also stand without these. In other words, the products of reason operate beyond the purely phenomenological realm and are not reducible to the evidence that our senses can provide. Arendt's focus on reason over truth represents a strand of process-based, as opposed to substance-based, philosophizing about human Being running through Western philosophical traditions, the latter being interested in what things are and the former showing concern for how things become what they are. In her meta-theoretical analysis of the history of Western thought, Hannah Arendt made the compelling case that proof, as an outcome of thinking, is germane only to a particular late nineteenth- and early twentieth-century subset of the enterprise of thought which postulates Being in terms of substance. I take up this analysis in ORGANIZATION and apply it to the field of training also.

Reason is at once Arendt's subject and her method; in writing on the subjects of 'time' and 'thinking', Arendt is intrinsically imbricated in her own materials and in a rather more self-conscious and necessary way than the general co-mingling of researchers in their own research materials. Arendt coordinates multiple historical accounts of thinking and enmeshes these within her own thought-process, isolating examples and illustrations that push out into the small 'track of non-time'[5] in which, as she has it, works are formed. In this work I am inspired by Arendt's observation that 'the need of reason is not inspired by the quest for truth but by the quest for meaning'.[6] The 'basic fallacy', she writes, 'taking precedence over all specific metaphysical fallacies, is to interpret meaning on the model of truth'.[7] I follow Arendt, again, in this book and look not to uncover the truth about training but to reason its meaning. For Arendt, thinking is moved by the quest for meaning, and reason is the rigour that thinking applies in order to pursue this quest. For me, the training done by individuals is also moved by this same quest for meaning and it too exhibits a rigour – rigour that moves out from our thinking processes and into the world of things, and back again. Training is, I argue, reason embodied and practised in the world.

Where I have departed from the participant-observation of my first book, these second two books have also kept distance from the historical and epistemological research templates of the subfield. As my professional role has shifted in emphasis from trainee to trainer, my research has taken a more overtly systematic-philosophical approach to training and also a more restricted anthropological-methodological approach. As I have become more ensconced in the institutional role of 'trainer', I have moved away from participant-observation in my training research and towards the ethnographic approaches of 'key informant interviewing', 'judgement sampling' and analysis of what might be called field notes. This move has been necessitated by the increasingly process-based ontological theorizing and questioning of my research and also by moral anxiety about what participant-observation-based theorizing might cause in terms of self-legitimating and self-substantiating reason.

The selection of key informants was guided by simple curiosity; an interest, formed back to 2012, to ask: who else designs and delivers programmes of training, and how do they do it? As I was preparing our new degree programme I was, from my time spent teaching at drama schools, already cognizant of the techniques and approaches to training actors common in the sector. I was also excited by the prospect that there were other approaches to training individuals, which I had glimpsed through the research for my first book, which might both offer alternative models of practice and, more importantly in the context of my research, reveal more about training itself – that is, reveal more about the philosophical category and ontic qualities of a thing called training.

Of course, being appointed responsible for someone else's training does not impute expertise but only responsibility. With a strong sense of this responsibility, I began, in 2012, a series of unstructured interviews with Theatre Royal Plymouth artistic staff and freelance creative theatre professionals, with the rather simplistic ambition of understanding how actor training married up to theatre practice in the twenty-first century. My research here was driven by the possibility of connecting the philosophical category of training, which I had been working on developing since the publication of my first book, in 2011, with what had been said and thought about the ontological nature of performance within the field of Performance Studies – the possibility of siting this theorization in the decidedly ontic conditions in which performance becomes itself. These interviews made forcibly clear to me a dissatisfaction with perceived mismatches between twentieth-century approaches to actor training and twenty-first-century theatre practice, and also a sense of frustration at what one interviewee called the 'stalled enterprise of actor training'. A unifying theme across these interviews was the belief that training is being done better in other fields; that institutions of sport in particular, but also music, medicine and aviation, among others, are training practitioners of these different crafts better than actor-training institutions.

The extent to which this is actually true seemed less significant than the fact that this belief was abiding, especially in light of the findings about a meta-disciplinary category of training in my first book. Accordingly, I widened out the scope of my interviews so as to address more fulsomely the ontic relation between training and performance. I started by considering what seemingly demonstrably effective training practices were available to me to research in the UK, and more specifically in the South West, in the expectation that I might at least discover the source of professional theatre's envious frustration. This led me to the Olympic dive team, some members of which trained in Plymouth and who had achieved global success in the games the previous year. From this first ethnographic site, I followed a very simple judgement sampling method whereby I took recommendations from an expert in each field, using the judgement of these trainers and trainees to determine the new sites of research. Accordingly, each training context analysed in the three years leading up to the publication of *Anatomy of Performance Training,* and on through the next four years to the publication of this book, has been derived from my interviews with key informants; I asked each key informant to recommend another key informant. Sometimes informants recommended their colleagues or collaborators and sometimes they directed me in much more tangential or esoteric directions informed by the research each had done in the development of her or his own training practice. This anthropological journey, which began with Olympic diving, led to new informants in the closely related swimming team, which, by 2014, in turn had led to cycling teams who had adopted various training approaches from the pool. Next, it led to informants who were dance and somatics practitioners and yoga teachers working with these athletes and therapeutic and creative professionals who were working with injured athletes and sportspeople, and also those with disabilities. Soon I could not establish from nearly a decade's worth of my field notes which discipline had led me to which, nor could I cogently establish any definitive order to the judgement sampling as the names of key informants popped up across multiple disciplines, recommended by several of the experts to whom I spoke. While some scholars, most notably Ben Spatz in his excellent book *What a Body Can Do,* have been motivated by the self-evident hybridity and bastardization of training practices to produce meticulous historical analysis and epistemological theorization, the questions prompted for me were not about where such-and-such a practice originated or how it was cross-fertilized or appropriated but more about what these intermarriages and widening gene pools, to use a social and a biological metaphor, might indicate about the category of training itself.

Never quite moving in one clear linear direction, my samples were idiosyncratic and often overlapping and intermingled, as with the case of Ben Dunks, whom I first met in the course of my research for *Anatomy of Performance Training*. Ben Dunks is a dancer and choreographer who was employed to assist Tom Daley in this 2012 medal preparations. Dunks also trained and worked with key informants I encountered while researching this book, such as Adam Benjamin, an integrated dance choreographer, and Ruth Way, the dance film-maker and somatics practitioner and now Co-Director of the Plymouth Conservatoire. Further overlaps came when I encountered Bob Whalley, an acupuncturist offering acupressure to combat stage fright, who was also the partner of key informant Lee Miller, himself also now a colleague at the Conservatoire. Lee is a yoga teacher practising advanced level yoga teacher training with Jim Harrington, a former yoga coach to the Indian national cricket team. Lee, with Jim, studied the practice of yoga with elite-level athletes and sportspeople, seeking to marry yoga's ideology of balance with the acquired disequilibrium of elite athletes, who obtain disproportionate bodies perfectly attuned to the specificity of their sport. Yet more overlapping occurred as my research for this book built on the field sampling research of the previous book and I met elite swimmer Russell Page-Dove, a compatriot of another key informant, Olympic silver medallist and pentathlete Heather Fell, who had, like Daley, come out of South-West-based UK sport-funded training programmes. Yet more connections came with Alex Cahill, a US competitive distance swimmer and actor-trainer specializing, like Bob Whalley, in well-being in performance practice and, like my key informant and collaborator on a number of research papers, Victor Ramierz lardon de Guevara, is also recommending a newly attuned ethics to actor training. Yet more with David Prescott, associate artist at Theatre Royal Plymouth spearheading the theatre's writer development programme, who grounded my training research both in the practicalities of training actors for employment in theatre today and in the social and cultural discourses of training across the numerous international context in which he operates.

In the first phase of my ethnographic research, from late 2011 to 2014, when I was analysing data for *Anatomy of Performance Training,* I was aware of how different training approaches might inform the design of the new Acting programme that ultimately was validated in the same year my book was published. In so many ways, the research for that book and the designing of the degree were coeval, and even this seemed to support the key findings of the book: this book, like *Anatomy of Performance Training*, uses ethnographic judgement-sampled accounts of training as the basis of methodic doubt about the philosophical category of training that I had established in *Training for Performance*. Sampling from the meta-discipline enabled, in *Anatomy of Performance Training*, a methodological scepticism about training as a philosophical category, which in turn enabled the forming of an argument about the interdependency of this category with what Hannah Arendt called the 'human condition'. In classic systematic-philosophical style, this gave rise to my dialectical proposition that 'we train because we're human and we become human because we train'.

My first book was motivated by the intuition that, wherever it was encountered across multiple disciplines and domains, 'training' was to a profound extent the same thing consistent of the same processes. The research findings that substantiated this intuition stimulated the further eclectic research journey I took through the various case studies of my second. The more interconnections and cross-currents I found between training practices in art, sport and medicine since this time, the more I have become aware that, especially in light of my new responsibility for the training of others, these various practices need to be subjected to the same systematic philosophy that had marked a key methodology of *Anatomy of Performance Training*. If training is, as I argued in 2014, indivisible from the human condition, and especially if it is co-constitutive of it, then training must bear a relation to the ontological status not only of performance but also of humans.

The research for *The Life of Training* has built on the field sampling up to 2014 with a further four years of key commentator judgement-sampling-led research into various and entangled training disciplines and practices located in the broad and often overlapping fields of art, sport and medicine. Where the human body provided a methodological device for the systematic philosophizing about the relationship between training and human beings in *Anatomy of Performance Training*, the seven characteristics of biological life – homeostasis, growth, stimulation, organization, adaptation, reproduction, heritability – provide the methodological framework for this book's philosophizing about the relevance of training not only to human beings but to the ontological concerns and qualities of Being.

With the lightness of touch that visual artists can achieve, Andy's marionette drawings, which accompany each chapter meditation, also emblematize its concerns. In the first chapter, the marionette sits, in Rodin-like contemplation, on a stool as wooden as its sitter. Three strings droop in seeming inactivity while two taught strings raise up the head and right hand in the deportment of thought. This illustration is an evocation of thinking and a touchstone to everything that Hannah Arendt writes on this topic, as well as an invitation to think differently throughout the chapter, and the book, about the relationship between training and thinking. The stillness of the figure in thought and the enduringness of whatever it may be thinking as it sits motionless are underscored by the intransigence of the natural materials from which it is made and counterpointed by the disposability of human products, such as puppets.

In Andy's second illustration, the marionette is cast in a distinctly theatrical light and the dynamic of growth is palled in the foot-light shadow of theatrical representations. In Andy's illustration for STIMULATION, the theatrical interplay between puppet-object and human-subject becomes richer still: a string is cut and falling, sending the puppet's limb falling too – seemingly an indicator of the unpredictability of the natural world, of contingency, change, disorder and accident, until one notices that the puppet is watching the limb fall. Either complicit in this apparent error or sufficiently self-aware to see it for what it is, the puppet reacts. Or perhaps the master reacts, or perhaps these two options are one and the same.

In the fourth illustration, the marionette is unworkably tangled but looks pleadingly, or perhaps in accusation, at the master who is implied above and just off the top edge of the page. As an image of organization, this illustration is at once exemplary and antithetical. The playfulness with which Andy has represented the various themes and images from within my manuscript is delightfully evident in his fifth image, in which the marionette imitates a famous and ancient strength-training exercise that I describe in ADAPTATION. Lifting a growing animal above one's head would be much harder, one would imagine, if that animal was not also suspended by strings.

By Andy's penultimate illustration, the marionette has already acquired some sense of character. The 'scene-setting' of the previous illustrations has accumulated for it a sense of identity which is juxtaposed in this image by the appearance of another identical marionette. It is, after all, just an object, albeit one made from natural things and handled by humans. This juxtaposition provides a comment upon the contradictions between the social reproduction of knowledge by training and training's facility to play a role in the reproduction of human life. Or perhaps this is not another marionette. Perhaps this is a double exposure or a kind of time-lapse illustration in which repetition has taken on a particularly visible form.

The seventh and final illustration is a salutatory and very theatrical leave-taking, a nod (or a bow) to the rituals of theatre events and a perspective on the relative insignificance of these codifications in the life of this figure. Through this book Andy's marionette is an illustration and an evocation of the preoccupations of homeostasis, growth, stimulation, organization, adaptation, reproduction, heritability, and each of the seven chapters that follow this Introduction provides a particular perspective on the temporal dynamics of Life, and of lives, and their formation and patternation by the processes of training. The first chapter, HOMEOSTASIS, and the last, HERITABILITY, also serve as a form of introduction and conclusion, the former being concerned to describe something ontological about training and the latter to consider training's ontic status in light of the findings of the chapters preceding it. HOMEOSTASIS forecasts the ways in which this book will utilize the biological framework of the seven characteristics of life to address different dimensions of training, and HERITABILITY meditates on how, having done so, it may be necessary to reconsider the place of training within the field of Theatre and Performance Studies.

As a figure connecting natural materials with human hands, and iconographically achieving near-perfect anthropomorphic transformation, the marionette also stands for the opposite of human. If training is, as I argued in *Anatomy of Performance Training*, indivisible from the human condition, and if the human condition is, as Arendt argued, an ontic proposition, then this book requires an analytical framework that can contain the scope of that proposition. Where Andy Park's woodcuts staked out the different vantage points of the chapters of *Anatomy of Performance*, his wood creature marks out the seven perspectives on training and time in *The Life of Training*. Part-nature, part-human and part-object, Andy's marionette dances and trills across this book and offers up a model, as did Kleist, for meditating on training and its role in attenuating the strings of fate.

1
HOMEOSTASIS

Training and thinking are opposites. This received wisdom is a ubiquitous and implicit social message that manifests in the various oppositional activities and attitudes relating to 'doing' and 'understanding doing'. 'That's fine in theory but it doesn't work in practice' is a statement that is heard in theatre rehearsal rooms, blue-chip boardrooms, science labs, building sites and each and every context in which human endeavour requires individuals to act. Training has historically been associated with technical acts of doing-of-things and has therefore been perceived in opposition to acts of cognitive perception and understanding of things-done and things-to-do. In the specific case of acting, which is the primary interest of this book, this differentiation is borne out in the oft-cited criticism by tutors that trainees are too much 'in their head' and not sufficiently 'embodied', 'present' or 'in-the-moment'. Examples of this attitude in practice and writing are manifold, and one recent example taken from the British actor-trainer John Gillett may serve as archetypal here. Gillett differentiates between feeling and intellect; willing and deducing; voice-and-body and 'cerebral' activity when he writes, 'if I do it all [playing an objective] cerebrally' and '"my objective" just sticks in my head like a piece of calculus', and 'if I try to implement … [my objective] in a self-conscious and over-controlled manner, thinking the words I have used to define it all the time I am trying to play it', 'it will of course be as useless as a disconnected plug'.[1] Taking some neurological licence, he even places a division between 'left brain logical analysis' and 'right brain-controlled imagination and intuition'[2] in his distinction between analysing and playing an action.

The problem of thinking is well played out throughout the canonical Stanislavskian writings, and indeed the differentiation between thinking and doing is frequently depicted as a central part of the actor's dilemma.

In *An Actor Prepares*, Stanislavski writes that it seems 'not only difficult but impossible to be thinking at one and the same time about your role, technical methods, the audience, the words of your part, your cues and several points of attention as well'[3] while also acting, and yet 'any simple juggler in a circus would have no hesitation in handling far more complicated things, risking his life as he does it'.[4] Indeed, the stultifying effect in action of the overburdening of the naïf Kostya's head with thoughts about units and objectives is a recurrent discursive strategy throughout this work. The more he thinks the less he acts, and the book expounds both explicitly and implicitly that thought and deed are related but differentiated things. The whole project of training, not only in acting but in each and every context of human action, has often been seen as centrally concerned with overcoming, bypassing or submerging conscious thought beneath an embedded, ritualized, instinctive and yet acquired unconscious 'doing' and crucially side-stepping the self-awareness of thinking.[5]

The commonly accepted differentiation between training as a process of acquiring the skills to do and learning as the acquisition of the skill of thinking about doing maps onto a socially and culturally much broader and older distinction. There are several genealogies of this broad sociocultural tendency in Western philosophy[6] but most relate back to Aristotle's differentiation between five virtues or attributes by which the soul arrives at the truth: *technê*, *epistêmê*, *phronêsis*, *sophia* and *nous*.[7] While *technê*, understood as 'practice', and *epistêmê*, conceived of as 'knowledge', have been both contrasted and conflated in subsequent theorizations,[8] it is Aristotle's primary distinction between the human capacity for a form of pragmatic reasoning about 'real-world' existence (*logistikon*) and for a species of knowing of transcendent facts about existence (*epistêmonikon*) that gave rise to this division in the history of Western thought.[9]

The opposition between training as a vocational preparation for technical tasks and education as an intellectual development of the capacity to establish a priori conditions by which the prima facie of technical operation come into being goes back at least to Aristotle.[10] His claim that 'men of experience know that a thing is, but they do not know why it is, whereas men of learning know the reason and the cause'[11] has since been used by both camps in this equation to signal the limitation of the other. In the realm of philosophy, theory, in its association with an objective view (from *theōros*, 'to spectate'), has asserted ascendency over practice (from *praktos*, meaning 'done, to be done'; verbal adjective of *prassein*, *prattein*: 'to do, act, effect, accomplish') since Aristotle's time, and this hierarchy has been renewed in the age of science just as the folk authority of practical expertise has been called upon to rectify those discrepancies uncovered in human endeavour between ideas that are fine in theory but unworkable in practice.[12]

Immanuel Kant drew this division into sharper focus as thinking was further refined and distilled into the process of judgement. With remorseless pessimism, Kant claimed that while the spectacle of humankind's actions 'may be moving for a while',

> the curtain must eventually descend. For in the long run it becomes a farce. And even if the actors do not tire of it – for they are fools – the spectator does because any single act will be enough for him if he can reasonably conclude from it that the never-ending play will be of eternal sameness.[13]

Kant appears to elevate the theatre critic's complaint that 'I've seen it all before' to new and more desperate heights. His rather uncharitable metaphor cleaves the wisdom of spectators (thinking) from the ignorance of actors (doing) with reference to an ancient parable ascribed to Pythagoras: 'Life … is like a festival. Just as some come to the festival to compete, some to ply their trade', but 'the best people come as spectators [*theatai*] so in life the slavish men go hunting for fame [*doxa*] or gain, the philosophers for truth'.[14] Although Pythagoras's substantive point would seem to be that only the spectator may see the 'whole' while the actor by virtue of enacting his 'part' may only understand partially, he also makes a very recognizable and seemingly contemporary complaint about actors hungry for, or psychologically dependent upon, the affirmation of an audience: *doxa* means both 'fame' and 'opinion' and in this parable the actor relies upon the spectator's 'it-seems-to-me' for her own sense of 'me' – the spectator's *dokei moi* for her *doxa*. Thus, the actor is not her own master; she is dependent upon the opinion of others and although Pythagoras is only using theatre as a metaphor we can see in the eternal wisdom that 'the audience is always right' about the quality of any given performance, a deeper reaffirmation of the superiority of thinking over doing here.

The division between thinking and doing, and the project of its dissolution, was a primary preoccupation of Performance Studies in the 1970s and 1980s. Here, body–mind dualism discourse stood as a proxy for a theatrical mise en scène at large where the apartheid of actors and audience – seers and doers, those with minds and those with bodies – which, seemingly was emblematic of division tout court, had become as distasteful in practice as it was in theory.[15] With seemingly scant regard for Pythagoras, Kant, Aristotle or even Stanislavski, Performance Studies adopted its own esoteric project of self-denial as if with great optimism it could be believed that wishes would become facts merely by stating them out loud.

Either in the form of Schechner's 1970s optimism and its much-desired 'end to dichotomies'[16] or Immanuel Kant's pessimistic eighteenth-century reassertion of Pythagoras's parable of dichotomous stage-relations, we may see, historically, thinking in association with reasoned inaction and training in association with thoughtless (or even foolish) action. Yet despite the seemingly eternal antagonism between the categories of thinking and training they have one thing in common. They both take time.

Thinking as a process related to but different from judgement (the forming of a thought) requires prior knowledge and an apprehension of future possibilities as well as a relationship to the reality of the present. Thinking as a practice is also refined over time as thinkers get more reliable, more accurate, more economical and less often wrong by the practising of thinking. Training as a process related to but different from acting (the manifesting of capacity) requires prior experience and cognizance of future outcomes as well as a relationship to the urgency of the present. Training as a practice is also refined over time as trainees get more adept, more effective, less wasteful and less often unsuccessful in the practising of doing. This would be a rather facile insight if all it is stating is that thinking and training, like all aspects of human experience, occur in a temporal context. The point is not that thinking and training happen in time but that the practising of thinking and training each give rise to the human experience of time, thereby placing our present endeavours in a relationship with our past and future thoughts and deeds.

In the history of philosophy, the differentiation between thought and action has been recapitulated by Hannah Arendt's use of the categories of the *vita contemplativa* – the contemplative life – and the *vita activa* – active life. While the differences between the two are stark, both lives are however just that: lives. They are vital and in the same way therefore inherent to human life itself. In Hannah Arendt's final work, the posthumously published *The Life of the Mind* (1978), she puts forth a compelling case that thinking is a process whereby we project ourselves, as humans, into existence. We establish continuity and contingency in our actions and relate ourselves to existential facts and phenomenological experiences. For Arendt, the life-giving essence of thought comes from the ubiquitous human capacity to conceive of actions in sequence and thereby to be purposeful, consistent, contiguous and thus 'whole'. In this book, my concern is with the purposeful, consistent, contiguous actions produced in relation to thought, or thoughtfulness, the means by which they come into existence and the consequences of them so doing.

The 'continuity of our business'[17] is evidently a matter not only of conceiving action but also of performing it. Acting, both in the limited sense of performing onstage and in the broader sense of human agency, is a matter of preparation in the present in relation to the past and for the future. The shaping of the 'everlasting stream',[18] as Arendt called it, into a more or less coherent experience of time is an activity well rehearsed throughout human history and performed everywhere in which humans undertake to act. The rigour of thought in its subjection to reason or, more accurately, to the 'imperative' – the law which commands that there should be reason – is manifest practically in the technical rigour of actions undertaken to achieve ends.

The imperative is usually described as the ontological force that commands human minds to thought and to action. In other words, it is the answer to the questions, 'How do we, as humans, know a fact?' and 'How do we know the right thing to do?' Levinas's translator, Alphonso Lingis, explains that the imperative 'is not a concept … is not a principle, or a law or an order' but rather it is a 'given, a fact' it is 'the first fact'.[19] The imperative 'is a command that there be principles and that our thought represent order – or that we represent the unprincipled and the chaotic correctly'[20] and it is met with at once in our encounter with the world and its things.

We may choose to see the imperative as a fact derived from itself or, put more simply, as the only explanation for the coherence and integrity of some thoughts and actions and for the efficacy of these thoughts and actions. However, positing the imperative does not mean accepting that human thoughts and deeds are transcendentally perfect only that they can be seen to conform and contraire with an ideal set of thoughts and actions which can be derived from whatever logical, moral, ethical or instrumental ends one may choose to posit. It has been my assertion hitherto that the refining of the capacity to act-to-achieve-ends, the remediation of deficient-acts-to-achieve-ends and the social reproduction of knowledge about acts-in-relation-to-ends are the concerns of training.[21] The political philosophy of Hannah Arendt has asserted something very similar about thinking and by aligning my assertions with hers I should like to contend for training, as she does for thinking, that training is a means by which humans generate and experience time.

In the post–Second World War context in which Arendt derived her theories, thinking was averred as a means for human civilization to be better or at least to avoid being worse. In the pre-apocalyptic context of twenty-first-century theorization, which Alan Read (inspired by the drive to extinction implied in Arendt's concept of the 'banality of evil') has called 'the last human venue',[22] training has arisen globally as a means for humankind to both postpone and prepare for its annihilation. In the lives of individuals and communities, training can provide an albeit transient sense of agency in the face of the indifferent and irresistible drift of time. The systematic and more or less sustainable increase in the human capacity to act in any given context and the transfer of that capacity down through the generations provide a pull against the increasingly new challenges of action in changing contexts, and thereby a means for human beings to insert themselves into the flow of sheer change, as Arendt calls it, and experience an albeit partial impermanent and perhaps illusory sense of mastery over it. Training, much like thinking, couples a preparedness for the future with an acceptance of the future's uncertainty and provides both a rehearsal and a requiem for tomorrow.

In the seemingly increasingly totalitarian global environment in which this book is being written, where political attitudes and their affiliates are seemingly hardening against each other, Hannah Arendt's philosophical predictions about the dangers of thoughtless action are beginning to seem all the more prescient. The new online spaces for thinking collectively derived in the late twentieth century are now showing a troubling tendency towards thoughtlessness. Arendt would, I think, have been positive about the emergence of social media and its potential for political (of the *polis*) action but I feel sure that she would have been concerned by its lack of rigour and its apparent openness to banality and to exploitation for personal gain.

Indeed, Arendt was highly critical of individualistic or unworldly modes of thought both in the form of 'pure thought' practised by philosophers and as the 'thoughtlessness' of totalitarians. For Arendt, thinking is a social or rather political activity and one that can only truly be said to occur when it takes place between individuals and is mediated by them in relation to immanent standards of goodness (even if these standards are tested and reconfigured in the process of thinking). Thinking in abstraction, in Arendt's redress of her former lover, the philosopher Martin Heidegger, withdraws from the world as does a fox to its lair,[23] while acting without thinking, which she attributes to Eichmann as a prototypical Nazi war criminal, is the banal root of evil. Thinking, willing and judging were all interconnected for Arendt, and freedom and agency are derived from the combination of these three in relation to the plurality of the world. Thinking, for Arendt, is integral to human Being, and human beings, but also, although she didn't put it in these terms, essential to *human-becoming* or *human-becoming-better*.

The Life of the Mind is a key reference point for this book and the title of my book recognizes my indebtedness to Arendt's writings. In her book Arendt asks,

> Could the activity of thinking as such, the habit of examining whatever happens to come to pass or to attract attention, regardless of results and specific content, be among the conditions that make men abstain from evil-doing or even actually 'condition' them against it?[24]

In posing this question, which tantalizingly goes without complete answer – Arendt died of a heart attack in 1975, following the Gifford Lecture series in the previous year from which her book *The Life of the Mind* was derived – Arendt is clear that thinking is 'not the prerogative of the few', the Heideggers of the world, but an ever-present faculty of everybody, and yet a complete 'absence of thinking' such as Eichmann displayed 'is so ordinary an experience in our everyday life, where we have hardly the time, let alone the inclination, to stop and think'.[25] In the contemporary context of the assertiveness of political ideologies of hostility, the function of human beings and human Being to become better through a collective and mutually respectful thinking is both attractive (to me, at least) and regrettably seemingly impotent.

Referring back to the time-honoured distinction between thinking and doing, in the realm of 'post truth' politics words and deeds appear to have fully parted company. To use an aphorism that probably owes some of its power to the legacy of this perceived division, it is unclear whether or not 'actions speak louder than words' and even less clear whether either can be corrective to the other anymore in the loci of political ideologies. For Arendt, thinking could be understood as the opposite of ideology: where ideology is predicated upon certainty, thinking is founded upon uncertainty; where ideology commands assent, thinking requires dissent; and where ideology determines actions in relation to predicated boundaries, thinking asserts agency and the transgression of illusory horizons.

Perhaps a part of the problem – part of the reason why Arendt's conception of thinking as humanizing appears to have lost ground – is that it is difficult to ground the kind of worldly thinking Arendt desires within the world. Indeed, a prerequisite for this thinking, for Arendt, is face-to-face togetherness and logistically this has its limitations, especially in a globalizing context. However, in this globalizing[26] context, training, as a rigorous, collective practice of thoughtful action towards open-ended goals,[27] might constitute a mode of the kind of thinking that Arendt heralded. It may in point of fact be indivisible from thinking or perhaps it is the material way this thinking is done. The argument I put forward is not the political assertion of later twentieth-century Performance Studies – the rallying cry that 'thinking' and 'doing', theory and practice, are equally rigorous and valid things. Nor do I assert that thinking and doing are the same thing, which has been the tacit message of 'mind–body' discourse in the subfield of training.[28] Thinking and doing are different phenomena; as Descartes puts it in his (unjustly maligned) writings on mind and body, thinking and doing are extensions of different substances.[29] 'Thinking substance' and 'extended substance', as Descartes has it, are quite evidently experienced as different things in each of our daily lives quite apart from the fact that they can be philosophically conceived from different concepts.[30] Following Arendt's theorization, 'doing' can be seen as the means by which 'thinking' shifts from the realm of individual contemplation and into a worldly context of plurality and consequence, for which, subsequently, thinking (and doing) must take account.

I feel that Arendt herself may have supported this assertion because in *The Life of the Mind* she writes, quoting Plato's *Meno* dialogue, that thinking would never 'be able to produce the good deed as its result as though "virtue could be taught" and learned – only habits and customs can be taught'.[31] She points out that our modern conception of morals and ethics is derived from the Latin and ancient Greek concepts of *mores* and *ethos*, customs and habits, and that, rather than pertaining to an abstract realm of categories, they relate to the very worldly domain of conduct.

With regard to the question of moral conduct and our human preparations for it, Arendt asks, with tantalizing reference to the representational space of theatre,

[W]as it not the discovery of a discrepancy between words, the medium in which we think, and the world of appearances, the medium in which we live, that lead to philosophy and metaphysics in the first place?[32]

Irrevocably imbricating thinking and doing in the human experience and encounter with the imperative Arendt displaces abstract philosophical thought from its presumptive primary position in the intellectual life of humans and situates it instead as a symptom or response to the more urgent crisis felt by human beings as actors in the world.

Thinking, in the sense defined by Arendt, and doing, in the sense of the 'action' of training,[33] are in a Möbius-like relation – a perpetual feedback loop, a relationship by which the self is embedded in the world. The materiality of selfhood takes form in the active situation of 'I' in relation to prior thoughts and deeds and future outcomes and actions. Training, as a conscious and conscientious response to experiential reality, produces and maintains self-identity by generating a temporal context for it to occupy. Training is a means by which we each can take account in the present of past experience and act in the present so as to prepare for and affect the future.

Furthermore, the rigorous, collective[34] practice of thoughtful action may be understood as definitive of human-being-in-the-world in the sense that it precludes both modes of unworldly being – the abstract and the thoughtless. Reducing this philosophical proposition further still, training may be the physical process by which human-being comes into existence precisely because the absence of this thoughtfulness would seem to give rise to definitively inhuman acts – the banality of evil, to which Arendt so famously referred – but also because it places human actions in a temporal context, because we, as humans, must have regard to previous effects, present experiences and potential future outcomes. Arendt writes

that we can shape the everlasting stream of sheer change into a time continuum we owe not to time itself but to the continuity of our business and our activities in the world, in which we continue what we started yesterday and hope to finish tomorrow.[35]

The 'continuity of our business' is a matter of preparation in the present, in relation to the past and for the future. The shaping of the 'everlasting stream' into more or less coherent experience is an activity well rehearsed throughout human history and performed everywhere in which humans undertake to act.

The theorization I am proposing, following Arendt, diverges from other common threads of discourse within the discipline in that I suggest that understanding training has little to do with understanding the forms of practice it produces. Self-evidently, study of the practices will entail study of the processes of training and vice versa but just as Arendt is concerned with thinking and not knowledge – process and not outcome – in this book I am concerned with training and not techniques. This is because I am interested to show how training as a process indivisible from thinking constitutes the temporal aspect of the human experience of living, which will necessarily be constituted differently in this life or that life. Time is a quite different thing to history and this is a fact not well represented in current scholarship on training. The assertion that training takes time is thoroughly uncontentious but the assertion that training makes time requires a little more justification.

Conceiving of and undertaking actions in contiguous sequence and amending of future undertakings with reference to present and past experience are integral to the phenomenon of training. For Arendt, conceiving of actions in thought may be enough to produce our experience of time and yet it is a self-evident phenomenological fact, acknowledged by Arendt, that in order for this thoughtfulness to differ from the abstract thinking that Arendt derides it will need to have regard to real experience – to the lived experience resulting from the enacting of our thoughts. It is in this very worldly respect that training emerges as the process whereby the human experience of time, produced from out of 'the endless stream of sheer change', is generated and maintained by the continuity of our actions and by the development and diminution of our capacity to act.

Training is productive of time and thus of Life, as Arendt has defined it, and at the same time training places terminal limits on lives. It is life-productive and death-directed. We may see it as the means of human self-determination in the face of the indifference of change and also as the planned preparation of human capitulation to the inevitabilities of mortality.

Thinking was, for Arendt, an onto-historical process which by its existence signified human existence as transcendent of history, which is not to say that human existence is not inscribed within and circumscribed by history. Rather, thinking is in a direct relationship with time, or more accurately, thinking produces time and therefore an envelope for all of our experiences of history.

Training, as the enacting of thoughtfulness, is indivisible from the process of thinking. Training is the mode by which thinking, if it is to be worldly in the way that Arendt desired and constituted in action and agency and not abstract contemplation, comes into being This is because our thinking, if it is to have regard to past, present and future effects and experiences, must be grounded in the existential, experiential and material nature of being.

A former student of Hannah Arendt, Richard Sennett, has also addressed the physical manifesting of the thoughtfulness that Arendt describes, most notably in his book *The Craftsman*. Here, Sennett takes up Arendt's categories of *animal laborans* and *homo faber*, each of which has an historical lineage to and through Arendt,[36] and takes issue with his teacher, arguing that '*Animal laborans* is capable of thinking'.[37] Sennett wishes to remediate what he sees as an error in Arendt's philosophy: where Arendt tended to see *the labouring animal* – humankind going about its business and producing stuff without much regard to the usefulness or appropriateness, morally, of the stuff – as unthinking and *human as (his or her own)*[38] *maker* as an altogether superior beast of contemplation, Sennett seeks to revalue the technical thinking done in the 'mere' act of making stuff. He suggests, rather compellingly, that 'people can learn about themselves through the things that they make'.[39]

My concern with the philosophy of Arendt is more directly aligned with the categories of *vita activa* and *vita contemplativa*, which relate to but are divisible from *animal laborans* and *homo faber* and less so with the things people make and more with the ways in which people make themselves. This has been a definitive aspect of my approach to conceptualizing training as a broad category of human experience[40] and, in this book, I am extending this approach to consider one very specific way in which training allows people to make themselves: as temporal creatures whose abilities and actions are stretched taut between past and future and are attenuated by the very urgent demands of *now*.

Time, in the context of Arendt's philosophy in *Life of the Mind*, is less occupied by the physical properties of the concept and more minded to enquire into the human experience of waking up again each day slightly changed and yet essentially the same right up until the last and lasting sleep. Some philosophers might tend to regard Arendt's attitudes as related to the concept of 'temporal consciousness' rather than 'time' in its strictest sense. Time is typically understood, philosophically, in relation to various theories – Fatalism, Reductionism, Eternalism and diverging cosmological theorizations about the expansion of the universe – and these bear often indirect relationship to the experience of temporal consciousness. Martin Heidegger, who conducted an intense affair with the young Arendt, provides one rather more direct bridge between human consciousness and existence itself in his seminal text *Being and Time* (1927). Heidegger is relevant here, not only by virtue of his personal relationship with Arendt but more specifically with how this relationship ultimately came to shape Arendt's philosophy, largely in opposition to his own. Arendt is profoundly concerned with ethics whereas Heidegger was occupied by the foundational grounds for ethics. Although Heidegger's 'foundational ontology' developed from a redress to Aristotle, it is driven to describe the existence of presence (*Dasein*) as the ontological basis for, well, everything, the concepts of 'care' and 'guilt' emerge only as preconditions of presence (*Dasein*) with temporality as the ontological meaning of Dasein's 'Being as care'.[41] His claim is that conscience summons and interrupts Dasein's everyday fascination with entities by grounding Dasein within its own finitude and what he calls authenticity.[42]

It would be erroneous to see Heidegger as concerned with guilt and care-taking as phenomenological and existential bases for ethical conduct and indeed Arendt's rebuke of him is chiefly centred on the esotericism of his ontology.[43] Nonetheless, via Heidegger, Arendt's attention to the temporal consciousness exceeds real-world ethics and moves into the ontological domain of presence. For Arendt, the human temporal experience produced through thinking is integral to and co-constitutively linked with presence as the fundamental basis of existence.[44]

For Heidegger, thinking and acting emerge from conscience; for Arendt, it is the other way around. When one engages in thinking, conscience emerges as a consequence of forming thoughts. The adjunct to conscience (which is to a large degree individualistic) is judgement (which is communal), which conveys conscience into the world – a world which, Arendt argues, is characterized by plurality.[45] Conscience is the 'inner' watchman of our actions whereas judgement is their agent in the world; conscience drives our focus inwards while judgement turns it on the world. Both are fundamentally temporal.

Temporality is crucial to Arendt's understanding of thinking and judgement. Writing of the context of political actions but in a set of statements equally true of each kind of action a human may take, Arendt states that 'without being forgiven, released from the consequences of what we have done [in the past], our capacity to act would, as it were, be confined to one single deed', and 'we would remain the victims of its consequences forever'. 'Without being bound to the fulfillment of promises [in the future], we would never be able to keep our identities', she explains, concluding, evocatively, 'we would be condemned to wander helplessly and without direction in the darkness of each man's lonely heart'.[46] Arendt's understanding of time, then, is not merely anthropological or sociological simply because it is existential and 'real-world' oriented. Time, for Arendt, is a measure of the state of appearance, which is itself the cipher for existence.

For Arendt, political action and indeed politics per se, as the collective experience of the *polis*, is described as the 'space of appearance'. This is the space 'where I appear to others as others appear to me, where men exist not merely like other living or inanimate things, but to make their appearance explicitly'.[47] Indeed, the making of appearance explicit through (in this case, political) action is, for Arendt, definitively human. Describing this space in terms that will sound very familiar to anyone conversant in the twentieth-century theorization of the ephemerality of performance events, Arendt depicts the space of appearance as fragile and brittle precisely because it depends upon the temporary (or temporal) interaction of plural beings.[48]

Arendt employs a theatrical metaphor to propose her conceptualization of life as a temporal event of appearance. She writes, 'the urge toward self-display – to respond by showing to the overwhelming effect of being shown – seems to be common to [humans] and animals', and

> just as the actor depends upon stage, fellow-actors, and spectators, to make his entrance, every living thing depends upon a world that solidly appears as the location for its own appearance, on fellow-creatures to play with, and on spectators to acknowledge and recognize its existence.[49]

'Seen from the viewpoint of the spectators to whom it appears and from whose view it finally disappears', she states, with reference to the ancient Pythagorian parable, 'each individual life, its growth and decline, is a developmental process in which an entity unfolds itself'.[50] It may be examined from many perspectives but 'our criterion for what a living thing essentially is remains the same: in everyday life as well as in scientific study, it is determined by the relatively short time span of its full appearance, its epiphany'.[51]

A human life then can be characterized as the (brief) process in and by which that living thing achieves its realization, by which it becomes fully manifest. This process is, according to Arendt, natural,[52] yet when looking around me I am increasingly made aware of the manifold ways in which in all areas of human living individuals are seeking to accelerate, prolong and even extend the boundaries of that realization through multifarious regimes of training, whether in 'staff development' activities at work, fitness and nutrition regimes at the gym and the sports club, routines and regimens of practice in the studio and the dojo or the diverse traditions and customs of self-improvement applied in retreat centres, places of worship, village halls and on the street. Each of these activities is at once in accord and opposition with that natural process of growth and decline described by Arendt: they are each a willful acceptance of and engagement in the ontological facts of mortality and a purposeful and consistent affront to these, a capitulation of agency to the drift of sheer change and a recalcitrant battle to rescue agents and empower them, and emancipate them from their mortal fate.

'To be alive', according to Arendt, 'means to live in a world that preceded one's own arrival and will survive one's own departure'.[53] Thus for life, 'appearance and disappearance, as they follow upon each other, are the primordial events, which as such mark out time, the time span between birth and death'.[54] Connecting the concept of time with the individual experience of it, Arendt claims, 'the finite life span allotted to each living creature determines not merely its life expectancy but also its time experience; it provides the secret prototype for all time measurements no matter how far these then may transcend the allotted life span into past and future'.[55] Indeed, ultimately life itself is subordinate to appearance because 'we, too, are appearances by virtue of arriving and departing, of appearing and disappearing; and while we come from a nowhere, we arrive well equipped to deal with whatever appears to us and to take part in the play of the world'.[56]

Taking part in the play of the world was, for Arendt, an urgent moral responsibility and possible only through the process of thinking. Just as time provides the stage for action, our actions provide the framework through which we understand, measure and conceptualize time. Dealing with time, as Arendt puts it, is something we are well equipped to do. This is because, for Arendt, in our nature – or rather, our human condition – is the capacity to connect and to effect past, present and future actions with thought. 'Training', I would contend, is the term we use to describe the schema of activities purposefully modelled to achieve this connection and effect upon our selves.

My conceptualization of training and its relationship to time diverges from the epistemological approaches within the discipline, which seek to address the basis of knowledge and practice and most often so by direct or indirect reference to the historical concept of technique. Technique and knowledge can be seen as the same phenomenon and, in point of fact, this is the central argument of Ben Spatz's book *What a Body Can Do*. 'Technique is knowledge that structures practice',[57] writes Spatz, who restates this point throughout the book in various forms: 'embodied practice is structured by knowledge in the form of technique'.[58]

To today's reader Spatz's point may seem self-evident. After all what could technique be if it was not knowledge in the form of doing. However, as Spatz explains, the discipline of Performance Studies has arrived at this rather tautological co-definition of the terms of 'knowledge' and 'technique' via a fairly circuitous route, taking in Mauss, Foucault, Merleau-Ponty, Bourdieu and Butler as well as the common-usage understanding, which is largely attributable in equal parts to Aristotle's concept of *techne* and Samuel Taylor Coleridge's description of mere technicians as a dismissive epithet of lesser poets.[59]

Conceiving of 'technique as knowledge' (the subtitle of Spatz's book) pushes theorists towards a sociological understanding of human actions in historical contexts and a tendency to ask, as Spatz does, 'where [regimes of training] come from and how they develop'.[60] Here, epistemological approaches become primarily 'concerned with the invention of technique [and] with its transmission and effects'.[61] Epistemology's salami slicing of history tends to fixate on the assertion that nothing can exist outside the episteme: as Spatz puts it, 'even something as simple as walking should not be reified as an ahistorical phenomenon, as this would prevent us from analyzing similarities and differences in walking across time and space and between individuals and cultures'.[62]

Arendt's 1946 assault on the 'terminological façade' cautioned against a linguistic word-play in theory that valorized concepts over the phenomena these concepts were seeking to describe. While there is much understanding to be gained from surveying walking, for example, from historical perspectives, Arendt would probably have suggested that walking, as with other 'practices', can be understood as onto-historical – not without history but within history, precisely because it occurs throughout all of recorded history.[63] With reference to the facts on the ground, she may have argued that bipedal motion is in fact used to understand and frame human history and that understanding certain phenomena as onto-historical does not prevent comparative analysis. It is precisely the similarity of walking in different individuals and cultures that allows one to analyse walking as different across times and spaces.[64]

Epistemology's interest in the 'substrate' – the material context of action – produces its objects for analysis as products of epistemes: as material 'things in context'. We could choose to see techniques as substrates or as of the substrate, present in the substrata of material life, just as we tend to conceive of knowledge as more-or-less fixed outcomes with a manifest material reality. There is significant value in epistemological and historical analysis of training, and I make use of these analyses in this book as in all my writings on the subject. However, by following a line of enquiry instigated by Arendt into the means by which our human lives come to be just that – human lives – I intend to pay heed to the processual and Möbius-like nature of human-being and human-becoming as onto-historical. In this way, I am unconcerned by originary myths of practice which are always by *their* nature caught up in both the politics of their own invention and the legitimization of the very idea of beginnings. Instead, as with Arendt's address to thinking, I am concerned with training as an onto-historical proposition and, like thinking, *sine qua non* human quality, which is not to say that training cannot or should not be surveyed epistemologically but rather that between and across epistemes it remains in key ways the same thing. This is what is meant here by homeostasis.

Homeostasis is the property of a system for remaining constant. It is the phenomenon of self-regulation to maintain constancy internally and/or in relation to an environment. My use of the term here is largely metaphorical given that training is not an organism, as such. However, as the metaphor of the seven criteria for life applied here reveal, training can quite reasonably be thought of as though it were an organism precisely because it operates in relation to Life and through the physical qualities of lives.

Homeostasis, or the phenomenon of a persistent sameness through the processes of living and evolving, is a useful framework to theorize what has been left out of the epistemological address to training. This persistent sameness to training and indeed to discrete disciplines of training does not preclude the study of the 'transmission'[65] of techniques; as with the example of walking used above, it pointedly enables them because it is sameness that qualifies and motivates comparative analysis. The homeostasis of training provides the basis of analyses of a thing called 'practice', and indeed of the concept itself, which has been promulgated throughout Performance Studies.

The fact that training is, at a fundamental level (or a meta-disciplinary level, as I have called it), always consistent of the same processes wherever we might encounter it was the central thesis of my first book.[66] I undertook to describe some of these processes so as to move towards a philosophical definition of training that went beyond the facile or the merely disciplinary. I theorized that training was irreducibly consistent of the processes of vocation, obedience, formation and automatization; the personal 'calling' to a craft or practice, the fidelity to its rigours and the judgement of its experts, the development of the individual in the direction of his or her own self-realization and the acquisition of specific forms of potential were characteristic of training and differentiated it from other categories of experience, such as discipline.[67] In my second book, *Anatomy of Performance Training*, I linked this category of experience to human embodiment – to the simple but profound facts that we have and that we are bodies – and described the ways in which these facts were prerequisites for the processes of training and yet also products of them.[68] In this third book, my undertaking is to consider the ways in which, because it is co-constitutive of embodiment, training is productive of our experience of time. By generating the past, present and future and connecting them by the practising of embodied (bodily; of the body) tasks, training has operated beyond the limits of human history to provide a means by which human beings can address themselves to the sociocultural realities and also the ontological facts of their existence – to their own growth, development and decline. I have already contended that training is an onto-historical process[69] but in this book I wish to show that it is indivisible from human's ontological being precisely because it has given itself as the means by which we may occupy, adapt and author and authorize our personhood and insert ourselves as agentic beings into an indifferent world.

In this way training is directly related to the phenomenon of the 'unity and persistence of the individual living being', which, according to the neurologist and writer C.U.M. Smith, Aristotle saw as the 'most basic [phenomenon] in the apparent flux of the world'.[70] Indeed, training, as I have defined it, may be seen as a cause for the apparent resilience of this basic unity amid the flux of the world or the 'stream of change', as Arendt, whose ideas proceed from those of Aristotle, puts it.

The concept of homeostasis is the vessel that I use to hold the claim that a persistent sameness in the processes of training despite variance in their practices is allied to, is resultant from and cause for human's temporality. Furthermore, human's temporality is the envelope for our experience of mortality and of the world – 'the secret prototype', as Arendt wrote, 'for all time measurements no matter how far these then may transcend the allotted life span into past and future'.[71]

By employing the biological metaphor in an analysis of training – by looking at training through the prism of the seven characteristics of biological life – I am, perhaps, muddying the philosophical waters. It is generally agreed that Aristotle is (surprise, surprise) the founding father of the classificatory or taxonomical approach to organism descriptions and that he greatly influenced the eighteenth-century taxonomist Carl Linnaeus. I am not seeing training as an organism and yet I am surveying the ways in which it corresponds to the life of the human organism, to the biological life (that we have bodies) and not just the social life (that we are bodies). Accordingly, the seven characteristics of *biota* – the super-domain of biological taxonomy – provide seven perspectives on the temporal structuration of life by the processes of training. Taking a taxonomical lead from Linnaeus and Aristotle and sequencing these seven characteristics to correspond broadly with the categories, or kingdoms, as Linnaeus would have called them, of past, present and future, each chapter that follows describes a different temporal property of training.

GROWTH describes the relationship of training to human development both in the sense of our biological maturation and with regard to our cultivation of specific abilities. It does this by theorizing from the moment at which maturation ceases and in which we glimpse what Aristotle called the 'abyss' of human potential.[72] Potentia is a Kingdom, as Linnaeus would have put it, of the future, yet the 'impotentiality' evident in the revelation of talent resides in the present. This 'impotentiality' erodes the divisions between the past, present and future and offers a glimpse of a world in which human beings were not subject to what Arendt called the indifferent flow of sheer change but rather in which we might effect it. This chapter addresses the question of 'talent' in relation to training for performance. Taking examples from famous historical stage performances and the rise and fall of famous actors, this chapter suggests a philosophical understanding of talent that can unify definitions and concepts across a broader range of disciplines. Mobilizing theory and concepts from the sports science subfield of talent development and aligning these with an Aristotelian understanding of the concept of potential, this chapter concludes by indicating that 'talent' may be a phenomenon that reconciles the future with the present.

STIMULATION is concerned with the present and the related concept of 'now'. With examples taken from contemporary dance and from European and American post-Stanislavskian traditions and techniques, this chapter examines improvisation-based exercises as a methodology by which training has helped and can help to consolidate and secure identity personally felt. In this way, this chapter shows how training practices such as these may perform the same function as the activity of thinking in securing the ego within its own self-produced domain. Stimulation is concerned with the human capacity for being effected by external forces and factors. This capacity has a special relevance to training in the case of complex examples of incremental and developmental acquisition of increasing sensitivity to the environment and growing capacity to utilize it not only to survive but also to thrive. This chapter situates training with reference to what Arendt describes as the two abiding time metaphors in Western thought – the cyclical and the rectilinear. From the latter arises our abiding sense of 'now', which has a particular currency in training practices, and from the former comes the promise of iterative development which holds a central ideological position in all training disciplines. These two time metaphors pertain to training as a concern of human beings and human Being, and as an activity of both doing and becoming. In the context of training, the 'now' gives and sustains the present as the space for our development, maintained within an environment characterized by uncertainty.

ORGANIZATION considers how the biological preparedness of species in relation to the facts of their environments provides a prototypical model for human strategy. At the macro level this has been the subject for not only evolutionary biology but also human history, and both thinking and training have been instrumental in the shaping of human history. In the modern era both have also been decisive in asserting the future as the primary domain of human endeavour. Just as thinking is an organizing principle maintained by humans to assert control in and over the unknowable and discontinuous flow of existence, training is the means by which our human actions, activities and capabilities can be modified in response to that flow. Taking examples from elite sporting competition in both swimming and cycling, this chapter considers how organization is exemplified within modern forms of training and also how it has secured the future as a near-certain and seemingly predictable realm of and for human existence today.

ADAPTATION reflects on our human capacity for modification, which has a strong sociocultural dimension especially today when we find ourselves having to adjust to environments produced by humans and to the various opportunities, challenges and dangers arising from what Arendt calls our 'work'. Adaptation is closely aligned with the ideal of progress that is explored in organization and also the futurological promise of training on behalf of human capacity. With reference to antique wrestling training, twentieth-century bodybuilding, somatic dance as well as theatre practices, this chapter weighs the near-certain control over the future obtained by training against the certain effect of contingency on all human endeavour and points to where training has lodged itself between potentiality and actuality and the kingdoms of the future and the present.

REPRODUCTION relates to the death of individuals and the 'life of species', and this chapter explores this juxtaposition via the examples of yoga and the globalized fitness industry. It also returns back to the phenomenon of the audition on which the next chapter, GROWTH, is centred but this time looks at it through the lens of beginnings rather than endings.

For social theory REPRODUCTION has described the process by which essences, in something like the form of philosophical 'substances', attain relative permanence by their reoccurrences in appearance. Time has clear and distinct relation to this process and to the phenomenologically evident fact that appearance is transient while essence is enduring. Appearance is therefore of the present and is, according to the 'ontology' of Peggy Phelan and Herbert Blau, the space wherein performance's essence is to be understood and located.[73] This strand of thinking posited the present as the realm of the immanent and also the illusory, and the past and future as the apparently more secure foundations for substantial meaning. Despite the fetishization of the evanescent in Performance Studies 'mere' appearance is reasserted as merely a cipher for 'true' essence. REPRODUCTION considers how training, despite this bias, may trouble this relation and invert it positing 'now' as the primary and most credible tense of our understanding.

HERITABILITY reflects back on the previous six chapters and on the effects of training in producing time and its three tense-concepts. Realigning the theorization in play with Arendt's ideas about thinking expressed in *The Life of the Mind*, this chapter suggests fresh ways of thinking on the ontic qualities of training. Meditating on training's ontic status in relation to human beings and human Being, this chapter makes some different propositions for performance ontology and suggests a relationship between performance and training on the basis of the ontic supremacy of the latter over the former.

2
GROWTH

Growth entails a leaving behind of the old and a development in the direction of a finite and terminal limit. While it is usually reasonably evident when one is 'grown-up' or indeed when any biological thing has attained its mature state, often the temporal point at which that maturity gives in to decline is only apprehensible retrospectively, and this has much to do with the mystery of human performance and what Aristotle called the 'abyss' of human potential.[1] Apprehending when the limits of one's ability or indeed the limit of ability itself has been reached only starts to become possible when I cease to be able to do today what I could do yesterday, and yet we each labour daily not knowing whether there remains any more promise of progress in the interregnum between today and tomorrow.

Locating this limit and testing its resilience are primary concerns of 'elite' performance training and while talented performers in all disciplines are made acutely aware of the tipping point between advancement and degeneration, whether or not they are able to 'leave on a high' or if they will 'go on too long' has little impact on their experience of growth and decay.

Growth is, it would seem, future-oriented although it takes its measurement from the past and from what has been left behind in the process of development. Shedding the skin is something that some creatures do literally and also metaphorically as they undergo transformation in the direction of what Arendt called their epiphany.[2] It is a rather poetic fact that almost the entire outer surface of the living human body by which we encounter the world and each other is actually dead; a significant proportion of the living human body, and certainly the majority of its outer surfaces, are dead or dying.[3] Growth is perhaps the most optimistic of all the seven characteristics of life and in almost all instances where we encounter the word it has positive connotations. The obvious exception to that rule being the metastatic growth that seemingly disobeys the given rhythms of biological development and pursues its development beyond the scope which 'should' have been set for it. The super-exemplary development of this growth and its seemingly unbounded processes plumb the biological chasm of the abyss of human potential. In relation to the more common and positive occasions of growth, we encounter fruition in its simplest and starkest form: the biological analogy of Arendt's understanding of epiphany. This is no open-ended development but development with inherent finitude, growth up to a point. In relation to expert performance both in theatre and in all realms of human endeavour growth obtains a relationship to pure possibility or more accurately to potentiality. Growth is the transformation of a being in the direction of its own full potential. It is an inherently temporal experience with fixedly natal and fatal implications.

In correspondence with the processes of training, growth is a measure of the proximity of a being to its own perfect realization and also therefore, emblematically at least, to perfection itself. The units of measurement applied entail the concept of talent which has both folk definitions and wisdom and also philosophical basis. This chapter is a discussion of the temporality of human experience produced by training via the concept of talent. It is also a concerted effort to state something about talent that has relevance to the onto-historical phenomenon of training and not merely to the disciplines through which it has passed into presence.

This is a fraught prospect seeing as talent is more often than not dismissed from proper academic discussions because of the apparent multivalence of its meanings. It is tempting to see 'talent' as one of the terms which the philosopher Isaiah Berlin saw as so slippery as to be almost meaningless: 'man' for example, wrote Berlin, might actually have no properly acceptable philosophical definition seeing as with 'enough manipulation' of 'the definitions of man … freedom can be made to mean whatever the manipulator wishes'.[4] Clearly, with enough manipulation of the definition of talent the concept can be used to justify almost any rigours of training and could perhaps has been used to rationalize or warrant mistreatment and even abuse of trainees. One sobering example may be found in the 'regime' of Headmaster Joukko Turkka and the Theatre Academy Helsinki (Teak).

According to Seppo Kumpulainen, a movement director who was in charge of physical training during Turkka's tenure at Teak (1983–1989), Turkka imposed an extreme physical training programme on acting students, demanding a 'willingness to suffer'[5] and inflicting demeaning experiences on students.[6] So worrying was Turkka's time in charge of Teak that 'enquiries were made, even to the level of Parliament and the Chancellor of Justice' about the extreme tasks he used in the entrance exams and teaching as well as the obscene language he used during performances and classes.[7]

Each student admitted to Teak had to complete a version of the Cooper test – a 1960s American military fitness test – and those who failed were expelled without ever having had the opportunity to present any artistic or creative task. According to Kumpulainen, Turkka 'told me that he hoped certain actor students with no talent would leave the school' and that the Cooper test would help to select these.[8] Kumpulainen would later write an article about Turkka's training methods and in it state that 'it felt entirely unethical to use a mechanical test of physical fitness to evaluate the artistic talent of a student'.[9]

Few academic accounts of training have grappled with our understandings and definitions of 'talent' perhaps for the same reason that Berlin was so circumspect in his definition of 'freedom' and 'liberty'. Over twenty years ago, writing in the *Australasian Drama Studies* journal, Kath Leahy asked for a thorough-going academic assessment of the meanings and definitions of 'talent' because she claimed many actors were being denied access to professional training, 'simply because of the underlying cultural values that inform "talent"'.[10] Ten years later, Mark Seton took up the challenge in this same journal referring back to Leahy's plea. 'Sometimes it seems almost improper to talk about "it"', he wrote, attributing this to the superstitious belief 'felt – often by actors and directors – that if one tries to reflect upon, measure or analyse "it" then "it" will disappear never to return'.[11]

This superstition has one point of origin in the influential writings of Heinrich von Kleist and his 'On the Puppet Theatre' (*Über das Marionettentheater*, 1810), which placed this dilemma in the context of a young bather once publicly extolled for the elegance of his figure exiting the bath who is later stripped of all bodily grace as a consequence of his self-awareness of his own beauty.[12] As Seton explains with close echoes of Berlin's cautionary notes about words, 'recognitions of having "talent" … also depend on whose interests – actors, agents, directors, producers, critics, audiences, academics, acting teachers, student actors, and so on – are at stake'.[13] Indeed, the well-worn groove in performance theory caused by analysing all relationships in the context of discursive power-relationships appears to have warded off attempts to respond to Leahy's request, perhaps for fear that any definitions offered would be pilloried for their allegiance to *this* or *that* enculturated subject-position. It feels significant that although ubiquitous in our theories and practices of and writings about performer training, 'talent' is not one of Simon Murray's twelve 'keywords in performer training'.[14] 'Creativity', 'rigour', 'skill', 'intuition' all feature, and even the more esoteric 'resistance' and 'neutral' appear, and yet talent, surely what Raymond Williams would have called a *keyword*, appears only under the heading 'vocation/vocational'.[15]

Aujla, Nordin-Bates, Redding and Jobbins, writing in the same journal – *Theatre, Dance and Performance Training* – in their three-year interdisciplinary longitudinal study of 'dance talent' are able to offer no definition of the object of study 'because of the problems associated with talent identification'.[16] The authors instead focus on 'talent development' and do 'not aim to define talent, or provide a comprehensive guide for its identification'.[17] While this may seem to be a methodological missed step, it may well represent the reality of professional conduct in dance and more broadly in relation to talent identification and development. Perhaps talent identification may itself be a talent, and this may be why it too has eluded definition.

In a somewhat elliptical description, which appears to fill the void where a definition might otherwise be, Aujla et al. write, 'dance talent has typically been perceived as something that can be intuitively recognized and not easily defined'.[18] Picking up Aristotle's (hugely influential) language about abilities and also following Walker et al.'s meta-analysis, the authors state that talent has something to do with an 'individual's ability – or their potential ability'.[19]

This chapter would be on safer theoretical ground if it undertook to analyse the 'interests at stake' in the (exclusively male) examples of talented performers that I will discuss – the actors Michael Gambon, Laurence Olivier, Peter O'Toole, Charles Kemble, Henry Irving and David Garrick[20] – and stop short of extrapolating any onto-historical parameters for the phenomenon of talent. I don't expect GROWTH will avoid the criticisms of discourse-analysts but I expect that it may produce something of use beyond the silos of discourse by way of a description if not ultimately a definition of talent. Producing such a description entails testing the folk assumptions about talent against philosophical concepts of potentiality, potentiality being a category with definitively temporal and human bounds. Utilizing the framework of growth as a lens by which to view talent, I am minded to reflect on both the positive associations of growth-as-development and also the terminal limits of fruition. Plotting the curve of ability in any instance of training would be a temporal undertaking: one axis reserved for the specific disciplinary measures of growth and the other always and compulsorily for units of time. Though I will later go on to refer to a prototypical image of such a 'development graph', this will be for conceptual purposes and to make connections with life-narratives proffered by Arendt, Aristotle, Sartre and Nietzsche. Graph lines are narratives after all: plotted between integers to produce familiar stories – linear, quadratic, exponential, rational, polynormal, logarithmic, sinusoidal – each one an orderly interjection, an assertive projection of meaningfulness into the spaces between otherwise disordered, discontinuous and anomalous values. Ascertaining the terminal limit – the uppermost values against the Y axis – is, in any experiment, only possible retrospectively. Knowing when, as an actor, one's best work is now in the past and not the future is often a judgement made on one's behalf.

Speaking about her contemporary, Sir Michael Gambon, following his retirement from stage acting in February 2015, Dame Maggie Smith said, 'it was about time he admitted [that he can't perform anymore], because it was hair-raising doing things with him'.[21] Although the story of Gambon's retirement broke in 2015, it had simmered since 2009 when Gambon pulled out of performing in a new Alan Bennett play, The Habit of Art, just weeks before its premiere. At the time Gambon told the press, 'I'm temporarily not firing on all cylinders', and 'this means must let the show go on without me.'[22] Six years later after numerous tests for various diseases, including Alzheimer's, all of which we returned negative, Gambon finally announced his decision to retire from stage acting because he simply could not remember his lines: 'It's a horrible thing to admit', said Gambon to a Sunday Times reporter, but 'I can't do it [act on stage anymore].'[23] Gambon's decision was hastened by a West End audition during which his lines were being fed to him via an earpiece by a 'girl in the wings': 'after about an hour I thought, this can't work. You can't be in theatre, free on stage shouting and screaming and running around, with someone reading you your lines'.[24]

At the age of seventy-four, Gambon finally concluded a stage career that had begun in 1963 when he was recruited by Artistic Director Laurence Olivier to his newly formed National Theatre Company. Given Gambon's public image as a sardonic wit one suspects that he might be perversely pleased that his career ended as it begun – with an audition. Gambon's audition for Olivier for a place in his newly formed National Theatre (which at the time was a theatre company without a venue) has been described by Daniel Rosenthal as a 'comic set piece': in 1963, primed to perform Richard III's soliloquy after the seduction of Lady Anne fully unaware that this was a 'high point of Olivier's most imitated performance',[25] Gambon proceeded to embarrass and offend Olivier and conclude matters by bleeding all over the Aquinas street rehearsal rooms where he auditioned.[26] Despite the disaster of his audition Gambon was invited to join the company as a 'walk-on'. During rehearsals, acutely aware that even the other walk-ons had been to 'RADA or Central or somewhere', 'it suddenly dawned on me', said Gambon, 'that I didn't have a right to be there'.[27]

As Kathy Leahy and Mark Seton have observed, auditions such as this, for an 'institution' rather than for a specific role, convey a very particular set of judgements upon auditionees. The selection here is less concerned with the suitability for a role and more concerned with suitability for a profession. Nicholas Ridout has indicated that stage fright generally, and perhaps also specifically the stage fright Gambon experienced performing in the presence of Olivier, may be 'intimately connected with the specific condition of theatrical employment'.[28] Gambon's sense that owing to his lack of training he may be deemed simply unworthy of appointment to the company may perhaps have been countered by a personal sense of his talent for acting, which may have ameliorated for his lack of training. Despite Gambon's self-effacing tale, it was no lesser figure than Gaskill who had arranged for Gambon's audition for Olivier after meeting the 22-year-old apprentice-engineer-come-aspiring-actor at the Royal Court Actor's Studio, London. Gambon's first appearance as a 'spear carrying boy' in the company was that same year in their first production, on 22 October 1963, at the Young Vic, in Olivier's Hamlet. It is an often overlooked fact that the production was not a great success. Peter O'Toole received lukewarm reviews as the eponymous hero. The *Birmingham Evening Mail*'s review is characteristic: 'the Prince's blondeness and his curiously comic trousers [were] disconcerting'.[29] The young spear-carrying Gambon also seemed to be captivated by O'Toole's physical appearance and, awed, described him as 'a god, with bright blonde hair'.[30]

Despite the fact that O'Toole, chastened by the whole experience, described *Hamlet* as 'the worst bloody play ever written'[31] – 'actors only do it out of vanity', he claimed, and, alighting once more on the theme of dress, 'I only did it because I was flattered out of my trousers'[32] – *Hamlet* was an obvious choice for Olivier's opening production with a National Theatre Company. By 1963, Hamlet was already a definitive role for young male actors, thanks in part to historic performances received rather better than O'Toole's. One of the more famous accounts in theatre criticism was Henry Irving's 1870 portrayal about which Yeats, who was in the audience, would write, 'he was a lean image of hungry speculation',[33] not mentioning his hair or his trousers once.

Irving, who – alongside fellow actor Charles Kemble, the writers Charles Dickens and Matthew Arnold, and the London publisher Effingham Wilson – made the first petition for a National Theatre in 1848, has been overshadowed only by his actor-manager descendent, David Garrick, in critical discussions of portrayals of Hamlet. This is perhaps in part because Garrick's portrayal is immortalized in a work of literature – Henry Fielding, a close friend of David Garrick, writes in his masterwork, *The History of Tom Jones, a Foundling* (1740), an account of a visit to the theatre to watch a production of *Hamlet*. The 'little man' (Garrick was very short) celebrated in the book was a close friend of Fielding whose novel has no doubt done much to secure Garrick's reputation as perhaps the greatest British actor. 'Hamlet', he writes in the book, 'is acted by the best player who was ever on stage',[34] contributing perhaps to the general and yet rather vague assumption that the role of Hamlet is the ultimate test for an actor.

Garrick's portrayal of Hamlet and especially his performance in the 'ghost scene' depicted in *Tom Jones* is perhaps one of the most written-of moments in British theatre. Some biographers have attributed Garrick's remarkable display of surprise at seeing the ghost to a wig-maker called Perkins who claimed to have constructed a mechanical wig for use in this very scene – one touch of the carefully concealed controls and Garrick's hair quite literally stood on end. The now mostly forgotten dramatist Fredrick Reynolds wrote that he had received a trim from his father's wig-maker, Perkins, on the morning of the same day he went to watch Garrick's hair-raising performance. According to Reynolds, Perkins beseeched the young man to celebrate the 'real cause' of Garrick's affecting display later that evening, 'approbation' being due to him, Perkins, 'as the artist of the most ingenious mechanical wig'.[35] Although Reynolds himself casts doubt on the truth of Perkins's claim, it was probably Reynolds who started this great rumour.

That Garrick could move audience members emotionally and profoundly seems beyond contention. As a herald of a coming and now still largely dominant genre of realist acting, Garrick is central to British theatre history and mythology.

Despite the diversification of acting styles and performance genres before and since it seems largely uncontentious to suggest that 'talent', as an attribute of an actor, is commonly understood to be associated with the (more or less conscious) generation of affects in audience members. As a definition of acting talent this is pretty limp and how if at all might it be tracked to a more generally applicable philosophical conceptualization of talent? If we can permit that all of the *Hamlet* actors mentioned thus far – Michael Gambon, Charles Kemble, Peter O'Toole, Laurence Olivier and David Garrick – have or had some talent, then what can be said descriptively about this talent that might have some more use to practice and theory?

I suggest approaching a definition of talent by asking not *what do talented performers have*? But what do talented performers, such as Gambon, *lose*? In other words, might we glimpse something of talent at the point at which we reach its terminal limits, at the point at which its epiphany becomes its epitaph?

At a biological and perhaps also at a practical level, Gambon has lost something of his memory facilities and arguably not any of his talent at all. However, accepting this fact doesn't account for the full 'horror' of his situation. The distress that Gambon reports, and which countless newspaper commentators share, is not the consequence of his loss of memory power but the result of the loss of his 'talent' from the stage. For commentators and audiences, this is a regretful situation because they can no longer extract pleasure from watching Gambon perform, but for Gambon himself the forfeiture is more complete because he is separated, and permanently it would seem, from his practice (of stage acting), which has evidently formed both a part of his professional life and also his sense of self-identity. Without wishing to infer too much into Gambon's comments the 'horrible thing' about his situation is not the loss of an area of professional employment − not to be crass but he probably doesn't need the money − it is the separation from the experience of being what he describes as 'free' on stage and separated from his experience of practising the art of acting and not only the profession.

So, more has gone or rather has been lost than a faculty of memory. The loss of the memory faculty may have precipitated or have been coupled with a more substantial and personal experience of loss. No commentators appear to suggest that Gambon has lost his talent whatever they may think that to be. None appear to suggest that he no longer has *It,* only that he can no longer *do It,* and this is accordingly an altogether more tragic situation.

Having it and *doing* it may be seen as two aspects of a common instrumentalist definition of talent that views talent as a form of potential for exceptionality. This conception defines the use of the word 'talent' to a description of aspiring performers in any discipline who show a strong aptitude for sustained high-level performances in the medium-to-long-term future, as well as experienced performers who exhibit the (highly bankable) potential to perform at a high level in short-term future performances. Gambon's talent, at least until recently, would fall into the latter category. This rather vague but nonetheless widely accepted conception of 'talent-as-potential' operates beyond the commercial world of theatre and has in fact been rather more heavily theorized in the field of sports science and the subfield of 'talent development'. The sports scientist Kenneth Aggerholm in a recent publication[36] has summated some findings about definitions and understandings of the term 'talent' within the field of talent development, and more broadly to conclude that although it is in danger of becoming a kind of 'empty concept'[37] the talent-as-potential definition is compelling and enduring. This is probably because it seems to encompass both our natural attitude towards the idea of talent and talented individuals and some more hard philosophical facts about *doing* and *having.* In professional sport, to 'be' a talent is not the same as to 'have' a talent, writes Aggerholm. Any individual that may be called a talent (being) will necessarily possess talent (having) but not all of those who possess talent will *be* a talent. To be a talent in sport is to be a 'young and promising athlete'.[38] Talent is a 'not yet' condition of being. A further complexity being that, 'to have a talent is not sufficient to be a talent'.[39] Having talent is a more general condition of being and while all 'talents' (i.e. talented performers) have talent-as-potential in a given area they also have a constellation of other necessary attributes – self-discipline, physical fitness, mental resilience, propensity to remain injury-free, etc. – which in combination with a talent for performance constitute their existential status as 'talents'.

Aggerholm's philosophical grounding is in the existential writings of Jean-Paul Sartre. Aggerholm links the 'negative' experience of performers who have talent but have not yet *become* talent to a *not-yet* condition which, in Sartre, is 'referred to the nothingness of what is not yet'.[40] This is, in Aggerholm's theorization, 'a general condition of human existence', which is 'intensified' in talented athletes because their status as such is determined by a 'lack of being'.[41] In Aggerholm, the performance of talented athletes is a practical example of Sartre's famous dictum, 'Existence precedes essence',[42] and Sartre's first principle of existentialism – 'man is nothing other than what he makes of himself' – might be seen to serve as a maxim for elite training where 'talent is related to what the young athlete makes of him- or herself'.[43] Indeed, Aggerholm finds an 'existential motto' for talent development in the writings of Nietzsche: 'everyone possesses inborn talent but few possess the degree of inborn and acquired toughness and energy, actually to become a talent'.[44]

Although rather unforgiving and judgemental (conditions which Aggerholm views as entailed in much talent development practice) Sartre and Nietzsche's assumptions about talent as a concept related to ability and potential reflect very commonplace understandings about talent and may even serve to justify the kinds of approach to training exemplified by Turkka. Even the distinctions between having and being a talent correlate, to a degree, with those operative within the field of theatre and more broadly performance. Sport may differ from theatre in the sense that once a talent has demonstrated exceptional performance in their discipline they are no longer referred to as a 'talent'. Indeed, professional theatre agents – often colloquially referred to as talent agents – will speak about the 'talent', in other words persons, that they represent. In the semantic field of theatre practice, 'elite' performers may still be referred to as talents but the differentiation between individuals with promise and individuals with evident abilities would seem to operate in the word-use of both fields and probably more generally too.

Talent development also has useful things to say about the event-hood of talent-as-potential. Aggerholm writes in his book *Talent Development, Existential Philosophy and Sport* (2014), 'when talent is something you are the actual level of performance is always seen in relation to a *potential*. i.e. what an athlete can potentially become'.[45] In this way talent has a temporal structure with regard to its relation to potential. '"Having a talent" is in relation between the past (or even the beginning) and the present, but is mostly described detached from temporality';[46] however, 'being a talent' 'is related to the future modality of existence as it describes a relation between present and future and is to a large extent defined by the temporal structure'.[47] In sport, the event-hood of talent – its phenomenal manifestation – is both the summation and the conclusion of talent. In this discourse one ceases to 'be' a talent at the point at which one manifests performing expertise in the moment of performance. There is in this sense, Aggerholm writes, 'performance oriented finality that determines the practical understanding of talent':[48] it is an 'existential condition that anticipates its completion'.[49]

This could be the finitude and fatal limit of potential that I wrote about in the beginning of this chapter but when these assertions are cast in light of Arendt's understanding of epiphany, a slightly blurry picture of talent emerges. In one sense, the sporting understanding of talent maps quite cleanly onto Arendt's conceptualization of the summative experience of epiphany. The moment at which talented athletes become elite performers suggests a rather binary and rather enduring alteration in selfhood which would seem to illustrate what Arendt may have been describing in the 'fruition' of individual lives. Where Arendt draws from the semantic field of nature for her descriptions of growth, Nietzsche and Sartre draw on the rhetoric of competition; however, all three tacitly acknowledge that alterations in individuals occur at the social levels of identity but also in relation to the technicality (techne) of embodiment and, presumably, in most if not all cases the intra-subjective sense-of-self. Or, to picture this from the disciplinary perspective of Performance Studies, the shift from having to being a talent may be seen to represent a threshold moment, and the exemplary performance that discloses the identity as 'being a talent' could be viewed as a rite-of-passage form of experience, perhaps. However, these 'professional' sporting classifications may be just that, semantic terms with a very limited and specific usage context. After all, Arendt would appear to be describing a broader experience of the blossoming of human potential, of the gradual realization of full development (whatever this may entail in each context), as opposed to the pivot in self-identity caused by the exemplary performance of talented athletes – beware 'the terminological façade',[50] Arendt might say. Athletes must surely experience the bull curve of potential just like everyone else must. In relation to our technical potential, the human experience (as opposed to diverse human experiences which, of course, vary considerably from this narrative) is ubiquitously one of development and diminution, growth and deterioration. If I had chosen to write my seven chapters in the framework of the 'seven ages of man' rather than the seven characteristics of biological life, then this narrative of growth and decay would be central: Jaques's speech in *As You Like It*, which has proved prototypical for the various dramaturgical strategies for understanding human conduct employed by Performance Studies, frames the seven stages of development and deterioration betwixt and between moments of entrance and exit. 'All the world's a stage', he says, and players play their parts, their 'acts being seven ages'. Within this quintessentially temporal account, epiphany perhaps arrives somewhere around the fourth or fifth stage: somewhere between the 'jealous' and hot-tempered 'soldier' 'seeking the bubble reputation' and the round-bellied and 'severe' justice full of 'wise saws'. Realization, only insofar as this might be seen as a form of perfection, is transient but we may have most to learn about talent from the 'last scene of all / that ends this strange and eventful history', 'second childishness and mere oblivion'. We tend to want our great performers in all disciplines to bow out before this scene – Maggie Smith would appear to like it that way. If Gambon is typical of a 'great performer' then his retirement is symptomatic of that condition too. Insofar as the lives of great performers are metonymic of the human struggle against the existential conditions of mortality, the dawning of their epiphany is the brief prelude to their heroic exit.

Returning this discussion to the 'abyss' of human potential, I observe that Aristotle writes that all humans possess two kinds of potential: generic and existing. Our 'generic potential' to learn new skills and get better at doing things has little to do with our individual abilities or aptitudes, but it is fundamental to our understanding of education as both a private and collective experience, as well as to our understanding of the means of social reproduction. By contrast, expert practitioners possess an 'existing potential', what Giorgio Agamben in his translations of Aristotle calls impotential, because of having (*hexis*) in an ongoing way specific abilities to do and not to do specific things requiring skill.

In one sense, Aggerholm's definition of talent via Sartre and Nietzsche may commensurate with Aristotle. Aristotle's categories are rather binary and if we place them in the temporal context of a human life they may describe a kind of event horizon in potential at which skilled practitioners leave the realm of generic potential and are conveyed, because of a learnt *having*, to the realms of impotential. As a narrative account this fits quite neatly with the use of the word 'talent' in sport to describe promising athletes rather than evidently skilled ones.

To view potential as a temporal equation is rather common, and this view has a very long historical precedent in Western philosophy. In both his *Metaphysics* and his *Physics* Aristotle opposed potentiality (*dynamis*) to actuality (*energia*), and, as Agamben puts it, 'bequeathed this opposition to Western philosophy and science',[51] thereby providing the foundations for Sartre's, Nietzsche's and Arendt's understanding of human development. 'The concept of potentiality', claims Agamben, 'has never ceased to function in the life and history of humanity, most notably in that part of humanity that has grown and developed its potency (Potenza) to the point of imposing its power over the whole world'.[52] However, in Aristotle's writing, the relationship between potentiality and actuality is not binary although these categories may be mutually exclusive, and yet we (i.e. you and me, here and now) tend to see this relationship as a mirror or even synecdoche of the relationship between existence and non-existence. Things that are or have potential are *not-yet* things and when they become *things* (or perhaps, *yet-things*) they will cease to be potential, and in this transformation they will move from non-existence and into being. This is, in almost direct terms, Aggerholm's description of the pervasive attitudes in talent development.

Philosophically, this reading may be limited and influenced probably by our instrumentalist tendencies, especially when considering commercialized endeavours such as acting or sport. These are areas in which money can be and is made and this money-making relies upon a consistency and predictability of production. If when we appreciate skilled performance we recognize its performers through their potential to meet prescribed performance outcomes[53] then our appreciation issues only from a simple satisfaction with means–end causation. The rationality of this causal link has benefits for commercial activity and perhaps also to that 'part of humanity' of which Agamben writes but what is celebrated is not potential but merely predictable causation. This means–end rationality is concerned with actualization, which we can permit is something different to realization. For those who enjoy or are moved or in some way value Gambon's theatrical performances, for example, I would suggest that these sensations come not from Gambon 'doing a good job' or even a 'predictably good job' but from his making present on stage something unique but apprehensible and, I would argue, valuable to the spectator beyond its economic function. The mimetic space of theatre, where all things can appear as and alongside something other to themselves, is an ideal space through which to decide what is being made present in moments of talented performance. Just as the stage prop appears in performance as the thing itself (a plastic dagger) and the thing it means (the knife used to slay) and all the things it doesn't mean (knives used in kitchens, woodcraft, other plays, etc.), the talented actor's performance is made present along with the absence of everything that it is not.

This is not to state a tautology, as it would be to say, 'mimetically, semiotically, a performance means everything that it means and contains everything that it means and contains and doesn't mean and doesn't contain anything that it does not mean or contain'. Instead, this is a reiteration of Aristotle's assertion that 'a thing is said to be potential if, when the act of which it is said to be potential is realized, there will be nothing impotential'.[54] In other words, and in this example, *the actor's performance is a realization of her or his talent when everything it does not represent or contain passes into presence fully and alongside everything which it does represent and contain.* It contains in actuality the potentiality to not-be itself, and this complex proposition is more readily understood in the example of theatre wherein which we can sense the utter immanence and possibility of the appearance of everything which 'this' is *not*.

To 'be potential', as Agamben writes, which in this case we may read as to possess certain faculties to act (or generate affects), is 'to be one's own lack'[55] or better, *'to be in relation to one's own incapacity'*.[56] Potential, as the capacity to both act and not act is, Aristotle argues, uniquely human and in fact the source of human power and the root of freedom: other living beings are capable only of their specific potentiality; they can only do this or that. But human beings are the animals who are capable of their own impotentiality. The greatness of human potentiality is measured by the abyss of human impotentiality.[57]

To be 'free' acting on stage, in the way that Gambon describes that experience, is in this context a specific example of the more generalized experience of being free to act per se, which is not simply to have the capacity to do this thing or that thing and nor is it the power to refuse to do this thing or that thing: to be free is to be in relation to one's own privation, to be capable of one's own impotentiality.[58] If we think about potential in this way and not only in a narrow instrumentalist sense, we may say that what Gambon has lost is his freedom, not in the broad human sense of the potentiality to act per se but in the narrow sense of his talent-as-potential to act on stage. In this way, the 'horrible thing' is synecdochical of the limits of human potentiality just as his retirement may be metonymic of the tussle between humans and mortality.

One might reasonably argue that I have not added much yet to the rather empty definition of talent except to say that talent, as a concept, can be credibly linked to the philosophical concept of potentiality and that we can see this in an individual case as well as in the abstract. Understanding talent via the concept of potential requires the disentangling of realization from actualization and also recognizing that talent, in our common-usage understanding, clearly does not only relate to a potential to do or to act but specifically to *do well* or to *act exceptionally*.

The word 'talent', like the philosophy of Aristotle, has its origins in ancient Greece. I should like to imagine that the Greek word *talanton*, meaning balance, or scales, and with an etymological origin as a term for a sum of money, was coming into usage at the same time that Aristotle's theories of potential were coming into being. Talent has probably always been associated, and still is, with a value or more simply with quality.

While everybody or anybody may be able to act in certain ways and in fact this is a definitive human attribute (generic potential), talented individuals act exceptionally in those ways. Recognizing this fact raises once again the danger of an instrumentalist understanding of talent: one in which the value of exceptionality – or its definition – is formed in relation to subjective and probably profit-oriented criteria and one in which actualization supplants realization in our proper conceptualization of potential. However, contained within Aristotle's writing on potentiality is the assertion that there is an efficacy to potentiality in and of itself or rather in relation to itself. Agamben has channelled this sentiment very effectively to annotate Aristotle by saying, 'there is truly potentiality only where the potentiality to not-be does not lag behind actuality but passes fully into it as such'.[59] What is truly potential, in other words, has exhausted all of its not-being bringing it wholly into the act of its being as such. In this way potentiality does not annul itself in actuality as is perhaps commonly thought but rather conserves itself or, as Agamben puts it, 'saves itself'.[60] Perhaps in the specific example of acting and more specifically Gambon's talented acting, in the integrity of the affect generated, there is a fidelity to itself and to its opposite which allows it to be itself. When I watch talented performers in whatever discipline, I recognize in their actions a realization of the very potential to act in that discipline such that there is nothing superfluous, extraneous or erroneous. What is more, I recognize in their performance all the possibility of and for superfluity, extraneousness and error, and in the non-presence of these qualities they remain existent within the representation of their other.

Now, perhaps, a more satisfactory philosophical definition of talent-as-potential is coming into focus. Talent could be that in which, in the fidelity of itself to itself in realization is also present and thereby contained its opposite. In more simple and perhaps less accurate terms, this conforms to our commonplace assumptions about talent: that we know talent when we see it because we do not feel any need to correct it. What is more, we can appreciate in how it is being done all the ways by which this *how* is not allowing the ways in which it should not be done to occur. This moves beyond merely saying that we have seen that which conforms to a means–end instrumentalism and towards saying that we have witnessed *the thing itself* in whatever form – theatre, sport, etc. – we encounter it. Talent, then, is in some way an encounter with the human attribute of potentiality. This is felt strongly as we encounter the limits of our individual potential. In the dead and dying surfaces of the body, we are brought into contact with the abyss of impotentiality, with the depth of our capacity to not-do.

As a criterion for talent, 'contact with the abyss of impotentiality' is rather impractical; if I were to add 'evidence of the fidelity of itself to itself in realisation thereby containing its opposite' to the checklist of attributes that I complete for all applicants to the Acting programme at Plymouth Conservatoire, I suspect it might raise a few eyebrows in our Admissions and Recruitment department. Alongside 'evidence of trainable vocal and physical skills' and 'ability to understand and interpret dramatic texts', 'contacting the abyss of impotentiality' seems rather grandiose. Expecting to witness impotentiality, so discussed, sounds perhaps rather unrealistic and yet despite the rather stark philosophical terminology this understanding of talent may encompass quite a wide range of the experiences produced when individuals set out to identify talent and, what is more, it may not be as rarefied a thing as it sounds.

Potential is in the domain, or Kingdom, as Linnaeus would have put it, of the future; it lives in a realm that we do not and will never properly occupy and yet impotentiality, such as we witness in the practice of experts and the revelation of their talent, resides with us in the present. In fact, impotentiality such as we witness in the performance of the talented undermines the cartographic division between the kingdoms of past, present and future precisely because it indicates, albeit partially, that the future may hold nothing that is not already in the present. In other words, when I watch a talented performer act, and when I am moved by their performances to say that they have talent or that they are talented or that they are a talent I may be seeking to express my sense that I have seen them do something as well as it can be done by human hands. That I have witnessed within whatever circumscribed definitions and attitudes about forms and genres and from whichever particularly enculturated perspective not perfection but the prospect of perfectibility and an image of how it may appear – not perfection as a transcendent state but perfectibility as the epiphany of an individual's potential and thereby the fruition of potential itself.

3
STIMULATION

The characteristic of life that pertains to stimulation is otherwise described as responsiveness to the environment; it is the facility of living things to react and not only to premeditate behaviour. Stimulation provides a very useful allegory for practices of training for actors because since at least the eighteenth century and what Joseph Roach has called a 'revolutionary paradigm shift'[1] in acting styles, and what contemporaries described as a 'new order' and 'transition'[2] from the ancient oratorical traditions to an emergent 'naturalist' sensibility, actors of the realist genre have been expected to premeditate at length their onstage actions as well as to execute these actions with an apparently spontaneous reactiveness in performance.[3]

Stimulation, understood as the capacity for being stimulated by external forces and factors, is essential to humans' biological existence. Although this facility may be illustrated through rather simplistic and immediate examples of fleeing from danger or moving to take advantage of resources in all living organisms this capability entails an incremental and developmental acquisition of increasing sensitivity to the environment and growing capacity to utilize it to not only survive but also to thrive. This is especially so in the complex example of humans. While this is understood to be the case in the context of species we can also see that developmental acquisition occurs in individuals and during their own lifespan and not only as a heritable species trait, and in the specifically human context we can see this dichotomy in the ways in which training ensures the social reproduction of knowledge and expertise as well as the individual attainment of these.

The ability to respond to external stimulation arising outside of the body is an innate and constitutive element of living organisms, and humans' apparent capability to learn new things and cultivate new abilities both as individuals and as a species would appear to be definitive of not only our human nature but also our human condition.[4] Responding to one another has long been seen as a foundational cause of humans' capacity for learning; as Aristotle wrote, 'imitation is a distinctive feature of man from his childhood: imitation separates him from the animals and it is through imitation that he acquires his earliest knowledge'.[5] When seeking the foundations of human development and fruition in *The Nicomachean Ethics* Aristotle proceeded from the question, 'whether happiness is to be acquired by learning or by habituation or by some other sort of training?'[6] Our seemingly innate ability to learn and to communicate learning to each other pertains to all areas of human enterprise. With reference to the business of actor training, the famous American actor-trainer Lee Strasberg wrote simply, 'the human being has an extraordinary capacity and can be trained'.[7] Perhaps all living creatures can get better at doing things even if these things obtain only to the survival and expansion of species, as evolution theory would seem to suggest. Human creatures, it would appear, can get better if not excellent at doing almost anything and many if not all of these things have little or no apparent survival advantage.[8]

This chapter explicates the time concept of *now* and its relationship to training through several 'cultural' activities which may appear to be of little relevance to the biological life of the species. *Now* may not be so simple a concept as its ubiquity would suggest. It is not, as we generally perceive it to be, the artificer of our human experience but rather the artifice of our cultural activities, which suspend us albeit temporarily from the flow of sheer change and which provides the environment for all of our undertakings, and most especially for our learning. *Now*, the present, is profoundly linked to uncertainty and to newness, the twin pillars of ignorance and innovation that support human endeavour and frame the stage of our actions. Twenty-first-century acting vernacular is littered with terminology valorizing a mode of being that is quintessentially or connotatively about the *now* – being 'in the present', 'moment-to-moment', 'live', 'alive' – and also about the oneness or openness of practising – 'reacting', 'available', 'unblocked', 'listening', 'open', 'giving'.

These aphorisms can be traced to what is reasonably regarded as the foundational text in the realist tradition of actor training theory and practice, Stanislavski's first published work, *An Actor Prepares* (in English, 1936). In this fictitious diary of the fictional young actor, Kostya, the reader finds 'the Director', Tortsov, frequently chastising his students for not being 'alive' or failing to 'live' their parts[9] and urging them to 'listen',[10] making multiple references to the task of acting in the 'present'.[11] In *Building a Character* (published posthumously, 1949), Stanislavski's second published work, the focus on reacting as a condition of present-ness is developed. 'A true artist should react to the stage all the time he is in the theatre' just as a 'true priest is aware of the presence of the altar during every moment that he is conducting a service',[12] Stanislavski writes. Developing a theme of the 'general creative state' as a golden ideal of practice, he asserts that 'when you are in this state every feeling, every mood that wells up inside you is reflexively expressed'.[13] It is 'easy to react' in this state, characterized by immediacy and spontaneity.[14] By the time of preparing his third and final canonical work on actor training, *Creating a Role* (published 1961, twenty-three years after his death), Stanislavski had become convinced that actors must be 'alive in a situation': 'one must be extraordinarily strict with oneself in this matter of feeling "I am" on the stage'.[15] Although Stanislavksi may be largely responsible for the centrality of this particular ideological tenet of twenty-first-century actor training, his thoughtfulness about the practice of acting is merely metonymic of thoughtfulness, or the practising of thought as such, wherein, as Hannah Arendt has shown, throughout history thinking has been required to maintain the 'sheer continuity of the I-am, and enduring presence in the midst of the world's ever-changing transitoriness'.[16] Indeed, training such as was proposed and promulgated by Stanislavski during his life and such as is propagated in his name posthumously is, in parallel with thinking, a means by which I-am takes form not only in the more or less realized characters of the stage but in the everyday reality of actors in all disciplines of performance.

Although the aphorisms of *now-ness* circulating through twenty-first-century acting practice and discourse may appear immemorial, they can be fairly accurately dated to the early 1930s and Stanislavski's formal research into acting technique. Their antecedents may be found in the seventeenth-century treatise of Rene Descartes on emotions (or *passions: Traité des passions*, 1649), and Denis Diderot's dramatic and philosophical works of the mid-to-late eighteenth-century Enlightenment, most notably the *Discours sur la poesie dramatique* (1758) and the seminal *Paradoxe sur le comédien* (written between 1770 and 1778; first published posthumously in 1830).[17] Descartes was a contemporary of the English actor David Garrick, whom Descartes called the English Roscius,[18] and who, as I observed in the previous chapter GROWTH, has been credited with bringing a more urgent and 'present' style of acting to the English stage.[19] The maxims of present-ness in acting that are ubiquitous throughout training practice today are both suitably old and, historically speaking, new. Despite scepticism of the various, new and old, discursive protocols within which these maxims operate, they evidently point towards a preoccupation with a certain kind of existential state-of-being that is across each of these traditions of actor training considered valuable to the practice of acting. This state of being is, it would seem, yoked to the concept of *now* as both a theoretical proposition and aesthetic claim. Despite my scepticism about these discursive protocols, in my professional role training actors at the Plymouth Conservatoire, I must acclimatize students to these terms and to the phenomenon that I think the terms are trying to describe. My experiences in the training studio suggest to me that this state, if indeed state is the proper term, is not fully accounted for by a description of alertness and preparedness for taking action – although these might be less problematic terms for us to deal with – but rather it is something more fully encompassing of the actor's selfhood and in line with the psychologist Professor Csikszentmihalyi's now iconic descriptions of 'flow' experienced by practitioners in numerous disciplines.[20]

Across the multiple and perhaps now incalculable disciplines of training, from acting to dance, martial arts to sport, gardening, cooking, typing, writing, game-playing and more besides, descriptions of practising (or perhaps, more accurately, practising *well*) contain a sense of dwelling-in *the now*. Csikszentmihalyi, the pre-eminent author on the subject of 'flow'[21] states of practising – experiences characterized by enjoyment and optimal performance – has observed that an altered perception of time is common to accounts of practising given by elderly German rose-gardeners, teenage Japanese motorcycle racers, Navajo horseback riders, Indian mystics and athletes of all disciplines right across the globe.[22] Despite this, Csikszentmihalyi's research suggests that there are 'few activities' that are 'apt to make flow happen',[23] and that among these sport and 'performing music, or drama' are foremost.[24]

There is an apparent immanence – in the strict etymological sense of 'indwelling' – to the temporal experience of the *now* that surpasses the experiences of past and future, which may be seen as (nonetheless very real) projections of the self beyond itself. We never actually live in the past or the future but always within what the philosopher Henri Bergson called *présent qui dure*, or the gap between past and future and among what Aristotle called 'nows'.[25] The cherished experience of present-ness in practice recalls and redoubles this phenomenological attitude that envelopes the self within itself and, experientially, would appear to have the effect of disrupting or intensifying the customary apprehension of time.

Csikszentmihalyi's foundational work, *Flow: The Psychology of Optimal Experience* (1990), is scholarly and evidence-based while at the same time being self-consciously poetic and deeply ideological. Flow, for Csikszentmihalyi, is not merely an optimal state of performing but also an optimal state of being, and one which is made difficult to obtain by the conditions of global capitalism.[26] Csikszentmihalyi characterized nine different aspects to flow states: challenge-skill balance, merging of action and awareness, clarity of goals, immediate and unambiguous feedback, concentration on the task at hand, paradox of control, transformation of time, loss of self-consciousness and autotelic experience – experience for its own sake. Csikszentmihalyi writes that 'one of the most common descriptions of optimal experience [flow] is that time no longer seems to pass the way it ordinarily does', and he goes on to contend that one of the reasons for the 'exhilaration we feel during a state of complete involvement [flow] is the 'freedom from the tyranny of time' that it entails.[27] 'The loss of sense of real time' that may occur during flow states is, according to Csikszentmihalyi, related to the 'absorption of attention' which can lead to 'forgetting the passage of time or to the perception that time is moving at a different speed to normal situations'.[28] One of the elite figure-skaters interviewed by Csikszentmihalyi for his book, *Flow in Sport*, explains that 'it seems as if it [time] almost bends at your will; this is the only time an athlete feels all God-like'.[29]

The 'oneness' caused by this shift in time-perception – the sense that the performer and the performance, the individual and the activity, are one – relates closely to the autotelic attitude, which is, it would seem, a term that Csikszentmihalyi may have borrowed from T.S. Eliot.[30] Eliot refers to autotelic (from *auto* and *telos: self* and *end*) art as being for its own sake, a conception that resonates with Immanuel Kant's sense of the function of art as purposeful purposelessness.[31]

With some seeming self-contradiction, Csikszentmihalyi cites both whole lives and moments within lives as examples of flow, stating, or perhaps proselytizing, that

> to change all existence into a flow experience, it is not sufficient to learn merely how to control moment-by-moment states of consciousness. It is also necessary to have an overall context of goals for the events of everyday life to make sense ... to create harmony in whatever one does is the last task that the flow theory presents to those who wish to attain optimal experience; it is a task that involves transforming the entirety of life into a single flow activity, with unified goals that provide constant purpose.[32]

According to Csikszentmihalyi, 'flow' experiences are frequently associated with optimal performance (in whatever disciplinary terms this may be defined), but this is not necessarily the case. Even if a certain indwelling present-ness may be experienced during acting practice, this will not necessarily be coupled to a deeply effected experience for audiences. Indeed, the narcissism of which actors have long been accused may, in the present context, be seen to relate to the self-absorption entailed by character-based acting techniques stemming from Stanislavski's published works. Even before the recent cultural stereotype of the self-centred *luvvie* histrionically in search of 'my motivation', with barely sub-textual self-loathing, Shakespeare chastised 'self-love' in his very first sonnet – it 'Feed'st thy light'st flame with self-substantial fuel' – mirroring the charge placed at beauty's door by Ovid in his *Metamorphoses* tale of Narcissus besotted with his own reflection. The slippage between subjective experience and objective perception also occurs within the mirroring and doubling that happens between stage and auditorium: as with anything that may be said about acting or performing more generally, it is necessary to accept the discontinuity between actors' *internal* processes and an audiences' apprehension of actors *externally*. Probably on numerous occasions when I have praised actors for 'moment-to-moment' performing, I have been projecting onto them my own particular reading of the scene or exercise in which they are playing. Especially when auditioning candidates for the few places available at the Conservatoire each year, I am reminded of the conversation recorded by Mark Seton between two 'assessors' auditioning candidates for the Victorian College of the Arts, in Melbourne: after one candidate's audition as Helena from *A Midsummer Night's Dream*, the assessors argue over whether or not she has '*It*'. One assessor, who is in favour of offering her a place says, 'I see [It]', 'I'm only responding to what she presented to me'; the other counters, 'I can't see it', 'wasn't it in her neutrality that you invested meaning?'[33]

The concept of 'neutral' in performance is, as Simon Murray has shown, a *keyword* with, like those terms above, multiple genealogies and understandings. Barba, Lecoq, Pagneux, Alexander, Feldenkrais and others each use the term to mean something slightly different and although no less deserving of the obligatory *air quotes* when used in speech – as an academic, my requisite shoulder-height, double-handed, two-fingered cub scout salute – some sense that neutral bodies are 'at that point of readiness, take-off and invention'[34] abides in each. If neutrality, in any of these traditions, can be seen to associate with the privileged existential state of present-ness, then this may be because of its connotations of indwelling-ness; because that which is neutral, conceptually at least, is unaffected by everything which is not itself. This self-absorption of neutrality appears analogous to the exclusiveness of present-ness and both may be associated with the optimal experience of flow.

I have been publicly sceptic about training practices and discourses that assert or presuppose a neutral state of embodiment, especially on the grounds that these presuppositions usually have an intercultural character.[35] The possibility for identifying what a neutral state would even look like when attempted from any given embodied and enculturated position notwithstanding there has been from the late 1960s to the present, in Performance Studies and more broadly, a questionable theorization propounded that sees various ailments and deficiencies as the material products of culture and which proposes remediation by the stripping away of layers of inhibitions to reveal the neutral and 'essential' self underneath.[36] Undoubtedly, there has been a trend from the 1970s onwards, both in performance practice and in culture more generally towards a revaluing of primal and essentialist ideals of human

Being over those (purportedly distorted and deficient) modes given by societies and cultures.[37]

Perhaps neutrality is, in part, simply a rather mystical way of describing the appearance and (economic, artistic, etc.) value of the smallness of the gap between intention and outcome in the practice of acting or indeed any other practice for that matter. What is neutral may be better described as that which is in closest accord with any given ideal but equally this may also be because readiness, as an aspect of something that might be called present-ness, is an existential condition which can irrespective of any discourse on practice be cultivated through training.

The cultivation of readiness might well be understood as a more encompassing definition of the fundamental custom of skill acquisition, which is commonly regarded as the prototypical or even ultimate function of training.[38] Developing a readiness to act both in the theatrical sense and the broader sense that pertains to the other contexts of performance in this book – sport, dance, etc. – is assuredly not a fully satisfactory reduction of the terms of present-ness implied by the aphorisms in discussion. Stimulation, as a definition of our human capacity to respond to our environment, assuredly entails a facility for reacting and implies reactions that occur at a greater speed and perhaps at a different conscious level to thoughts. The largely outward-facing qualities implied by readiness, which appear to signify a capacity for response while inferring a largely 'neutral' internal state, don't encompass the existential spectrum of qualities implicit in, for example, being moment to moment. Nonetheless, most regimes and schools of actor training include exercises in improvisation, one aim of which would appear to be the cultivation of a form of present-ness by the refinement of a readiness to respond.

Improvisation-based exercises feature largely in what may be called the canonical traditions of actor training in the UK – various regimes that form loci about the predominant methods of Stanislavskian actor training. It is, of course, a well-accepted fact that there is no one method or system but rather that Stanislavski's approaches to training and rehearsal varied during the course of his career.[39] The committed focus on improvisation as both a training and rehearsal tool appears to have emerged in Stanislavski's later work, beginning with preparations for *Othello* in 1929 and developing through productions of *The Three*

Sisters and *Carmen* in 1934, culminating in what came to be known as 'the method of physical actions' after Stanislavski's death in 1938.[40]

This method of physical actions (as I will call it, following the precedent) signifies a shift in focus away from the emotional inner life of characters and towards the broader structure and action of the drama.[41] The 'active analysis'[42] of this methodology cut short the lengthy readings and preparatory discussions of playtexts that had characterized Stanislavski's earlier approaches and put actors on their feet from the outset of rehearsal improvising scenes within the basic structure of the plot and the given circumstances.[43]

Definitively, practicing, in acting and every other discipline, s a performing in the *now* that which has precedent in performances of the past and that which must express and regard the past (structures) while being contingent upon an unprecedented present (improvisation). While all forms of practising – gardening, motorcycle-riding, singing, dancing, acting, etc. – entail a level of improvisation within the given structures of disciplinary forms and tenets, and while there is assuredly learning to be had from the simple and profound act of 'merely' practicing ('learning by doing' as this is colloquially described) many training regimes self-consciously employ the model of the structured improvisation to adapt and modify the conduct of practitioners for performance. This model, or methodology – the structured improvisation – is utilized in various guises, from the drills of team sports to the kata of martial arts, the scales of music-playing to the Active Analysis of actor training, to reduce and delimit the experience of performance and to focus training experience on a select element or elements of the encompassing performance experience.

For example, in the method of physical actions approach, actors improvise small episodes from within larger scenes and acts, refining through the process their practical knowledge of the objectives, tactics and actions of the character they are playing. They build up scenes, acts and, ultimately, plays by accumulating episodes and improvising progressively larger sections of the narrative without interruption. While all this has a practical rehearsal function as it causes the play as a whole, and the actors knowledge of it, to take form, it also has a very particular training function which arises through the exposure of actors to uncertainty by the stripping away of supports – the words of the text, direction, and often set, props and costume – that enable actors to premeditate their performances.

Many, although not all, of the actors that we train at the Conservatoire find improvisation exercises harrowing and reject these in favour of the relative comfort of *performing again* tasks and games. Inexperienced actors are often intimidated or embarrassed by improvising in this approach precisely because they have been stripped of the assets that they would normally use to effect 'entertaining' performances – scripts, direction, etc. When the objects from the past – scripts, direction, set, etc. – are removed, the route to affects and effects in the future is entirely unclear and *now* becomes the realm of total unknowing. Indeed, it can feel rather like throwing a student to the lions when, as a teacher, I set up an improvised episode for two actors to play in front of their classmates. This is, in part, no doubt because of the cultural pressure actors feel to not only perform but to perform *well* and to surprise, delight or entertain. In the context of this pressure they may feel that they have been thrown into an intense problem-solving task in which they must gather all of their resources in order to survive in the coliseum of public approval that, without due care, the studio can become.

Perhaps some, such as Jouko Turkka,[44] may consider that there is a pedagogic value to forcing this experience upon actors even if only to acclimatize them to the horror of that inevitable moment when they will forget their lines on stage, but this would be a very narrow appreciation of the purpose of structured improvisations such as those entailed in the method of physical actions approach. With reference to what Simon Murray has said about the widespread sense of a 'point of readiness, take-off and invention', we might see improvisation, as a training methodology, as directly related to the inherently creative nature of uncertainty; our human reactions to the unpredictability of *now*.

The condition of uncertainty is sine qua non the condition of the present. The past has a strong degree of certainty and the future has no dimensions by which to encompass the concept. Nothing of the future is certain except for that which is assured for it by the present. From an evolutionary perspective, Csikszentmihalyi has placed a high value upon creativity which 'involves the production of novelty',[45] and as trainers we may often secure the value of novelty in performance scenarios – the delight and thrill of originality, freshness and unexpectedness – from the imperative of novelty associated with the survival of species. This would seem to characterize training as the (perhaps sadistic) pedagogy that concerns itself only with cultivating a survival instinct against inevitable future failure were it not for the fact that the improvisation exercise may also rest upon two incompatible, if not mutually exclusive, metaphors of time which have, throughout human history, been employed to produce the gap between past and future. The rectilinear motion of time presupposed by both performance and narrative theory – that theatre events, like plays, have a beginning, middle and, crucially, an end – appears in perfect accord with the linear finality of each human life; the inexorability of what Bergson described as the gap between past and future, between birth and death. This accord is strongly asserted in this much-quoted passage from Peggy Phelan, 'performance's only life is in the present … [it] becomes itself through disappearance',[46] as well as in the almost-as-popular, and earlier, statements from Herbert Blau about performance's 'vanishing point'[47] and a theatre whose 'subject is disappearance'.[48] More recently, in 2014, Rebecca Schneider has indicated that 'the definition of performance as that which disappears … has gathered added steam over the last 40 years'.[49] In her critique of matters archival, Schneider questions whether, by fixating on the terminal disappearance of performance events as a unique characteristic when compared with other artworks, for example paintings, 'we limit ourselves to an understanding of performance predetermined by a cultural habituation to the patrilineal West-identified (arguably white-cultural) logic of the archive?'[50] Schneider sees the archive as 'habitual to Western culture' and of 'societies which articulate (mythic) descent from Greek antiquity'.[51]

However, the foundational assumptions about time of such a 'performance ontology' derive not from Greek antiquity but from Medieval theology and its conception of time in space. Schneider's sense of an alternative image of the 'vanishing point' as various moments of 'body-to-body-transmission' rests upon a cyclical metaphor for time which, as Arendt has shown, has origins in Babylonian, Persian and Egyptian thought, emerging 'almost inevitabl[y] once the philosophers had discovered an everlasting Being, birthless and deathless, within whose framework they then had to explain movement, change, the constant coming and going of living beings'.[52] The archival pre-requisite for disappearance derives from the historically newer metaphor proposed by a 'radical break in temporal cycles' announced in Christian doctrines which, as Max Deutshcer has contended in his book, *Judgement after Arendt* (2016), 'require the break from a cyclical to rectilinear sequence' to support the proclamation of 'Christ born, crucified and resurrected' as 'unique and unrepeatable'.[53]

Both metaphors assume spatiality for time, in the form of a circle or a line. Schneider may well be right in contending that performance theory has built its house upon the space assumed by rectilinear time concepts but practices of training for performance (despite their congruity with Christian asceticism)[54] have always predicated and necessarily predicate both rectilinear and cyclical time concepts by assuming a prototypical function as our human means for cultivating readiness in a context of uncertainty.

Arendt explains that 'it is due to the thoroughgoing spatiality of our ordinary life that we can speak plausibly of time in spatial categories':[55] that the past is something lying behind us while the future lies ahead. However, this gap only 'opens up in reflection': it is a product of human thought and the insertion of 'I' into the world; it is not inherent in time itself. Rather, 'time itself and the constant change it implies, the relentless motion that transforms all Being into becoming instead of letting it *be*', 'incessantly destroys its being *present*'.[56] The present is an invention, if you will, of the rectilinear metaphor and spatial conceptualization of time. It is the product of what Arendt repeatedly calls the 'fighting presence' of humankind in the context of past and future. Arendt cites Kafka's parable of a man fighting two antagonists, one who pushes him forward from behind and the other who blocks the road ahead of him, as well as Nietzsche's image of the gateway bisecting two roads, each leading to an infinitely distant origin over opposite horizons, to illustrate one account of the meaning of *now* as the *nunc stans* – '*standing now*' – of medieval philosophy, wherein existence only comes into being because of humans or, more precisely, human thought producing a 'small non-time space in the very heart of time'.[57]

This image and understanding of *now* as a kind of time-out-of-time is itself a product of thought *in thought*. 'The chain of "nows" rolls on relentlessly', writes Arendt, such that 'the present is understood as precariously binding past and future together'. The moment we try to grasp it, it transforms into a 'no more' or a 'not yet', and yet 'the enduring present [which] looks like an extended "now"' is a 'contradiction in terms – as though the thinking ego were capable of stretching the moment out and thus producing a kind of spatial habitat for itself'.[58] The seeming spatiality of a temporal phenomenon is, according to Arendt, 'an error, caused by the metaphors we traditionally use in terminology dealing with the phenomenon of Time',[59] and yet, in the context of training, it may be a most productive error and perhaps even a necessary one.

That central aspect of training which is concerned with getting better at doing things can be understood in relation to what Arendt has described as 'the old dream of Western metaphysics': an 'eternal presence in complete quiet' away from 'human clocks and calendars'.[60] In this 'region of thought'[61] we may contemplate our self and make plans to maintain, amend, correct or develop it because, like Pythagoras's spectator, it is only in the 'disinterested, uncommitted, undisturbed' position of reflection that we can become 'intent only on the spectacle itself'.[62] We 'find our place in time', as Arendt puts it, 'when we are sufficiently removed from past and future to be relied upon to find out their meaning', to assume our positions as 'umpire' over the 'manifold and never-ending affairs of human existence'.[63] The improvisation exercise, such as may be found in the episodes of the method of physical actions approach apply the same human qualities to change (to 'time') as do thought, producing and opening out a region of *now* and thereby imagining a 'spatial habitat' for self – the actor's self and also, perhaps, the character's self, in this instance. These improvised episodes allow actors to reside in and return to a *now* from the narrative of a play and to contemplate its possibilities, but they also enable actors to dwell in the very presentness of their activity, of their acting craft and of their selves.

For Arendt, the function of human thought in producing and elongating the sense of a region of the 'time-out-of-time' can be theorized by first principles but, she insists, also by the datum of her (or indeed, your or my) own experience: 'the constitution of an enduring present' is the 'habitual, normal, banal act of our intellect', performed in every kind of reflection.[64] Indeed, the abstract theorization of the effect of this mental activity appears to have found substantiating evidence in the accounts of 'flow' experience supplied by Csikszentmihalyi – a demonstrable manifestation of the fact that, owing to the 'medieval interpretation' of time (the rectilinear), we 'are forced to conclude that not just spatiality but temporality is provisionally suspended in mental activities'.[65]

Training actors, just as with training in general, is predicated upon the more properly ancient cyclical time metaphor because of its provision of developmental experience linked to the very materials of biological life. Repetitive and iterative action is a conceit as central to training ideology as the premise that it provides for a withdrawal from or suspension of everyday experiences of the passage of time and an immersion in the *now* through a reflective form of practising. Embracing two seemingly juxtaposed time metaphors, training can be seen as that which predicates and which is predicated by both our human nature and our human condition; by the biological facts of our existence and the existential reality of our biology. Although one's development – getting better at things – requires or presupposes a linear sequence of time in which abilities can be cultivated and modified, guided by the reflections of an imaginative and imagined present, getting better at doing things is equally predicated upon the repetition of tasks and concomitant accumulation of abilities, a cyclical spatiality commonly characterized as the virtuous cycle.

The seeming paradox of the two spatial metaphors of time within training relates to both the 'naturalness' of our biological existence and the 'fighting presence' of our human condition in nature; the act of will, as Arendt would have it, that carves time out of the mass of sheer change and produces the present out of the rectilinear metaphor thereby reconfiguring nature's indifferent cycle into a feedback loop of experience. Both forms of our existence as humans – our biological status and our 'fighting presence' – provide the materials for training, and training requires and responds to the interplay between these two in the generation of both our abilities and our sense of our self as, if not stable then at least consistent.[66]

The sense and experience of the present as a time-out-of-time are only made possible because of the 'I' inserting itself into the metaphor of time.[67] As Arendt explains, the sense of the present does not apply to 'everyday occupations' but only to the 'thinking ego' to the 'extent that it has withdrawn from everyday life'.[68] The present opens only 'in reflection', whose subject matter is 'what is absent-either what has already disappeared or what has not yet appeared'.[69] Put simply, it is only because we stop to think, as they say, that we are no longer carried away by the continuity of everyday life in the world of appearances. Past and present manifest as 'pure entities' only in the practice of deliberate cessation, in thinking. The thinking ego – the 'I' – is not the same thing as the 'incarnation' of body and mind and yet training, and more specifically in this example, exercises such as those based upon improvisation grounds the thoughtfulness of the 'I' in the material 'I am'.

We may see the present, produced by what Arendt has called the thinking ego, as facilitating an exchange between past and future in the repetition of training exercises – a form of feedback between past outcomes and future potentialities. Feedback is an integral part of both training practices and also a definitive characteristic of the flow states described by Csikszentmihalyi. In training, feedback can be both interpersonal and intrapersonal, arising both between trainees and teachers and 'within' trainees themselves. These dichotomous forms of feedback are sedementized in Stanislavski's now canonical actor training texts which follow a grand philosophical tradition, often associated with Socrates, whereby the author develops ideas through a fabricated dialogue of questions and answers between fictitious, although reportedly real, characters conducting thought by a dialogue with the self.

These forms of feedback, which Arendt's might call face-to-face 'political' action, might also be understood as synecdoche for the process of feedback between past and future abiding within training and occurring as the context for *now*; a time-out-of-time in which changes and change itself can be both contemplated and experienced. Exercises such as the improvisatory episodes of the method of physical actions described in Stanislavski's final work, *Creating a Role*, produce in the studio a kind of perpetual present – a time-out-of-time in which the succession of *nows* within a play can be suspended, opened and contemplated. This occurs through the labour of the thinking ego and its enrapture with and by the rectilinear metaphor of time; the metaphor most suited to our prevailing conceptualization of narrative structure.

Somewhat paradoxically, the intention of this late method in shifting focus from a character's inner life and feelings to the broader and more structured dramatic journey of the role was, it would appear, to move closer to the apparent spontaneity of everyday action.[70] In Jean Benedetti's compilation and translation of Stanislavski's 1930s writings, entitled *An Actor's Work on a Role*, Stanislavski states, 'the most important thing is not the actions themselves but the emergence of natural impulses towards them'.[71] He writes:

I try to find physical tasks and actions in living, human experience. To believe they are true, I have to give them a psychological base and justify them within the given circumstances of the role ... when

I have discovered and felt that justification, then my psyche, to a certain extent, merges with the role.[72]

The idea of impulsive action, and impulse more generally, has featured in Stanislavski's writing and practice from his earliest experiments influenced, most probably, by the emerging science of psychology and more specifically by what Rose Whyman calls the 'Soviet Science' of reflexes.[73] Impulse was, for Stanislavski, a key concept and touchstone in acting practice to the state or condition of present-ness, and remains so today. The acting teacher, John Gillett, is just one individual who has placed emphasis on the impulsive nature of acting (or rather, acting *well*) and attributed this to Stanislavski, stating, 'he [Stanislavski] stresses that the most important thing is to create the impulse to action. All actions should not be planned and contrived because that creates mechanical, clichéd acting'.[74]

Living, human experience – the present-ness of everyday life – is, I might suggest, for many of us, frequently, if not always, characterized by the premeditation of our actions. These actions are not 'for the first time' but are self-consciously performed with the expectation of particular effects (and affects). This has been a primary finding of the foundational social theory of Irving Goffman and Victor Turner as well as the attendant performance theory of Richard Schechner and Judith Butler, to name but two influential theorists. The present-ness in actors that is seemingly demanded by realist traditions of theatre – that their rehearsed actions will appear spontaneous and for-the-first-time – it has been argued, has more to do with the stylistic preferences of this form than any genuine study of *real* behaviour. Colin Counsell has called this the 'style without style' 'misconception'; the mistaken belief that realism's apparently 'neutral' presentation of reality is anything more than a material fabrication – a 'repertoire of themes and images which, far from being neutral, reproduce constructions of the human subject and the world it inhabits'.[75] One of the central 'misassumptions' that Counsell challenges is that the proponents of Stanislavski's methods have failed to notice that the 'signs of good acting *per se*' – the present-ness under discussion – are only constituted as good because they are self-legitimated by the ubiquity of the realist orthodoxy which has 'been at the heart' of 'western performance training for a substantial part of the twentieth century'.[76]

Taking this debate out from the narrow context of performance theory and into the terrain of existential and phenomenological experience more generally, one cannot help but note that our everyday lives occasionally feature unexpected emotional experiences that cause us to act spontaneously, or rather to behave in ways that are not governed by our self-conscious plans. Such episodes are undoubtedly the stylistic stock in trade of realist dramatic narratives while, paradoxically, the conscious plan of the through-line of action remains the basis of realist character. The nineteenth-century writer Gustav Freytag left a lasting impact on dramatic theory and also dramatic writing with his pyramidal analysis of ancient drama in which what has come to be known as a play's 'arc' unfolds over five phases (exposition, rising action, climax, falling action and dénouement), peaking in emotional upheaval in the middle.

However, despite the apparent stylistic specificity of 'for the first time' acting impulsive and seemingly un-pre-planned behaviour has considerable currency in other forms of performance and performance training too. From at least the 1970s onwards structured improvisation has come to be a key choreographic methodology and from around this same time it has featured in the training protocols and practices of contemporary dance, a form which 'foregrounds a responsive dancing body'[77] and which for many scholars is exemplified by the Contact Improvisation form.[78]

A proponent of structured improvisatory scores in training and choreography as well as of improvisation as a performance form in and of itself, the choreographer, Adam Benjamin, speaks of 'impulse' as guiding principle in his practice. 'It's very layered', he tells me, 'but I generally tell students that, whatever they're feeling is the right feeling. The more difficult thing is helping them to understand when and how to respond to those feelings'.[79] In Benjamin's practice training dancers, he unpeels the layers of his concept of impulse and spreads these apart into four, albeit overlapping definitions. 'You've got feelings', he says, 'the senses', 'the body's motion, which is also to do with contact', and the 'idea'.[80] Benjamin's training practice, which consists of elemental 'scores' – spatial and temporal rules and structures for improvised movements – functions by providing dancers with parameters within which to experience feelings, physical motion, physical contact with others and contact with others' ideas, as well as to generate their own, and thereby to act within, act upon and react to new and un-pre-planned situations.[81] The purpose, according to Benjamin, is to attain and to train a 'sensibility' which is concerned with being at peace with and being able to act within performance environments characterized by uncertainty.

This sensibility appears to be congruous with what Lee Strasberg called 'sensitivity', which is where, in Strasberg's actor training ideology, 'the talent of an actor lies'.[82] Both practices, Benjamin's and Strasberg's, are concerned with the idea of impulse and how impulses, whether defined as feelings, motion, ideas or some other and more ineffable combination of these and other elements, can be either acted upon or stifled within the *now*. In a passage that may sound to many readers like a loose paraphrase of Grotowski's famous essay on the *via negativa*, Strasberg states, 'human beings, by the time they start their training with us, have already been conditioned to respond, react and express themselves in a particular way'.[83] He says, 'an impulse may begin to rise within an actor' and 'his conditioning says, "No. I shouldn't express that"'.[84] This, he says, 'has no value on stage'; 'in life you're trained not to react', but in the environment of the stage, and through a process of training, actors learn *to react*, within the restraints given by 'technique' and acquired by 'technical procedures'.[85]

Benjamin's exercises, like Strasberg's, are perhaps not intended merely as a preparation for the (decidedly not present) practice of specific genres of acting or dancing: of performing again and again situations as if for the first time. These exercises may be about maintaining the sense – for performers and audiences – of performing for the first time in entirely pre-planned situations and, perhaps, more accurately about bringing a certain sensibility or sensitivity to pre-planned situations (of performance) such that they can be experienced, by performers and audiences, as if for the first time.

Despite Colin Counsell's valid criticisms of the 'style without style' misconception in relation to the realist genre of theatre, as Phelan, Blau and others have contended for over forty years, the liveness and aliveness of performance and the inherent uncertainty and ephemerality of the *now* within which it occurs may pertain to performance *tout court*, even if, as it would seem, the specific discourse on impulse and social conditioning may be a specific late twentieth-century phenomenon. Indeed, in the case of Benjamin's improvisation performance practice with the company 5 Men Dancing and with other collaborators, including Russell Maliphant and Kirstie Simson, the highly valued essence of the *now* in performance situations becomes the quintessence of the performance form itself. Governed by various 'strategies' for encountering the other performers on stage during an improvised performance, including 'benign provocation or neglect' and 'sabotaging any material that another performer appears to have pre-planned',[86] Benjamin's improvised performances are conceived as a playground for the sensibility cultivated through training and as a genre that takes the sense of for the first time-ness of performance as a formal predicate.

Taking perhaps the most apparently superficial material fact about performance events – that they have a rectilinear form which necessarily means that they happen *now* and only *now* – while this may not properly constitute an ontology of performance, it does entail that practising facilitates and perhaps ultimately means a particular encounter with *now*. Training, in its multiple forms, valorizes this encounter and situates *present-ness* at the fulcrum of past experience and future possibility in its ideology of human fruition. The diminution by scholarly sources, such as Counsell, of concepts pertaining to an actor's present-ness may relate to the apparent reification of the state or condition of being present as typifying good acting per se without apparent regard to the cultural materiality of practice.

The activity of the thinking ego which finds it worldly correlate in training practices transcends culture because, as Arendt writes in explication of Kant and Aquinas's philosophy of selfhood, 'the thinking ego is sheer activity and therefore ageless, sexless, without qualities and without a life story'.[87] In acting or dance or indeed the sporting contexts within which 'flow' experiences pertain, present-ness or a hyper-absorption in the here-and-now in moments of practice may represent a countermotion against the everyday sense of time. The immediacy of the present as is asserted through flow or impulsiveness and the various forms of what I have been referring to as present-ness appear to undermine or at the least displace past and future concerns from the experience of practising. Or, to constitute these as extra-terrestrial domains providing content for the thinking done within the imaginatively constructed habitat for thinking, which is the present. If the *now* is, in our everyday lives, ordinarily regarded as substantially immaterial and enduringly ephemeral in contrast to the facticity of the past and the causal certainty of the future then the sense of present-ness given by training through improvisatory tasks may invert this relationship and assure an enduring materiality to *now*, emptying past and future of their meaning and fixedness and solidifying the I-am amid the ghostly entities of I-was and I-am-going-to-become.

Valorizing the phenomenon of present-ness in, for example, the idea of moment-to-moment acting may recuperate and resituate emphatic experience within the temporal context of training which is more usually characterized by a fixation on information from the past and an obsession with the potentiality of the future. On a practical level, this may aid the justification (to the self, and more broadly) of the relentless and often arduous continuity of training.

The seeming contradiction between actor training's central conceit of contiguous and repetitive action and its implicit aim of deriving for-the-first-time practice finds an allegory in the individual's experience of time throughout the processes of training: the remorseless rigour of repetition, which, experientially, may augment an experience of the present that feels interminable, is bound ideologically to an experience of present-ness that is incessant and unbounded.

Performance theory and the narrative form of performance rest firmly upon a rectilinear time metaphor, as does our abiding sense of *now* as a real domain or habitat, as Arendt called it. The purpose of *now* as a reflective space for self-identification and assessment is, evidently, as central to training as it is to thinking and may be identified most clearly in the structured improvisation methodology common to training practices. The incremental and iterative development of capability forecast by training and its production of a coherent temporal modality sequencing subjective and collective experiences through practice rests upon the cyclical metaphor of time which concerns itself with rhythm and intransience and the biological materiality of bodies and the body. These two contrasting time metaphors pertain to training to the extent that it is a matter of human being and human Being; a matter of both doing and becoming and an experience issuing from and self-substantiating the I-am of our existence. Looking down the other end of the telescope, so to speak, we can see how Stanislavski's commitment to the strictness of the

I-am of the character when on stage is metonymic of the stringency of the I-am of the self more generally. Both formulations – the I-am of character and the I-am of self – arise through the human labour of thinking which produces the *now* and which, in the context of training, gives and sustains the present as the space for our development, maintained within an unpredictable environment characterized by uncertainty.

4
ORGANIZATION

As a characteristic of biological life, organization refers to the fact that organisms are complex and consist of cells. They are comprised of units which together form systems and processes. Life, by its nature – or perhaps that should be simply, by nature – is a composite. Organization is, as the name suggests, not only a definitive but also a quintessential aspect of organisms. The complexity and coordination of biological life is, as evolutionary biology has made clear, a result of the past, but it is also a response to the future. The organized and organizational nature of biological life represents preparedness and provides a prototypical model for human strategy which, at the macro level, has been the subject for not only evolutionary biology but also human history. Both thinking and training have been instrumental in the shaping of human history and, in the modern era, both have been active in predicating the future as the most urgent domain of human endeavour. The life of the mind, as Hannah Arendt has shown, is also complex just as its mode – thinking – is a composite organization of information and rules.

In the modern era when science has established progress as an end in and of itself, thinking has taken the guise of scientific thinking or 'organized knowledge', as Arendt has it.[1] Practitioners of thought have always 'insisted that there was something that refused to lend itself to a transformation' that would 'allow it to appear and take place among the appearances of the world',[2] she wrote in *The Life of the Mind*. Philosophy, and specifically metaphysics, with its 'ever-recurring' attempts 'to warn the reader' that what is being offered comes in the shape of 'thoughts, not cognitions, not solid pieces of knowledge which, once acquired, would dispel ignorance',[3] has in its pursuit of what escapes human knowledge and haunts human reason nonetheless discovered many things that are 'indeed knowable, namely, all the laws and axioms of correct thinking and the various theories of knowledge'.[4] Scientific thinking – an historical subset or methodology of the enterprise of thought – has instead sought to delimit the terms of enquiry to such an extent as to generate irreducible facts and to situate knowledge in the citadel of human wondering that once housed thought.

In her subtle history of thinking, Arendt is too careful a historian to put in place a crude conflict between philosophy and science but rather views philosophy as 'the mother of the sciences', 'itself the science of the beginnings and principles of science'.[5] Rather, science is a particular characteristic or quality of thinking allied with the idea and ideal of progress that 'sprang up with the rise of the sciences as the natural response of every thinking' person 'to the enormous and enormously rapid advance in human knowledge'[6] – an 'advance that was bound to make the previous centuries since antiquity appear as sheer stagnation by comparison'.[7] With this there came an 'important shift' in 'the understanding of time': 'the emergence of the Future to the rank formerly occupied by the Present or the Past'.[8] This shift was produced by the notion that 'each subsequent generation would necessarily know more than its predecessor and that this progressing would never be completed', a conviction that, as Arendt foresaw, 'only in our time has found challengers'.[9]

This shift in our sense of time also came about with scientific thinking because of the simple matter-of-fact perception that 'scientific knowledge' has been and can be attained only 'step by step through contributions of generations of explorers building upon and gradually amending the findings of their predecessors'.[10] Arendt claims that the 'rise of science' began with the new discoveries of astronomers – scientists who 'used most systematically' the findings of their predecessors and who without records of these findings from the past would have been unable to make any 'progress' at all,[11] especially since the lifespan of a single astronomer or even one generation of astronomers 'is evidently too short to verify findings and validate scientific hypotheses'.[12] Astronomers were, according to Arendt, the first scientists to pay full heed to the future, composing star catalogues to be used by future astronomers and thereby laying 'a basis for scientific advances'.[13] For Arendt, astronomers are the first and most rigorous of futurologists – a sweet irony given the prophetic claims of their committedly unscientific celestial companions, astrologers, and also in light of the fact that their very objects of study and fascination have a material existence only in the past, light years hence.

In the realm of practice as opposed to conjecture, craftsmen too used the method of trial and error and 'were keenly aware of certain improvements in their crafts', although the guilds 'stressed the continuity rather than the progress of craftsmanship'.[14] Progress, which has 'dominated every other science', ultimately became 'the dominant notion of the equally modem concept of History', which was originally based on 'the pooling of data, the exchange of knowledge, and the slow accumulation of records that were the requisites of astronomical advance'.[15] As far as history is concerned, it was after the 'world-shaking discoveries of the sixteenth and seventeenth centuries' that the science of progress 'came to the attention of those who were concerned with the general human condition'[16] and thus even while the 'new philosophy' was proving the inadequacy of our senses and giving 'rise to suspicion and despair' the equally 'manifest forward movement of knowledge gave rise to an immense optimism as to what man can know and learn'.[17] Knowledge, despite the intellectual challenge to its basis in perception, was inherently optimistic because of its futurological premise. While it was of relatively little use to 'men in the singular',[18] its application to successive generations and to humankind as a whole was its chief ideological premise.

Pascal, whom Arendt sees as the first to detect the emergence of the idea of the new temporal order, came to see progress as a

> particularly [human] prerogative [distinguishing man from animal] that not only each human being can daily advance in knowledge, but that all men together progress continually while the universe grows older ... so that the whole succession of men throughout the centuries should be considered one and the same man who lives forever and continually learns.[19]

'Progress became the project of Mankind',[20] writes Arendt, and today training has become the technology of this project.[21]

Both thinking and training exhibit and require organization. They are each characterized by processes that deconstruct complex phenomena into units and which sequence and re-sequence units – of information, action, activity, etc. – into flexible and complex sequences and systems. Training has, in the modern age at least, leant heavily on a particularly rigorously organized version of thought. It has, in many fields, become increasingly goal-directed and data-driven as it has sought to both utilize the findings of scientific thought and emulate the process of scientific thinking. Adopting this methodology has allowed training in all its forms and disciplines to attain a status as quasi-science and to propose itself as the mechanism by which human beings will bring their own futures under their own control.

This has meant that training has been able to offer to individuals what science can only offer to groups. While individuals may apply knowledge acquired by science to aid their own lives, they must each wait for the pace of progress to yield results favourable to their own aspirations and ambitions. Training has placed aspiration firmly in the hands of everyone, for good or ill.

In the particular field of sporting training, the modern age has seen the rise of attendant fields of scientific thinking – Sports Psychology, Sports Nutrition, Sports Physiotherapy and the encompassing Sports Science – producing data for and acquiring data from sporting practice and exerting an ever-growing influence on training practices. The impetus driving scientific thinking in the modern age has been felt beyond this particular (and particularly commercial) field also. In the workplace, training has sought to become and to show that it has become better – more effective and efficacious – by showing itself to be more sensitive and responsive to data generated by appraisal, performance review, performance management and through the provision of increasingly specific 'packages' of learning tailored to ever more discrete aspects of worklife: Managing Conflict, Recognizing Unconscious Bias, Working Safely, Valuing Diversity and Performing Value-based Behaviours.[22]

In the arts, where the influence of commerce on the 'product' is often more indirect or circuitous than in sport or the workplace, the modern age has also seen an increasingly organizational approach to training wherein the methodology of scientific thinking has displaced the judgement of experts from its central position in discourse even as it has co-opted expert judgement as one of its engines for data production. The theatre industry in the UK provides an illustration of the ascendency of 'scientific training' in the modern age as well as of a juxtaposition between this and its opposite. Professional actors in the UK can be divided into two groups – those who received formal actor training at one of the UK's conservatoires and drama schools and those who did not, with the former often representing an informed, rigorous and dogmatic approach to acting and the latter typically a naïve, haphazard and flexible attitude towards the task of performance. Irrespective of the relative merits of the scientific data-driven approach to actor training in the arts, one of its key contributions in this field, as in all other fields, is to diminish and undermine its opposite – an approach based on feelings rather than data and predicated by thoughts rather than knowledge, diminishing the sense of temporal movement in the direction of improvement as rhythmic, or even arrhythmic, and reconfiguring it as (optimally) consistently linear.[23]

This modern state of affairs in training notwithstanding, the normative history of actor training in Western civilizations is co-natal with the history of Western philosophy and the practices of training and thinking are, in European societies, coeval with one another. While these two practices have in the modern age been drawn centripetally together in ever-decreasing concentric contraction in the direction of a shared, scientific, centre-ground, their fundamental nature retains its premise in the terrain of metaphysical thought. While it might be common to think of training as an attitude taken towards certain tasks and activities – that what 'elevates' practising to the status of training is that it is done with a certain intention and commitment to *improve* – I have argued in *Training for Performance* (2011) that this 'commitment' cannot be reduced to a cognitive attitude.[24] Evidently, the 'sense of vocation'[25] experienced by practitioners of all kinds towards improving their practice is fully encompassing of their personhood and in large part definitive of their self-identity, training being the means by which they can become 'more perfectly what they already feel themselves to be'.[26]

Training is systematic. It is increasingly systematic across more disciplines of practice. It is concerned with processes that anatomize practice, isolate aspects of practice and seek to cultivate and coordinate increasingly specific and discrete expertise in a complex reintegration of elements as performance. Such rigorous systematization has profound effects on individuals' sense of self-identity, in both positive and negative ways. The swimmer Russell Page-Dove, a national-level athlete and competitor in 100 metre fly, spoke both of the feelings of empowerment and 'achievement' that his training gave him and described to me the psychological challenge of completing programmes of training without being in control of their design: 'I'm not a performing seal, I'm a swimmer',[27] he said.

Routines and interval regimens provide the foundation of many sporting training programmes. In most elite sporting practice, routines are themselves units within a higher-level organization that also prescribes technique exercises, psychological conditioning and, in group sports, 'drills' and 'plays' – set-piece rehearsals of specific instances of practice. Page-Dove's training regime involved two pool sessions daily, 07:00–09:00 and 16:00–18:00, six days a week, with rest periods in early morning and gym work in the afternoon. Pool sessions involved drills, such as swimming with only one arm or swimming as slowly as possible with perfect technique – 'your stroke is everything', said Page-Dove, 'it is in everything, in the water, in the gym, everything'.[28]

Perhaps a more accessible example of organization within training and one that may be quite familiar to many is the fitness routine. Whether practised with gym equipment or unaided routines involve repetition of a single exercise task, for example, lifting a weight or sprinting a distance and sets of repetitions such that the routine consists of x 'reps' performed in y 'sets'. The routine, consisting of units within units, may itself be organized as part of a more complex regime wherein high intensity and lower intensity routines are interspersed; this is usually called 'interval training' and comes in various forms and guises, including Fartlek training (a Swedish method for training runners), Sprint-interval training or Walk-back Sprinting, or CrossFit, a branded and trademarked high-intensity fitness regimen registered to Greg Glassman of CrossFit Inc., which is among the latest fitness crazes and fads.

When one starts to look at the institutions that cultivate habits of thinking – schools, colleges, universities and certain workplaces – the organization of units into increasingly higher-level systems is readily apparent. In the higher education sector in which I work, undergraduate degrees are composed of levels which are comprised of modules each with individuated aims, objectives, tasks and assessments. The accumulation of expertise is charted by the accretion of 'credits' from assessment tasks, and accrual of multiple credits entails graduation between levels. Each volume of credits is recognized at terminal moments by the award of different degrees – certificate, diploma, undergraduate degree, postgraduate degree, doctorate. These terminal awards amass the outcomes of numerous assessment tasks, each of which test discrete and specific skills and abilities – component parts of a thing called performance.

Within many workplaces, staff will encounter systematic performance training programmes and courses, CPD (continuing professional development), performance development, appraisals, performance reviews and numerous other interventions and initiatives that anatomize job roles and cultivate discrete and specific 'competencies' and 'behaviours' within them. Owing to its ubiquity across disciplines and professions today, the systematic or scientific approach to training practice appears quintessential to training per se rather than characteristic of training *now*.

The pre-eminent Stanislavski scholar Jean Benedetti takes a familiar approach to historicizing the practice of acting now in his book, *The Art of the Actor* (2012), by tracing a narrative line from 'the present day' back to 'classical times'.[29] Professor Joseph Roach takes the same approach in his seminal work, *The Player's Passion* (1985), deriving a point of origin for the art of acting amid the practitioners and treatises of rhetoric and oratory in Greek and Roman antiquity.[30] Within this Western-centric narrative of the practice of acting, Cicero, 'Rome's greatest orator',[31] and Quintilian, author of the paradigmatic textbook for public speakers, *Instutio Oratoria*, appear as stock characters – expert practitioners of a proto-acting art form capable to differing degrees of providing didactic and pedagogic guidance on the practice of public performance.[32] Quintilian's treatise (which is, conceptually, a more fulsome explication of the five canons of rhetoric laid down by Cicero in *De Inventione*) figures in Roach's account as archetypal of acting textbooks, and in scholarly discourse, *Instutio Oratoria* has, as Quintilian claimed that it would, rendered *De Inventione* obsolete[33] and provided the Ur-model for actor-training pedagogy. Systematically anatomized, Quintilian approaches the practice of oratory from numerous perspectives each kept hygienically separate from the other until their glorious re-coordination in performance. Building on Cicero's model which requires the conceptual division of the practice into five categories of activity – invention, arrangement, style, memory, delivery – Quintilian adopted an encompassing educational mission in his book. Seeking to provide practical advice on numerous aspects of the performance of speech, including vocal delivery and gesture and not only composition, which was the primary focus of the five canons, Quintilian re-weights actor training discourse to focus on the elements of style and delivery.

Quintilian wrote that even the great Cicero 'is content to speak merely of the kind of speech to be employed by the perfect orator',[34] while his own purpose was to 'form the orator's character and teach him his duties'.[35] With zealous immodesty Quintilian wrote, 'I have no predecessor to guide my steps and must press far, far on, as my theme may demand.'[36]

Quintilian's rigorously taxonomical approach to the practice of oratory – *Instutio Oratoria* is divided into twelve parts covering, in isolation, various aspects of performance including childhood education (Books I and II), types of oratory, structure of speech and methods of persuasion (III, IV and V), laughter (VI), arrangement (VII, VIII and IX) extant approaches to oratory (X), subject matter for speeches (XI) and the career of the trained orator (XII), and is further subdivided to tackle topics such as gesture,[37] imitation[38] and memory[39] – is exemplary of antique philosophy and also prototypical of the various acting manuals that burgeoned forth during the Renaissance. Among the authors of these, John Bulwer is foremost, according to Roach, and the 'most systematic theorist' of rhetoric in seventeenth-century England, best known for his 1644 double-volume *Chirologia* & *Chironomia*.[40] Bulwer took Quintilian's taxonomical approach and didactic impetus to its logical conclusion subdividing the task of acting to the smallest possible units and including series of 'chirogram' plates showing line drawings of specific hand gestures to be used to convey precise emotions. To today's reader, Bulwer's work, which draws heavily on Quintilian's, seems both quaint and oddly topical. The obsessive anatomization of the task of performing appears equally futile and productive, and his obsession with the composite units of performance seems both prescient and misguided.

While Stanislavski's 'uniting' of playtexts can be easily understood as a dramaturgical reverse-engineering of the canons of *elocution* (style) and *disposition* (arrangement), the taxonomical subdivision of the practice of acting within his three major works owes much to Bulwer and Quintilian. Despite the strong influence of modern science in Stanislavski's writings of the sixteen sections of *Building a Character* at least eleven – dressing a character, characters and types, restraint and control, diction and singing, intonations and pauses, tempo-rhythm in movement, speech tempo-rhythm, stage charm, physical characterization, making the body expressive, plasticity of motion – could very easily be subheadings of *Instutio Oratoria*.

While Joseph Roach has rightly pointed out that to 'the modern reader' Quintilian's 'rules for delivery' seem 'the most inhibiting and affected sort of artifice',[41] there is on many themes considerable continuity between *Instutio Oratoria*, *Chirologia*, *Chironomia* and the three volumes that comprise the Stanislavski oeuvre: *An Actor Prepares, Building a Character* and *Creating a Role*. On the subject of restraint and verisimilitude in gesture, for example, the reader may struggle to insert a cigarette paper between Quintilian's advice that an 'orator should be as unlike a dancer as possible and his gesture should be adapted to his thought rather than to [miming] his actual words'[42] and Stanislavski's assertion that 'an excessive use of gesture dilutes a part [in a play]'.[43] While one may caution against un-historicized readings of Quintilian, there is a great deal within his seminal text that, Joseph Roach's criticism notwithstanding, chimes as wholly contemporary in its appreciation of acting style. On the subject of mimetic and 'annoying restlessness of gesture',[44] Quintilian comments, 'esse hanc negotiosam actionem', which is typically translated as 'there is too much "business" in such delivery'. It may sound to some, such as Roach, perhaps, that something has been added in translation here giving the word 'negotiosam' a modern and anachronistic definition. However, Quintilian's notion of 'negotiosam' (*nec* ('not') + *ōtium* ('leisure')) on stage may equally be the etymological root of our understanding of 'stage business' and 'busy' actors who like so many playing Francisco in *Hamlet* Act I Scene I walk out on to the battlements of Elsinore shivering and hugging themselves saying, 'tis bitter cold!' However, more striking and less continuous than such points of correspondence between *Instutio Oratoria* and *An Actor Prepares* is the formal similarity between these key texts and the pedagogies that they proscribe. Each approach the subject of training performers as a task requiring deconstruction, subdivision and reorganization: systematic observation and discrete analysis and anatomization of the practice of public performance in the composition of a training method-of-parts. While many have credited the emergence of science with producing this affect in Stanislavski and largely via his influence more broadly throughout twentieth-century approaches to actor training – Alison Hodge, for example, views Stanislavski's research-based process of actor training as emblematic of a 'widening influence at the turn of the century of objective scientific research'[45] – it is clear that, historically, the organized and organizing impetus of training predates the scientific age and while its hyper-realization within public life may be associated with the blossoming of modern physics, its incubation occurred within a decidedly ancient metaphysical context.

The complexity of training systems, which consist of discrete and specific exercises and tasks, would appear to be a more or less universal characteristic of training today and arguably a fundamental and definitive trait differentiating training-for-practising from practising itself. One may choose to read Quintilian thus when he writes that he has produced a method in response to what his 'theme may demand', or, in other words, we may be minded to consider the vivisecting approach to practice as indivisible from the activity of training.

If complexity is an ontological condition of training, it is also one that has asserted itself most clearly in an historical development of training. The anatomization of practice in the activity of training would indeed appear to have achieved new impetus in what Arendt called 'the rise of science in the modern age'[46] of scientific analysis. During this modern age and up to the present, training has increasingly come to reflect thinking, especially in the paradigmatic form of scientific analysis, but thinking was and remains a metaphysical art even as it has been co-opted as the foundational premise of the new practices of science. Thinking is systematic. More starkly, if it is not systematic, it is not thinking. This understanding of thinking differentiates the activity from the involuntary activity of the conscious mind which does not bear the requirement for systematization. Systematization is the cogent response to the rigour that predicates thinking and which is predicated on thinking and which distinguishes it from other activities of the conscious mind such as imagining. For Martin Heidegger, rigour entails a responsibility or a 'care-taking' just as for his ex-lover, Hannah Arendt, thoughtlessness entailed a deep ethical implication because it is 'something entirely negative' and the 'banal' root of evil. Evil, such as displayed by the Nazi Adolf Eichmann, she would conclude, was not 'stupidity but thoughtlessness'.[47]

Although Arendt was critical of Heidegger's withdrawal from a realm of worldly ethics,[48] it is very tempting to read much of his writing on the subject of thinking and care as ultimately ethical: 'what calls on us to think', he states, 'demands for itself that it be tended, cared for, husbanded in its own essential being, by thought'.[49] While for Heidegger, this dictum applied to the purity of thought rather than the ipseity of others, there is something bequeathed (albeit in the form of a challenge) here to philosophers, such as Levinas, which gave rise to a sense of care for essential differences in the manner in which one responds to different things and different people.[50] It was Heidegger who wrote that 'we are capable of doing only what we are inclined to do', and 'again, we truly incline toward something only when it in turn inclines toward us, toward our essential being'.[51] 'We learn to think by giving heed to what there is to be thought about',[52] he claimed, and by thinking about it in the way it requires for itself to be thought.[53] 'If he is to become a true cabinetmaker', Heidegger contends (using, in the Aristotelian tradition of philosophical example, a very practical illustration), 'he makes himself answer and respond above all to the different kinds of wood and to the shapes slumbering within wood – to wood as it enters into man's dwelling with all the hidden riches of its essence'.[54] 'In fact', he asserts, 'this relatedness to wood is what maintains the whole craft' because 'without that relatedness, the craft will never be anything but empty busywork, any occupation with it will be determined exclusively by business concerns'.[55]

This is what Andy Park's exemplary woodcuts in our previous collaboration, *Anatomy of Performance Training*, illustrated; as I wrote of them then, 'he must find the *right* cuts to make, working with the limitations of the wood, the grain and textures its depth and imperfections. He *knows* the right cuts to make, from experience, expertise, imagination and his sense of taste but he only *finds* the right cuts in concert with the wood'.[56] An artist and an artisan, I suspect Andy would agree with Heidegger that without the summons of the wood or, in the case of his illustrations for this book, of the paper and the ink, 'every handicraft, all human dealings, are constantly in that danger' of subordinating to 'business concerns'.[57]

The 'philosophy of mind' – the subfield of philosophy concerned with thought, thinking and mental activities – has, unsurprisingly, suggested numerous definitions and understandings of 'thinking'. Some of the foundational ideas of this field include (to simplify, greatly) Decartes'[58] and Locke's[59] senses of thinking as a process involving bringing concepts and ideas before the mind, Berkeley[60] and Hulme's[61] versions of thinking as a sequential series of ideas or images in the mind and Hobbes'[62] notion of thinking as a process of forming verbal images in the form of an inner monologue. Each of these, just like the many other definitions built on and in opposition to these, are unified by the agreement that thinking whatever it might be must be internally organized – that it must have rigour in some form – process-based and at least internally coherent.[63] As Jaegwon Kim explains in *The Philosophy of the Mind*, 'when coping with the myriad things and events that come our way at every moment of our waking life, we try to organize them into manageable chunks', and we do this by 'sorting them into groups'.[64] We seek to define categories-of-things by defining their shared characteristics and then to apply our definitions of these characteristics to identify and understand each 'thing' that we encounter. We may extract rules or principles from this process and then test these rules with the evidence of our sense, and these fundamental activities of our thought-process as humans are both definitive of our categorization of ourselves as humans and imperative to our survival. Perhaps for this reason, few philosophers have doubted that thinking is something at which one can and in some cases should or must get better. For Heidegger, 'we come to know what it means to think when we ourselves are thinking. If our attempt is to be successful, we must be ready to learn thinking' and yet, 'as soon as we allow ourselves to become involved in such learning, we have admitted that we are not yet capable of thinking'.[65] This may be one more way in which thinking and training have in the modern age co-mingled and displaced and replaced each other's discourses.

Thinking is unavoidably and integrally radical because it can only be driven by a movement against orthodoxy: 'we can learn only if we can unlearn at the same time … we can learn thinking only if we can radically unlearn what thinking has been traditionally'.[66] Herein lies a paradox, identified by Arendt in *The Life of the Mind* – the paradox of thinking as a process at once both passive and active, both motivated towards an end-to-thought and predicated upon thinking's unendingness. 'Thinking aims at and ends in contemplation', she writes, 'and contemplation is not an activity but a passivity; it is the point where mental activity comes to rest'.[67]

Charting a history of thought in *The Life of the Mind*, Arendt argues that 'with the rise of the modern age, thinking became chiefly the handmaiden of science, of organized knowledge' and herein 'thinking then grew extremely active, following modernity's crucial conviction that

I can know only what I myself make'.[68] While the human capacity for thought can be inferred and substantiated in our species prehistorically, our conception of thinking, and indeed the foundational assumptions that Heidegger and others have debated, is a decidedly historical phenomenon. Indeed, the so-called Western canon of philosophy only exists because of broad agreement about the fact that from at least two and half thousand years ago human beings (in this lineage, in Europe) have been engaged in an activity called thinking.

Arendt wrote that philosophy, and indeed history, has typically taken 'for granted man's need to think'[69] and while 'we cannot date the moment when this began to be felt', the 'very fact of language and all we know of prehistorical times and of mythologies whose authors we cannot name give us a certain right to assume that the need is coeval with the appearance of man on earth'.[70] Language, or rather speech in its supreme organizing and organizational qualities, represents what Arendt saw as the mode of thought: 'thinking', she writes, 'in contrast to cognitive activities that may use thinking as one of their instruments, need speech not only to sound out and become manifest', but rather 'it needs it to be activated at all'.[71] Since speech 'is enacted in a sequence of sentences, the end of thinking can never be an intuition', or, in other words, the resolution of a sequence of thought cannot be 'confirmed by some piece of self-evidence beheld in speechless contemplation'.[72] Language is integral to the organization and systematization of mental activity – of thinking – and is the fulcrum for an historical pivot from theory to logic.

Both Greek in origin, 'theory' – a way of *seeing* – has been gradually diminished and displaced by 'logic' – a way of *saying* or of *the word* – in the history of thought and of Western civilizations. Logic – perhaps deriving from the proto-Indo-European *leg* (the hypothetical source of the Greek *legein* – to say, tell, speak or, in Homer, to pick out, select, collect) – subordinates theory to speech in the form of axioms or as statements about phenomenal facts. Language, which evidently predates and predicates logic, consists of units and rules together comprising systems with internal cogency and while we cannot, as Arendt explains, date the origin of language or thought, 'what we can date is the beginning of metaphysics and philosophy'.[73]

The emergence of metaphysics in the ancient world, and its modern repackaging as 'philosophy', is an historical phenomenon well discussed by Arendt in *The Life of the Mind*. Therein, Arendt charts the emergence and development of three 'answers' in response to what she calls man's need to think, the last of which has proved the most enduring and most influential in the emergence of the scientific age. 'The Greek answer', writes Arendt, holds that 'virtue was what we would call virtuosity'.[74] In other words, 'whatever existed was supposed, first of all, to be a spectacle fit for the Gods'[75] and to be both exemplary and exemplified on a high plane of existence. The 'Roman answer', by contrast, has 'an existential root in unhappiness'.[76] Thinking, apparently, is motivated by the inadequacy of human existence – 'how often indeed must the first thought-impulse have coincided with an impulse to escape a world that has become unbearable'.[77] The Roman is, as Arendt puts it, 'essentially practical'[78] and resonates with personal experience. Here, 'thinking has become *technê,* a particular kind of craftsmanship, perhaps to be deemed the highest – certainly the most urgently needed because its end product is the conduct of your own life'.[79]

Finally, 'the Socratic answer' is bound first and foremost to language. It is 'concerned with the transposition of adjectives to nouns'. One can see and recognize a happy individual, a just person and a bad one, and one can even see and recognize happy conduct, just and bad deeds. The difficulty arises – and philosophy emerges – when we seek to translate this information into nouns – happiness, justice, evil – and this is where logic, an internally coherent language-based system choreographing units of information into structures of knowledge, properly emerges. The foundational assumption of language – the transcendent or immutable character of entities denoted by nouns – is akin to and reasserted by the ideological premise of training, that expertise is consistent of more or less fixed and attainable elements and that the cultivation of these units shall enable their ever-increasing complexification in routines and ultimately performances, whether sporting, academic, vocational or recreational. What thinking has offered to this ideology, and offered more assertively and urgently since the scientific age, is the compulsion for units to be directed towards a cogent objective: that routines of practice, like routines of thought, are required to be consistent of organized and internally coherent elements. Furthermore, that just as with trains of thought these routines may seek and motivate *better practice.*

Alison Hodge writes in her introduction to *Twentieth Century Actor Training* that while 'Western culture has enjoyed a long history of actor apprenticeship', it has not exhibited 'the systematic traditions of actor training that are integral to Eastern performance cultures'.[80] She cites Noh theatre (c. 'fifteenth-century Japan') and 'the ancient cance-theatre form' Kathakali as examples of such systematic traditions.[81] While Hodge may be overlooking the systematic traditions of ancient oratory that, as Benedetti and Roach have shown, are antecedent to contemporary acting styles and forms in Europe, Russia and America today or whether she may be dismissing these proto-acting forms is unclear, but she is as one with other scholars in seeing the beginning of the twentieth century as an 'explosion of interest in the power and potential of actor training … in the West'[82] due to the 'widening influence of objective scientific research'.[83] Hodge describes a hungry search by 'Western European practitioners' for 'absolute, objective languages of acting that could offer models, systems and tested techniques to further the craft'.[84] This attempt at 'rationalising the acting process' typified by Stanislavski's 'seminal texts' led to 'increasingly pedagogical aims' and 'to the opening of a number of new studios, schools, academies, laboratories and theatres throughout Europe and the United States'.[85] In Hodge's view, the burgeoning of systems and schools of actor training was due to three factors: 'knowledge of Eastern traditions', 'the influence of objective scientific research' and 'the rise of the theatre director'.[86]

What has become apparent through the postmodern age – and to the present day, an age for which, as far as I am aware, no sound 'ism' has yet predominated – is that science has in many instances established itself as metaphysics' opposite. 'Modern science', writes Arendt, 'relies on Being and Appearance having parted company' such that the 'philosopher's special and individual effort is no longer needed to arrive at some "truth" behind the appearances'.[87] Scientists depend upon appearances, she explains, so as 'to find out what lies beneath the surface' and by the means of 'sophisticated equipment' the scientist 'deprives' appearances of 'their exterior properties' in 'order to find out what lies beneath'.[88] 'Modern science's relentless search for the base underneath mere appearances' has given 'new force' to the 'old argument' of philosophy – the 'logical fallacy' or the 'dichotomy of Being and Appearance',[89] Arendt opines.

As Arendt contended, the first 'entirely new notion' brought in by the modern age of science was the seventeenth-century idea of 'an unlimited progress', which 'within a few centuries became the most cherished dogma of all men living in a scientifically-oriented world'.[90] By the twentieth century it would seem that training had emerged, in the Western world, as the means that would transpose this futurological promise into the lives of individuals. Just as the sciences could forecast humankind *getting better*, training emerged across numerous fronts as an accessible means by which individuals could *get better now*. As I discussed in *Anatomy of Performance Training*, the role of training as an 'emergent ideology' must be seen 'in the context of the volume of research into globalised culture, and more specifically the international New Age movement and its relation to "mainstream" media and workplace culture'.[91] As 'personal growth', 'self-development' and the realization of one's 'individual potential' have become core principles of a globalized culture ever-expanding across the globe so too has, as Paul Heelas puts it, 'to change for the better' become so 'widely adopted' that it may be said that 'our culture amounts to the "age of training"'.[92] Steve Bruce has shown that the expansion of this culture can be measured by the extent to which all people are influenced by these principles in all areas of their everyday life.[93] Andrew Ross and Wendy Parkins have shown how these values permeate culture explicitly, through business management and consultancy training cultures.[94] Paul Heelas,[95] Richard Roberts,[96] Hildegard Van Hove[97] and Adam Possamai[98] all emphasize the global reach of these principles, and I have discussed in my previous book how these 'propositional' values are circulated and entrenched by training activities in the twentieth and twenty-first centuries.[99]

For Arendt, scientific thinking is not thinking as such – it is an 'enormous prolongation of common sense reasoning'.[100] This is not to say that scientific thinking is deficient but rather that it is a particular order of thought attached to the ancient dichotomy of Being and Appearance and allied with the seventeenth-century ideal of progress. Similarly, training forms as they have proliferated during the age of science are not deficient but rather a subset of the training genus especially concerned with progress and the completion of specific objectives and aims as opposed to an open-endedness. What scholars such as Hodge are seeing as the emergence of actor training in the Western world in the modern age is actually the predominance of a hyper-rationalized and hyper-rationalizing subset or subspecies of the training genus. This 'modern training' has been characterized by activeness and goal-directedness and is especially preoccupied by progress. In other words, this is training in modernity and training as an engine for modernity.

Despite scepticism about modernity and the project of progress as such, many training practices, including actor training, seem to be largely immune or indifferent to this countermovement and are continuing to thrive and to proliferate a very specific training doctrine and ideology of 'self-improvement'. This doctrine is exemplified by the already-legendary (and actually non-existent) 'marginal gains unit' in British Cycling. Over two successive Olympics (Bejing 2008; London 2012), British Cycling (the main national governing body for cycle sport in Great Britain) went from being 'King of the Qualifiers', or, in other words, as British cycling legend Sir Chris Boardman put it, not up to it 'when it mattered',[101] to being the most successful British team in any sport at a world and Olympic level. Although there was never a marginal gains 'unit' as such, the 'philosophy' of achieving 1 per cent increases in performance in every possible area of competitive cycling so as to deliver definitive aggregate effects in competition was, and is, central to the efforts of the coaching team. Often associated with Performance Director (or Head Coach) Sir David Brailsford, the marginal gains approach also extended to technical advancements and the (actually existent) Secret Squirrel Club, headed by Sir Chris Boardman. Boardman travelled widely and consulted with 'the military, F1, academic, [and] aviation [experts]' to seek out relatively small improvements to cycling technology which accumulatively would add to the competitive edge of British Cycling.[102] Accusations that the British cyclists rode on 'magic wheels'[103] and that their plasticated skinsuits – now banned – were securing anti-competitive advantages abound, but the Secret Squirrel Club always stayed within the guidelines of the International Cycling Union. Team Sky, the all-conquering professional bicycle racing team established by Brailsford, has extended the marginal gains approach to as many aspects of cycling and cyclists as possible. Team Sky rider Tao Geoghegan Hart revealed in a recent interview with *Cyclist* magazine a Howard Hughes-like attention to personal hygiene – 'a bloke attempted to take my smartphone off me and scan in the flight's barcode. No thank you – he's touched a thousand of those in the past couple of hours'. 'Pass me an infection', says Geoghegan Hart, 'and that could be two weeks off', but 'it's even worse when you're on the plane ... just think how many people have flicked through the in-flight magazine – although that's nothing compared to the food trays. They're rarely washed and are purportedly 10 times dirtier than your average toilet seat. Would you eat lunch off a toilet?'[104] Summarily, in support of Team Sky's new focus on hygiene control, he remarked, 'tell any bike rider that if you do this [follow hygiene protocols] you'll reduce the chances of being sick by 50% and they'll do it'.[105]

Scientific approaches to training, exemplified by Brailsford and Team Sky, are reliant upon knowledge acquisition and application. They are obsessive of control and thus address not the wholeness of practice but rigorously delimited domains within it about which knowledge can be generated and applied. 'The thirst for knowledge', as Arendt calls it, 'never leaves the world of appearances altogether; if the scientists withdraw from it [the world] in order to "think"', this 'is only in order to find better, more promising approaches, called methods, toward it'.[106] Science, in this respect, is indeed an 'enormously refined prolongation of common-sense reasoning in which sense illusions are constantly dissipated just as errors in science are corrected',[107] and this description of scientific thinking is an exemplary description of Stanislavski's approach to the problem of acting throughout his three major works on the subject.

Lessons and adages in Stanislavski's writings are invariably derived from problems in practice just as pedagogic principles in the work of his followers invariably present themselves as solutions to difficulties in performance. While the idea that actor training should be pedagogic is at least as old as Quintilian and Cicero, the idea that it should be 'coherent, logical – systematic'[108] comes fully into being, as Jean Benedetti writes, with Stanislavski who establishes his approach as primarily remedial, as opposed to instructional, and eminently scientific. The first lesson of Stanislavski's first book, the only book on actor training whose editing and publication was overseen by him during his life time, regards the performance of a scene from *Othello*. The 'exhibition performance', as Stanislavski calls it, is in intent an audition for the 'great director'. Perhaps significantly Stanislavski returns to this same performance of *Othello* in his third and final book as the source material for his latest methodology – the method of physical actions – and in both his first and last teaching on the subject of acting he uses the metaphor of a train journey: 'my favourite places [in the performance of the scene] flashed by like telegraph poles seen from the train',[109] he has Kostya recount in *An Actor Prepares*. In *Creating a Role* and the 'improvisation on *Othello*', he has Tortsov observe that the various 'intermediate objectives' 'flashed by like so many telegraph poles'.[110]

What began as merely the 'extremely complicated creative work'[111] of actor training, which must 'create consciously and rightly'[112] because 'to play truly means to be right, logical, coherent',[113] to develop 'conscious technique' and 'the intelligence of an engineer',[114] is consolidated, in *Creating a Role*, into the programmatic form that Stanislavski appears to have been seeking from the outset: one role consisting of one 'superobjective which contains in itself all the other units and objectives', five objectives in each act 'with a total of twenty to twenty five for the whole play'.[115] Perhaps, with reference to the engineer, the organization of these units and objectives is achieved for the actor in the metaphor of a 'railway [map] with its large and small stations, flag stops'.[116]

There is little doubt that Stanislavski 'wanted his ideas to be scientifically valid',[117] as Jean Benedetti put it, and was at pains to emphasize what he saw as the scientific virtues of his work – its logic, coherence, systematism and reference to new quasi-scientific ideas about the subconscious. Furthermore, all of Stanislavski's writings on the subject of acting and all of his exercises for actors are remedial. They typically begin with the expression of a problem, its description and analysis. The illustration (the problem) is an image of something that should not be so or, in rarer cases, of something as it should be. The perfect example (the solution) is already known, albeit in most cases in Stanislavski's writing only to the director and not to the performer providing the illustration. The trope introduced in his first book, *An Actor Prepares*, whereby the neophyte, Kostya, makes countless naive errors and achieves the odd accidental success under the watchful and expert eye of the director, Tortsov, is one that persists into his later works. Even in the final vignette of the final book – an appendix entitled 'Improvisations on Othello' – Stanislavski depicts the hapless Kostya alongside his ineffectual colleague, Paul, both failing to convincingly play Iago and Othello under the sagacious gaze of *the Director*.

The literary device of the trainee-actor-as-negative-example is embodied by Kostya's various descendants. To give just four examples, where there are many: Grotowski's 'courtesan actor',[118] Brook's practitioners of 'deadly' acting,[119] Donnellan's 'blocked' performers[120] as well as in Uta Hagen's redress to 'formalism',[121] among players. These actor-trainers, and their literary outputs, are explicitly goal-directed, working within a discourse wherein the objective (of 'good' acting) is both known and knowable and identifiable objectively. The fatalistic causality and extreme irreducibility and reproducibility that are key tests of scientific endeavour – doing *x* will result in *y* in all cases – survive in some form within these works even though an apology must be made at some stage for the vagaries of artistic enterprise. Benedetti laid down the archetypal formation of this apology in his 1984 publication, *Stanislavski: An Introduction*, which begins by stating that 'anyone who imagines that the System will yield results' in and of itself without the proper application of input 'will be disappointed'.[122] While with a little more rhetorical subtlety but entirely the same intention, Declan Donnellan, in his introduction to Benedetti's edited *An Actor's Work*, cautions actors to 'slow right down' because results will never come for those who demand, *'just show me the steps and I'll follow the plan!'*[123] Later, Donnellan appears to push this apology for art's capriciousness to desperate heights when, with a thinly veiled comparison between dogma in art and '[religious] fundamentalism of the present century', he writes, 'great spiritual leaders stress that, when there is a conflict between the letter of the law and the spirit of the law then, without exception, it is the spirit that must prevail'.[124]

The promise of actor training in the modern age, and indeed of training more generally today, appears to be precisely this – learn the steps, follow the plan and you'll get results. This is reflected in 'the growing desire of students', as Donnellan puts it, 'to acquire skills'[125] and the 'stashing of qualifications and information'.[126] As Donnellan acknowledges, this is 'fair enough'[127] in today's context, but for him, 'the current consumerist tendency in education which prizes only the acquisition of visible skills' is not 'as worrying as the increasing clamour for certainty'.[128] Returning to the trope, he writes that there is no 'step-by-step or fail-proof process to act well or make good theatre … there simply isn't', and returning to the comparison, 'just as no religion with a first-you-do-this-then-you-do-that system can guarantee redemption'.[129] 'Stanislavski was', according to Donnellan, 'at pains to point this out'.[130]

This may be an unwelcome state of affairs for many, including Donnellan, but it is perversely a product of Stanislavski's desire for actor training to be scientific. The futurological promise of scientific thinking is precisely that of certainty or, to use scientific terminology, causality, to detect in the present an immutable principle and to provide an unbroken and unbreakable chain-link to tomorrow. This is integral to progress, which by definition is a consolidation and a motion inexorably forward. This is not to lay blame at Stanislavski's door but in his own desires for training, and in the appropriation and co-opting of his desires, ideals and approaches by subsequent generations the fundamentalist clamour for certainty was bequeathed as a corollary of highly efficacious methodologies for generating predictable results.

With apparent disdain for the open-ended thinking of philosophy, Stanislavski wrote, 'art ends where philosophy begins',[131] and yet, paradoxically, Stanislavski's methods for and approaches to training artists rest not only upon the scientific ideal of progress but also upon the most central intellectual premises laid down at the beginnings of Western philosophy, which are, as Arendt noted, at odds with scientific thinking. Although training of all sorts is founded upon an ideology of the 'unending perfectability of the human species' which, according to Arendt, first became prominent in the eighteenth-century Enlightenment,[132] actor training from Stanislavski until now has represented a means to both grapple with the real-world limitations of our human abilities and to transcend these limitations.

This dichotomy finds a parallel in Kant's distinction between intellect (*Verstand*), which 'desires to grasp what is given to the sense', and reason (*Vernunft*), 'which wishes to understand its meaning'.[133] 'What science and the quest for knowledge are after is *irrefutable* truth, that is, propositions human beings are not free to reject',[134] wrote Arendt. Our 'desire to know, whether it arises out of practical or purely theoretical perplexities, can be fulfilled when it reaches its prescribed goal', and this activity 'leaves behind a growing treasure of knowledge' for generations and civilizations.[135] 'The thinking activity, on the contrary, leaves nothing so tangible behind', she goes on to state. However, 'the most that we can expect from it' is to extend our horizon (or use of reason, as Kant had it) beyond the horizons of appearance (or 'the limitation of the sensorily given world', in Kant) and that would be to 'eliminate the obstacles' by which a scientific thinking restrains itself.

In Kant this distinction risks meaninglessness precisely because of the unfalsifiability of a 'thinking activity' that requires no connection to the so-called real world of sense perception.[136] Nonetheless, even if the differentiation cannot hold as a proper distinction the description of scientific thinking as a particular branch of thought obtaining fulfilable desires is credible to Arendt.

Thinking is both experientially and in its various philosophical definitions open-ended. This is because we can only properly think about that which we do not already know and because we do not already know it we cannot anticipate it, plan or account for it. Thinking is done by degrees; it is done by accretion. What Arendt calls 'thought trains' arrive at more or less cogent conclusions and depart from the more or less cogent conclusions of other trains of thought. This timeless process – as Arendt has said, we have always taken for granted humankind's need to think – is both systematic and wholly unpredictable. It is organized and rule-governed without being bound to causality or certainty. It is reliable and yet cannot be relied upon to ever reach any given end. While it would appear to be possible to become better at thinking, thought, as Heidegger wrote, begins with its own inadequacy and can perhaps at best only represent its efforts to grapple with a world which may or may not incline itself towards our own human understanding.

Scientific thinking has adopted the rigour of thought and utilized it within a proscribed domain that may ensure knowledge generation precisely because the domain prescribes the existence of knowledge. Where thinking begins with a problem – *why is this so?* – scientific thinking begins with a hypothesis – *this is so because of …* or, tacitly, *is this so because of … ?* – and by the various procedures of experimentation and testing the hypothesis is either proven or disproven. Scientific thinking cannot fail to generate knowledge even if it may or may not ultimately find the cause of *this*.

Akin to the ancient philosophical method of deduction, scientific thinking is a method of negation. Knowledge it generates may be in the negative form – *this is so not because of* – and the accrual of negatives will, within its own ideological premise and conceptually at least, produce a positive answer. In differentiation from thinking, scientific thinking proceeds from that which we *do* know. Each enquiry into why *this is so* develops its hypotheses in the spaces left between all the negative answers hitherto accrued. Scientific thinking is goal-directed. It precedes by asking specific and answerable questions and by applying cogent and stringent methods that will, within its own terms, permit the question to be answered. It is, as it were, a subspecies of thought, not deficient but capable only of asking about what is already known. It is thinking maintained within what Arendt called the world of appearances.

Certainly the rise of what Eugenio Barba called 'the age of exercises'[137] in the twentieth century has coincided with the insurgence of scientific thinking across more domains of human life, since the Enlightenment and even more intensely throughout the last century. Training for sport, for the workplace, for actors, dancers and practitioners of all kinds has demonstrated an increasing inclination towards scientific thinking during this period. Indeed, in the arts and in sport this would appear to be especially so and perhaps this has helped to legitimate practices that have faced criticism for their non-empirical and non-utilitarian nature and to secure their value to a society increasingly enthral to empiricism, utilitarianism and functionalism.

Training has also been able to transpose the futurological ideology of progress integral to science into the lives of individual humans and to deliver progress, which is otherwise the preserve of generations, to and into the human lifespan.

Despite the diversification and dissemination of training ideology during a period of globalization,[138] training also maintains an ontological connection to the open-endedness of thinking per se. With reference to Benjamin Spatz's excellent work, while each context has delimited and determined 'what a body can do' in every case training remains an open-ended and experiential investigation of what *this* body, *my body*, can do.

Scientific thinking – data-driven and goal-directed – has, evidently, been greatly beneficial in competitive environments of practice both in the sporting sense and in a broader social sense, for example, in competition between individuals in the job market. As scholars, including Seton[139] and Leahy,[140] have shown, the acquisition of specific competencies (and especially their acquisition from specific institutions) has secured 'professional advantages' for actors and performers. Some, such as Leahy, have suggested that at a social level this has been especially harmful both to practices and to individuals.[141]

Just as thinking is an organizing and organized principle maintained by humans in response to the seemingly disorganized or simply unknowable and discontinuous flow of existence, training is the means by which our human capabilities can be modulated in response to that flow. In the generation by humans of a time continuum out of what Arendt calls the indifferent flow of sheer change, organization – the accretion of small things and their patternation as larger, complex things – has secured the future as a certain and in some way knowable realm of and for human existence.

5
ADAPTATION

Adaptation is a readily recognizable trait of biological organisms from the cellular level through the organs and systems and even conspicuously so at the most perceptible levels of surface appearance. The findings of evolutionary biology have been so thoroughly dispersed across and integrated by the systems and institutions of twenty-first-century civilizations that an understanding of adaptation as a survival trait of species has become a principle of business success and social progress, as well as a personal mantra for citizens and notably performers. Literary examples of this abound, ranging from business to showbiz and from the tongue-in-cheek to the downright bad-taste, including Eric Mark's *Business Darwinism: Evolve or Dissolve, Adaptive Strategies for the Information Age*,[1] Alex Symon's *Mel Brooks in the Cultural Industries: Survival and Prolonged Adaptation*[2] and Arnalee Newitz's *Scatter, Adapt and Remember: How Humans Will Survive a Mass Extinction.*[3] The literary genre of the survival handbook would appear to have proved especially popular in professional fields where employment is scarce or precarious, such as acting, where one can read *The Actor's Survival Kit*,[4] *An Actor's Survival Guide*,[5] *The Actor's Survival Handbook*[6] and countless other treatises on the necessity for adaptation amid a hostile employment environment. Pierre-Michel Menger has focused scholarly attention on the hostility of this employment environment in relation to the 'unusual nature of artistic labour'.[7] Menger notes that art and sport are distinct from other professional fields to the extent to which they each depend 'heavily on the format of the tourney of comparison'.[8] Menger also notes that art has 'many more temporal scales for weighing merit [even when compared to sport]':[9] *daily*, by box-office receipts and downloads, *weekly* with lists of best-sellers and hits, *annually* with prizes and *very long term* or *indefinitely* 'when the most famous or accomplished artists are invited into the various pantheons that celebrate and consecrate art as a great and enduring human achievement' and one 'worthy of universal and eternal admiration'[10] down through the generations. Art, it would seem, is both a personal survival project and a heritable commodity.

There is a fine distinction to be made between the biological traits of adaptation and heritability: adaptation denotes the facility of organisms to change (typically advantageously in survival terms) in response to environmental factors, whereas heritability describes the capacity for species to pass changes on to future generations. Although adaptations in species can arise and apparently have arisen as the result of genetic mutation, as a characteristic of biological life adaptation refers to the more or less purposeful changes made by organisms in response to their environments. In this sense, adaptation is a largely behavioural phenomenon although behavioural choices will by their nature impact on various aspects of organisms and their social groups from diet to feeding, rearing, hunting, resting, sleeping, inhabitation, grooming and also, especially in the case of humans, performing.

In the human species our capacity to adapt has a strong sociocultural dimension given that humans are living in increasingly complex cultural environments. Adaptation, for humans, often concerns adapting to the environments produced *by* humans and to the various opportunities, challenges and dangers arising from what Arendt calls our 'work'. Work, according to Arendt, is the process that produces 'use-objects'[11] and is closely associated in our present moment with the ideal of progress, discussed in ORGANIZATION. The frantic advancements of technology in what has been called our 'digital age' were foreseen with trepidation by Arendt who, as early as 1958, suggested that 'the question [regarding technological progress] … is not so much whether we are the masters or the slaves of our machines but whether the machines still serve the world and its things' or whether, 'on the contrary, they and the automatic motion of their processes have come to rule and even destroy the world and its things'.[12]

Margaret Betz Hull has suggested that 'had Arendt lived to see our present reliance on computers – both actual and psychological – there is no doubt that she would have strongly disapproved'.[13] Daren Barney has observed, in *Community in the Digital Age: Philosophy and Practice*, that Arendt was decidedly positive about the durability of things made by human hands and about the need for the fabrication of a 'common world of enduring things about which disappearing beings are gathered'.[14] Nonetheless, Arendt's abiding argument about the products of work – the various use-objects cluttering up the world as they become obsolete and increasingly un-useful – would appear to be that they may be diminishing the sociality of humankind and driving humans towards a form of self-annihilation from which even the protocol to *Scatter, Adapt and Remember* will not bring salvation. The perils to life and the imperative to survive would appear, according to Arendt, no fewer in these contemporary self-generated environments than they were in the imagined realm of prehistoric nature where humans competed directly with other animals for resources. In fact, as Arendt appeared to forecast, humankind has, through the relentless progress of modernity and the 'victory of the *animal laborans*',[15] brought its own destruction firmly within its own control. Whether humankind's extinction is wrought directly by choice, as in mutually assured global nuclear destruction, or indirectly by irredeemable planetary neglect it would be largely incidental to the causal root of our demise in the deeds of our own hands, and this perhaps gives context to Annalee Newitz's exhortation to humans to adapt.

Training plays a crucial role in both the probability of extinction and the possibility of salvation for humans amid an increasingly threatening environment that humans themselves have helped to create. The myopic fixation of *animal laborans* on progress at all costs, which Arendt describes as a threat to our species survival, counterpoints the sociality of *homo faber* which has anticipated a check on *technê* and proposed 'consequence' as a more ethical alternative to 'outcome'. With regard to our animal and ethical nature training has, since at least antiquity, given itself as the means by which humans have brought the biological trait of adaptation within their own control and driven adaptations not in the direction of environmental pressure but in the direction of human expectation and desire.

Milo of Croton, the fabled wrestler of antiquity, was said to have developed his unrivalled strength by the precocious application of the principle of adaptation. As a child, Milo would lift the same calf each day thereby loading himself with extra weight as both he and the calf grew. Ensuring a continual 'overload' by systematically lifting progressively heavier weights, Milo apparently provides the first (and seemingly isolated) historical example of a rigorously systematic strength training programme.[16] Overloading is a specific methodology of training forcing adaptations at the level of systems and cells by the application of behavioural changes and patterns. While some adaptations may be painless or indeed serve to make living less painful, in general overloading the body is always and unavoidably painful and in the fields of sporting competition overloading is regarded as 'a basic principle of training'.[17] As Thomas Reilly writes in *The Science of Training*, this basic principle entails 'that the biological system to be affected is overloaded … otherwise there is no requirement for the body to adapt'.[18] Adaptation, for athletes, is the characteristic of life that allows for not only improved practice but also competitive superiority. As the swimmer Russell Page-Dove explained to me, the difference in technical ability between top-level athletes is very minimal and swimmers will typically perform within split-seconds of their personal bests at competitive level, and so the adaptive capacity of a body and the suitability of a training regime to exploit that capacity are instrumental in determining success in competition. In the sporting context of swimming, training, like most athletic training programmes, is managed in schedules or 'cycles': in this case, six-week cycles with the first two weeks being, in Page-Dove's words, 'deepest darkest training'[19] during which the body is most seriously and consistently overloaded. At this elite level the overloading is extreme. Page-Dove told me of training to the point of vomiting daily and this is by no means an atypical response to overload.[20]

In sporting contexts, overloading brings benefits to strength, power and endurance which when coupled with technique, tactical and strategic practice can deliver competitive success. In recreational fitness practice, and in what Alphonso Lingis calls the 'cult' of bodybuilding, overloading may serve to be not only the basic principle of training but the seeming sum total of training activity. Lingis describes bodybuilding and to a degree by extension the booming recreational fitness industry as producing musculature to provide a 'second[ary], expressive role for which the other animals have evolved distinctive organs-to-be-seen … peacock tails … crests … coiled horns' and 'lustrous pelts'.[21] As Wolfgang Fuchs writes, Lingis 'points to a clear distinction in contemporary culture' between practices, such as bodybuilding, with an 'inherent goal of turning the body into a spectacle' and the 'virtuous body' obtained by athletes.[22] The first 'we find grotesque and the latter noble', because it is 'ready to undertake tasks' while the former exists only for purpose of its own display.

Arendt might challenge this hierarchy in light of her observations that a readiness to perform tasks is not inherently good, especially given the disastrous potential of both work and action.[23] She would no doubt also question whether the 'metaphysical fallacies'[24] that value depth over surface might be inversions of the proper order in light of the evident primacy, value and necessity of a world of appearances. As Arendt asked provocatively, 'could it not be that appearances are not there for the sake of' depth but rather the contrary, 'since we live in an appearing world', 'is it not much more plausible that the relevant and meaningful' should 'be located precisely on the surface'?[25]

Wolfgang Fuchs notes that Lingis describes bodybuilding as a kind of 'evolutionary feedback effect', 'strangely incompetent and counterfunctional'.[26] Perhaps thereby, Lingis reiterates on behalf of contemporary society the tenacious resilience of what Arendt calls the 'two world theory'.[27] In this theoretical view, 'true' being resides beneath 'mere'[28] appearance, and this 'metaphysical hierarchy', although intellectually reversed by the revaluing of appearance, remains strong in the collective consciousness of Western societies.[29] If, in light of the resilience of the metaphysical hierarchy of depth and surface, physical training for sport and more latterly for a thing called 'fitness' have had to suffer a phenomenological prejudice against non-functionalism,[30] then the training of actors has also been impelled to justify itself on utilitarian grounds. Paul Roseby, the artistic director of the National Youth Theatre, was reported in both *The Stage* and *The Guardian* as saying that drama school training was a 'waste of money' for the 'majority of actors' because 'you don't need to learn how to act, you need to learn how to sell yourself'.[31] Instead of a formal three-year training, Roseby suggested that all most actors require is what he called 'modular courses' and only 'every so often' in order to obtain employment. Pilloried by Edward Kemp, the director of the Royal Academy of Dramatic Art, for suggesting that 'improved marketing skills are all that are required to make a talented young person capable of performing *Hamlet*, or playing a lead in a West End musical or a major movie',[32] Roseby promulgated a popular and tacitly accepted view that 'you can either act or you can't'[33] and that actor training might only be worthwhile insofar as it can ensure employment.

Nic Ridout, commenting on the conditions of employment for actors in 'the modern city', has rather un-bathetically described these workers as 'professional specialists'[34] – wage slaves who must secure their 'livelihood by the acquisition of specialist training'.[35] In the terms in which Ridout describes them, these actors appear to fall between the two stools of the grotesque and the noble – a 'group apart', yes, 'more beautiful, perhaps, more agile, more powerful and subtle of voice', and yet also mere 'representatives', 'actors' rather than 'human beings, in all their diversity'.[36] In somewhat derisive prose, Ridout depicts these creatures as almost sacrificial – 'chosen on the basis of some initially describable attributes' – and heavily processed, 'honed and refined by means of professional training'.[37] Actors appear in contrast to their more authentic-seeming animal counterparts – dogs, horses, bears, birds – all of whom although pre-historically imbricated with humankind via systems of training and husbandry would appear to maintain for Ridout a kind of nobility elusive to most actors. Animals, for Ridout, are representative of a kind of semiotic integrity because of their recalcitrance to being 'naturalised out'[38] of the theatrical scenario.

From the perspective of the human imagination, the apotheosized functionalism of animals – their sheer capacity to *do* which, as Ridout explains, undermines their ability to represent – provides them with an ethical advantage over humans who do not know how to act but instead must make an effort of will in order to act well.[39] As I contended in *Training for Performance*, animals cannot be unproblematically included in any ontological consideration of training because their inclusion would require assigning to them consenting-powers which would also obtain ethical responsibilities that, as Roger Scruton showed, would 'weigh so heavy on the predators as to drive them to extinction'[40] and even for their prey would be a 'gross and callous abuse'.[41] Owing to the perfect functionalism of animals, they cannot be agents in the philosophical sense pertaining to humans. Ridout and Scruton's excellent writings on animals and agency notwithstanding, Squire Gordon, a character in Anna Sewell's prototypical 'animal autobiography' narrative *Black Beauty: The Autobiography of a Horse*, has expressed this impasse most elegantly: 'God had given men reason by which they could find out things for themselves', but 'He had given animals knowledge which did not depend on reason' and which 'was much more prompt and perfect in its way, and by which they had often saved the lives of men'.[42]

Reason and willing are inseparable functions of human action and agency and responsibility accrues to their compound. Responsibility is, as Arendt has detailed, a concern of both the means and the ends of human action. It is an intriguing historical fact that Thomas Aquinas, the influential theologian of the Middle Ages and a key reference point in Arendt's study of thought, should omit from his philosophy of willing the antique fact that 'there could be an activity that has its end in itself and [which] therefore can be understood outside the means-end category'.[43] According to Arendt, this fact never 'enters Thomas'[s] considerations' because for him, 'every agent acts for an end ... the principle of this motion is in the end'.[44] Aquinas's view that 'it is that the art, which is concerned with the end, by its command moves the art which is concerned with the means', just as the art of sailing 'commands the art of shipbuilding' comes directly from *Nicomachean Ethics*, Arendt writes.[45] Yet, for Aristotle, this is true of 'only one kind of activity, namely, poēsis, the productive arts, as distinguished from the performing arts', where the 'end lies in the activity itself – flute-playing, compared with flute-making', or 'just going for a walk, compared with walking in order to reach a predetermined destination'.[46] This fact that the end-in-itself justification gets lost or perhaps deeply and invisibly embedded in the Western philosophical tradition during the Middle Ages may have something to do with the influence of Aquinas. The end-in-itself principle is a foundational one of the Christian religious orders of which Aquinas was a member but a principle perhaps somewhat peripheral of the new orders to which Aquinas aspired – the Franciscans and the Dominicans. These orders, and especially the Dominicans whom Aquinas joined, cherish lives of religious devotion outside the walls of the cloister and beyond the daily control of an abbot. This may, at least in part, explain why Aquinas did not attend to actions wherein the end lies in the activity itself; Aquinas could be master of his own ends and was, perhaps, less familiar with the existential need to make sense of his purpose in a life of asymmetric subjection.

The remorseless teleology of medieval drama – the sheer fatalism of liturgical dramas, mystery and morality plays and even the farces and masques – suggests a particular fascination with endings both good and bad. The fatalistic narrative form survived into the drama of the Renaissance, as it would seem did Thomas Aquinas himself. Scholars, including Steve Sohmer, have suggested that *Twelfth Night*'s

Quinapalus is a compound of the names of saints Paul and Aquinas, two theological authorities on foolishness and wisdom.[47] Foolishness and wisdom are not, as Aquinas pointed out in *Summa Theologiae*, opposites because 'folly is the way to arrive at wisdom',[48] but rather both have qualities pertaining to reason whereby humans must find answers and make decisions about their means and their ends.

In Aristotle, 'it is quite clear that praxis must be understood in analogy to the performing arts', Arendt explains, 'and cannot be understood in terms of the means-end category', and so it is 'quite striking that Thomas [Aquinas], who depended so heavily' on Aristotle and especially the *Nicomachean Ethics* should have 'neglected the distinction between poēsis and praxis'.[49] Aristotle opposes poēsis and praxis many times in the *Nicomachean Ethics*, most often on the grounds of their different *ends*. Poēsis, as a form of making, entails the producing of things whereas praxis, as a kind of doing, does not produce anything other than itself. Although Aristotle's categories are not concerned with utility as such and yet herein, perhaps, there is the root of a functionalist bias in favour of a particular kind of production that makes 'things'. In Aristotle's examples of the two activities, frequently one serves the other. In the above example, the flute-maker's poēsis is only functional or useful insofar as it serves the flute-player's praxis and yet the flute-player's praxis is categorically secondary to the flute-maker's poēsis precisely because it is reliant upon it. Aquinas carries this causative relation forward and situates poēsis as causal of praxis even if praxis summons and entails poēsis. Training poses something of a problem to these categories and their already slippery mutual exclusivity seeing as its end is both in itself and yet not of itself. Training is not wholly identical with practising (praxis) although it involves it and yet it is not wholly causative of practice (poēsis) although it is precursory to it. What is more, these categorizations become less fixed given that, in the performing arts, the materials involved in production (poēsis) and performance (praxis) are oft the same rather than, in the strict physical sense of poēsis, resultant from one another.

Pierre-Michel Menger, in his book *The Economics of Creativity*, notes that Aristotle justifies or rather valorizes human labour via three different principles, 'individuation', 'contingency' and 'self-realization, in a productive activity that has itself as its own end'.[50] For many people the idea that a practice may be valuable in and of itself is not difficult to grasp or indeed that this value may accrue to a process of self-realization.[51] Equally it is evidently true that the value of a training – such as for football or swimming – can be secured upon the economic outcome of its practice, for example in competition prizes, ticket sales or sponsorship deals and television rights, in the globalized economies of the present day. These two perspectives notwithstanding it is apparent that, as Menger explains, Aristotle 'elaborates [his whole] philosophy of action (*praxis*) and production (*poēsis*) based on the principle of contingency and the indeterminacy of the future'.[52] As Menger sees it, humans live in an 'incomplete world' in which 'human action can modify its course'.[53] Owing to this, 'change is a possibility that always remains open and human action is situated in the gap between potential and actual being'[54] because the 'domain of contingency makes it possible to invent and produce something new'.[55] This domain is, as it were, the playground of 'action'. Tacitly acknowledged throughout Arendt's writings, it is the field in which natality (the production of new *things*), as a philosophical concept, is grounded. However, despite the massive power this domain appears to offer human action, it does not presuppose a causal certainty but rather predicates a gap between cause and effect, an 'obstacle to the actualization' of human potential.[56] This is the nature of contingency and would appear to be the kind of principle that Benedetti and Donnellan refer to in their apologies for actor training.[57]

Time is integral to the principle of contingency, seeing as the cancellation of this principle would entail handing over all human potential to time given that, in this case, the individual could 'express the totality of his potentialities provided that he has enough time to actualize them'.[58] Individual 'failure or incompletion would exist only for lack of time'.[59] However, contingency cannot be cancelled because of the manifest authority of uncertainty in the natural world which, as Menger explains, 'is the bearer of the success as well as the failure of action'.[60] In other words, the indifferent flow of sheer change, as Arendt describes it, disrupts the activity of both praxis and poēsis while also being the backdrop for each. Indeed, it is 'the test of uncertainty that gives creative work its human depth and its greatest satisfactions'.[61] Although not said with reference to the profession of acting or the fraught question of talent addressed in GROWTH, Menger's observation that, therefore, this 'is what explains the social prestige of occupations whose success is uncertain' is pertinent.[62] In this matter, uncertainty about the course of the action and 'the existence of differences in ability between individuals, even if minimal, are essentially linked'.[63]

The manifest reality of the domain of contingency shifts the power and promise of potentiality from the realm of time and places it into human hands. Seeing as time alone cannot ensure or permit actualization with any degree of certainty the human will inserts itself as a bridge between what is *not yet* and what *will be* and, as an expression and activity of the human will, training removes the futurological promise of progress admitted by its organization from the realm of the future and situates it within the present. In this way progress is wrestled from time and brought within the purview of human agency and not only our speculation or memory. While human history would suggest that this movement has given humankind a power not enjoyed by other animals, it has also made the human into an ethical being and one whose, albeit contingent, ability to control the future must be checked and balanced.

Organization in training, the accrual of 'marginal gains' and the application of scientific thinking can be seen as the project of contingency's negation. This will have the desired effect of not so much reinstating potential to the realm of time as suturing the break caused between potentiality and actualization by the unpredictability of the natural world and the fallibility of human actions. The rigorously goal-directedness of organization postulates the end in a direct and uninterrupted continuum with the means. It postulates a causal relationship in which, at least hypothetically, all interruptions between cause and effect can be removed. This has the effect of positing the *end* as a fixed thing and a thing in and of itself to which the *means* can become identical, and this is quite different from the process of an *end unto itself* provided by Aristotle in his valorization of human labour. 'The mental agent cannot be active except by acting, implicitly or explicitly, back upon himself',[64] Arendt tells us, and adaptation can be used to describe the reflexivity with which human beings, through training, are embroiled in an unending arrow-flight towards a constantly moving target. Training is the means by which the human will acts upon itself and is acted upon by itself in the open-ended re-evaluation of self and selfhood.

In training's various discourses, the discourse of the will is paramount. Lay accounts of training, such as those associated with recreational fitness practices and the 'cult' of bodybuilding, amount to homilies for a thing called 'will power' and despite the softening of the 'no pain no gain' rhetoric in more recently burgeoning 'alternative' fitness regimes the implicit requirement for wilful self-overloading remains. Professional athletes take this requirement to an extreme but while it may be relatively simple to comprehend the principle of overloading in the context of sporting trainings appreciating whether or not Thomas Reilly's claim, that overloading is a 'basic principle' of training, is true more broadly is less straightforward.

There are several European and also non-European twentieth- and twenty-first century actor training programmes and regimes that have rather conspicuously and self-consciously adopted the principle of overload. Several of these are described in Alison Hodge's edited collection, *Twentieth Century Actor Training*, and most trace a lineage to Jacques Copeau and or Konstantin Stanislavski.[65] Paul Allain has remarked on Copeau's 'rigours physical, mental and educational training'[66] delivered in rural isolation and on how this has provided a model for Etienne Decroux, Michel Saint-Denis, Jacques Lecoq, and Włodzimierz Staniewski's Gardzienice Centre for Theatre Practices in Poland, as well as for 'Theatre de Complicite [in the UK], Odin Teatret [in Denmark]' and for the archetypal actor-training taskmaster, Jerzy Grotowski.[67] In America, with the Group and in Japan with Tadashi Suzuki, Allain gives further examples of training programmes of 'demanding rigour'[68] and 'exactness'.[69] According to Kameron Steele, an actor who performed in Suzuki's *Dionysus*, 'the training is most useful as a tool to test your own will as an actor, because it's hard to get up and do it everyday',[70] and this certainly resonates with the feelings of some of my own students at the Conservatoire who must begin training classes at 8.30 am.

Classes at the Plymouth Conservatoire begin early and finish late and while this is not a timetable designed to 'overload' students, it does cause them to adapt. If adaptation were only about hardening actors to working unsociable hours its worth in a scheme of training would be minimal and also perhaps questionable. Somewhat paradoxically committed training requiring some level of obedience that entails subjection to the will of others may, in numerous training systems and methodologies, be beneficial to an individual's sense of self-realization.[71] It is this paradox and the dichotomous relation between 'negative' and 'positive' notions of freedom – the 'degree to which no man or body of men interferes with my activity'[72] and the extent to which I am a 'subject not an object ... self directed and not acted upon',[73] as Isaiah Berlin put it – that characterizes training and differentiates it from its close cousin, discipline.[74] The training schedule is not the only aspect by which actor training at the Conservatoire, and generally in drama schools and conservatoires in the UK and beyond, causes a form of overload enabling actors to adapt their own abilities and expand their potential. Stress, and especially the stress caused by emotional exposure, disclosure and public vulnerability, is also an implicit aspect of realist-actor training.[75] It is commonly accepted that an athlete must push her body to its physical limits in training and it would appear to also be tacitly acknowledged, from at least the turn of the twentieth century onwards, that an actor, whom Artaud called an 'athlete of the heart',[76] should push herself to the limits of her emotional capacity. As Susan Sontag puts it, Artaud shows his 'inveterate taste for physical and spiritual effort' in this epithet and also, through his iconic writings, provides a touchstone to the ideal of 'art as an ordeal'.[77]

Grotowski, who, according to Lisa Wolford, 'resisted the pervasive [scholarly] tendency to view his work as part of an Artaudian lineage'[78] made much of his 'inductive' method of actor training – an 'eradication of blocks'[79] rather than an accumulation of skills. Many, including Declan Donnellan in his *The Actor and the Target*, have adopted this rhetoric and also understood it as a totalizing paradigm for understanding actor training per se. Donnellan writes, 'we [as actors] can be taught how not to block our natural instinct to act'[80] and he goes on to assert that 'rather than claim that "x" is a more talented actor than "y" it is more accurate to say that "x" is less blocked than "y"'.[81]

The tautological discourse of detraining[82] has predominated in the latter part of the twentieth century and has tacitly asserted the requirement for a form of emotional or psychological overloading to rid actors of bad habits. As I have argued elsewhere, this 'stripping away'[83] can be seen in context of a broad sociocultural trend in the West, from the 1960s onwards, that tended to pose various back-to-basics therapeutic responses to the perceived corrupting effects of society on the body and self. In the field of late twentieth-century actor training, the personal journey of the fictitious Kostya, constantly wracked with anxiety and feelings of inadequacy throughout Stanislavski's oeuvre, has provided a liturgical figurehead for actors in the realist tradition everywhere. The immolation of the totemic Ryzard Cieslak in Grotowski's *The Constant Prince* has produced an historical record, in vivid imagery, of the ecstasy of the overloaded actor; woken unexpectedly n the middle of the night by Grotowski to be tested on his lines,[84] Cieslak is described by Taviani as a 'miracle actor' whose 'impulse was not to succeed but to go beyond', to 'scale a theatrical Everest',[85] anc he is archetypal for the actors of the Odin Teatret, such as Roberta Carreri, who has described her training as a 'dialogue with tiredness'.[86]

In the 1960s, Cieslak taught 'plastique' exercises to students of the Odin Teatret[87] and left an imprint on the attitudes to and ideologies of training within that group. The commitment in training to 'push beyond exhaustion',[88] and to experience 'what lies beyond exhaustion',[89] and thereby develop new physical, mental and creative skills and abilities is something that, as Carreri says, 'those who do sports ... know ... very well'.[90] 'Transcending the state of exhaustion is the result of an effort of will', Carreri explains. As well as necessary for adaptation, Carreri also sees this effort of will as 'proof of the authenticity of an actor's motivation',[91] verification of an actor's vocation to performing.

Certainly the presupposition that the practice of acting was perilous, physically and psychologically, dates back even beyond the emergence of the seeds of the realist style in Garrick's eighteenth century[92] and the appearance of an English-language lay tradition of public acting during Betterton's seventeenth century. The apparent psychological precariousness of acting and the emotional burden of performing have been witnessed in productions featuring David Garrick and Thomas Betterton and right back to the Ur-actors at the fabled origins of *drama* in ancient Greece. Aulus Gellus testifies to the authentic tears of grief cried by the actor Polus, who, as Electra, mourned an urn containing the ashes of his own dead son.[93] While the belief that acting was an excessive emotional experience is ancient, the contention that actor training must also be excessive emotionally appears to emerge, in the West, with Stanislavski and take proper hold in Europe with Artaud and Grotowski, and in America in the work of the Group.[94] The playwright Arthur Miller, deeply affected by a production by the Group – so much so that he claimed that sixty years on, 'I could still restage certain scenes I saw from the Group ... they were so vivid'[95] – wrote of the time-honoured concept of overloading actors psychologically or emotionally in inverted commas, so ubiquitous is the conception that even the literary master resorted to air quotes when he wrote about how directors might '"break them [actors] down"'.[96]

With reference to the Group, Colin Counsell has joined other scholars in noting Lee Strasberg's 'preoccupation with the expression of emotion'.[97] Counsell has also recorded the largely anecdotal justification for this in the departure of Boleslavsky to America from the Moscow Arts Theatre at a time when 'Stanislavski's interest in emotional psychology was at its height'. This chance occurrence, in Counsell's words, confers 'upon America a lopsided System'[98] despite or incidental to Strasberg's predisposition towards an emphasis on emotion in training anyway.[99]

The psychological burden of performing, and more latterly of training, has also received commentary from scholars such as Mark Seton[100] and Kathy Leahy,[101] who have focused on the socio-psychological effects of institutional values and practices on actors. Some, such as Seton, have made recommendations for improved, safer institutional practices in this regard.[102] My friend and colleague at the Conservatoire, Alex Cahill, whose primary directing experience has been in America, has developed practical pedagogic approaches to addressing the psychological burden of performing and especially for young actors-in-training. Adopting and developing certain applied theatre strategies, Alex has developed a form of shared ritual whereby at the end of rehearsals, actors can disavow and hold at a critical distance the characters they play and thereby obviate some of the emotional baggage accrued through emotion-based workshop exercises.

Overloading alone will not bring about adaptive change. A period of recovery, or 'taper', to use a term from the context of sport training cycles, is necessary to enable overloaded systems and tissues to repair and regenerate effectively overcompensating in their production and causing adaptations in response to the stress of overload. Although swimmers will be pushing themselves towards 'peak' consistently during the earlier phases of the training cycle, peak performances cannot be achieved because the body's systems are so thoroughly overloaded. Peak performance is achieved after a managed period of taper – of slowdown and recovery – and for a six-week training cycle a taper might last two weeks. Swimmers, or rather coaching teams, time tapering and the cycles of training to coincide with competitive events ensuring that maximal recovery and adaptation has occurred in time for competition. The training of actors, even in those exacting approaches described by Allain, does not tend to follow such a systematic approach to tapering in preparation for performance. This is, in part, because of the comparative discontinuity between training and performing as an actor when contrasted with training and performing as an athlete. While athletes embed performance events within training programmes and cycles, professional actors in the UK will typically conclude formal ongoing training upon graduation from a given school and instate a new bipartite relationship between rehearsal and performance. Many actors will pursue more or less formal and organized career-long training, taking classes or workshops with experts and practitioners as they see fit. Many actors working in companies such as Odin Teatret or Suzuki Company of Toga may maintain a more direct relationship between training practice and performance events but many 'jobbing actors' will, by virtue of the professional necessity described by Ridout, find training displaced by the bipartite relationship between rehearsal and production in which any sense of 'tapering' becomes commercially impractical.

Tapers are not, in the case of professional actors, those lulls in between jobs. If the taper is the time during which adaptation takes place, then this time would need to be as purposefully modelled as would overload and not merely the uncontrollable occurrence of interruptions and lacunas to professional employment. The timetable at the Conservatoire permits a kind of 'taper', although, in the tradition of theatrical production that will only finally come together and be 'alright on the night', the taper tends to come after performance and its sometimes frenetic rehearsal period. Class time leading up to second-and third-year productions may increase considerably, with students uncertaking additional rehearsals alongside but following production these hours may 'taper down' and the focus of our pastoral efforts switches to supporting students' self-analysis and auditing of skills and development. Much of the adaptive effect of the formal training of actors is brought about during periods of comparative rest but especially so when these rest periods are deliberately modelled as times for self-reflection. Reflection in training feeds further training and development and in the case of elite sport the reflection is often undertaken as an act of science also, with the analysis of performance data and retrospective assessments of the efficacy of various exercises and drills. Cycles of training, such as Page-Dove's elite swimming programme, are designed to 'taper' towards competition, easing off in the run-up to competition so as to give time for physical recovery as well as tactical and strategic reflection. In the case of actor and performer training, this tends to be less data-driven – in fact it may be omissive or dismissive of data in the form of reviews and grades – and centred on self-realization and awareness. As a good example of this, my colleague and the co-director of Plymouth Conservatoire, the dance film-maker Ruth Way, has written about how her 'main aim' in training performers is 'to shift the focus away from the more goal-oriented training systems and [towards] nurturing students' creative potential and developing reflective practical scholars'.[103] Indeed, writing specifically of yoga practice but stating something broader about training, Way writes that the cycles of 'breath hold such conscious and relaxed modes of being' and that through a focus on breath in training one can 'learn to accept … rest and [to] acknowledge times … when more rest is needed to maintain wellbeing'.[104]

Whether under a discourse of well-being, tapering or of recovery or reflection or self-knowledge, training protects a time of inactivity within the cycles and rhythms of its hyperactivity. In the context of elite sport, this is a moment for data analysis. In somatic movement and contemporary dance training, this is an opportunity for subjective introspection. In actor training at the Conservatoire, this is a period of recovery and reflection and for slowing down to absorb knowledge acquired during the breakneck pace of rehearsal. These times provide for some discernment, by trainees and trainers, about progress and also for the discerning of the likely future limits of possibilities.

The cyclical rhythms of training – their scheduling and their ritualization – position tapering as a terminal and a natal phenomenon. The outcomes, either as objective data or as personally felt and tacit knowledge, become the input for the next cycle of training, informing, guiding, motivating and determining the activities and objectives of the near future. This cyclical pattern is, at the level of generations, perpetual and yet at the level of individual experience it is decidedly finite. This is not only because ultimately Milo's calf will grow to full size but also because Milo himself will also stop growing. As Arendt observed, human life projects itself into the future, into the past and occupies the present by the production of temporality as such and whether conceived in cyclical or linear form the limit to that temporality is purely hypothetical, humankind's apparent drive towards extinction notwithstanding. Individual lives, however, follow a rather more succinct arc, characterized, as Arendt wrote, by 'growth and decline'.[105] The 'developmental process in which an entity unfolds itself in an upward movement until all its properties are fully exposed' will be followed by a period of 'standstill – its bloom or epiphany'.[106] This phase, followed as it is, according to Arendt, by disintegration and complete disappearance, stands in defiance of the flow of sheer change and of the inexorability of human mortality. Glorious in prospect as this time-out-time presents itself to be, in the lived experience of many performers the epiphany is less the summation of all potentiality and more volubly the announcement of an end to training.

In each context that we find training, we may also see the principles of overload and recovery in operation, to greater or lesser and to a more or less self-consciously organized extent. Despite the powerfully teleological nature of training, the massive potentiality delivered to humans by training's exploitation of our adaptive capacity, which obviates the vagaries of contingency, the spectre of the limitations of human potential as such haunts every training enterprise. This is not the capricious gremlin 'uncertainty' that, as Menger observes, is apt to interfere with human endeavours but is the conceptual ceiling atop of human facility that, although in the doctrine of progress remains seemingly untouchable and unreachable, can and does press down upon each individual human. This phenomenon goes by many names across the various fields in which we can experience and identify it. The name used to denote it in the context of elite sporting training has probably achieved the most currency, socially – plateau.

Russell Page-Dove explained it to me like this: 'inevitably, swimmers, like all athletes will reach plateaus in their training, and that's hard'; 'it's hard because you don't know if is the final one or not'.[107] Despite rigorous cycles of training, the improvement to peak performance can be minimal, non-existent and in some cases even negative, and plateauing occurs when no external explanation can be found for why peak abilities have stopped increasing. Plateaus can sometimes be overcome by the modulation of training cycles and exercises, and a process of continual improvement in peak performance kick-started again. Plateaus can also be surpassed when nutritional science or sports psychology, for example, is able to unblock an obstacle to peak performance or when improved technique can be achieved or a 'marginal gain' obtained and elite sporting training is, it would seem, rather good at finding these hidden pathways to a higher ground. However, each of the practitioners of these remedial disciplines, and every athlete too, is also aware of the conceptual limit to an individual athlete's abilities which, whether absolute or circumstantial, will ultimately determine their all-time personal best. Retrospectively, for all performers whether in disciplines of objective standards of attainment or of subjective judgements about achievements, we shall be able to see the total value of all that each person was able to actualize out of the potentiality offered to them by training and by the adaptive capacity of humans which is associated with our own agency amid a contingent world.

The promise of training on behalf of human capacity will forever be futurological. Training has since antiquity brought the future within our almost perfect control and only just beyond our fingertips, knowable and accountable in the most systematic ways and predictable almost to the degree of becoming certain. The longevity of training protocols, exercises, regimes and methodologies, and the epistemological road maps of lineages of 'schools' and 'systems' charted by Ben Spatz[108] and others, is an historical trace of the tantalizing near-certainty obtained by training over the future and the near-supremacy of human will over actuality. And yet in the space of intersection between future possibilities and past achievements wherein training has lodged itself, the past shall be forever hurtling forward in readiness to overtake the *now* and to cast all of its future promise of potential in the immutable light of actuality.

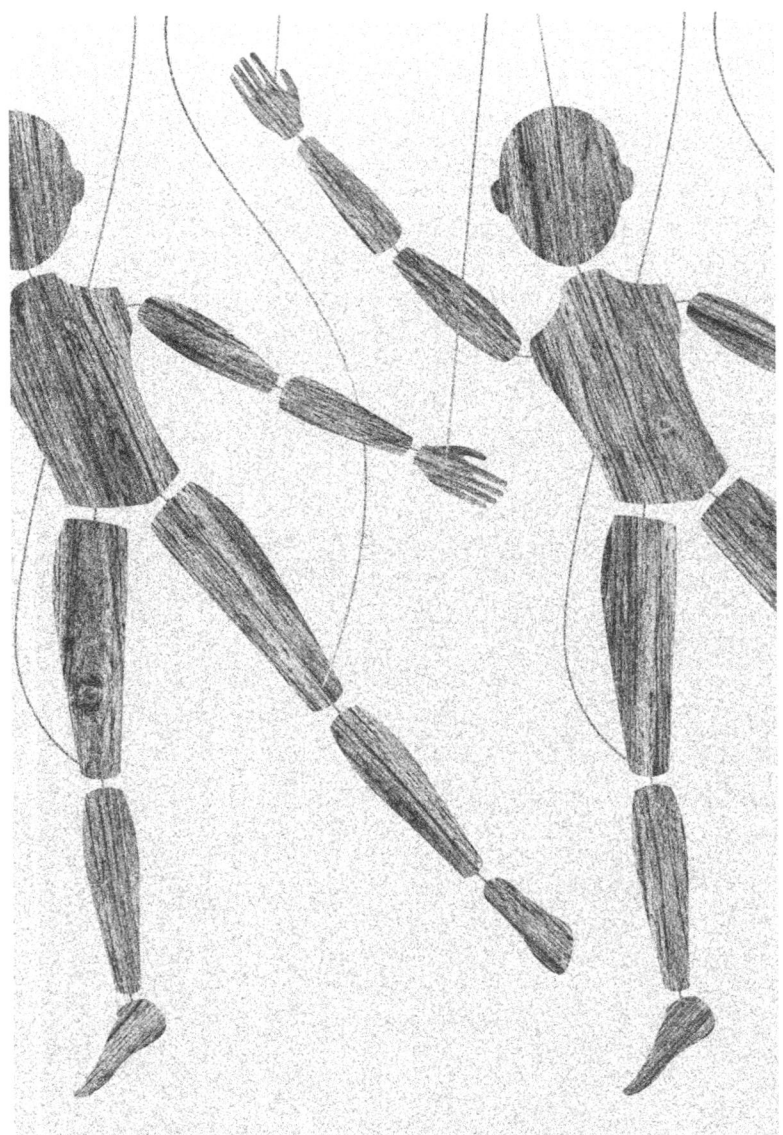

6
REPRODUCTION

When biologists speak of reproduction as a constitutive characteristic of Life and of living organisms they refer to the simple and profound fact that creatures die and species live. Social science has made use of biological reproduction as a metaphor for the facility exhibited by social institutions to maintain themselves throughout successive generations and also for the capacity for values – ethical, political, ideological, aesthetic, etc. – to sustain themselves throughout time via these institutions and even beyond the lifespan of social institutions. Social reproduction has acquired a definition as the means by which deeper currents run through the shallower waters of appearance, the means by which the fundamental and motivating principles of human existence endure covertly beneath surface structures that are more or less superficial, artificial and pertaining to *appearance* rather than *essence*.

Time has clear relation to this phenomenon. Appearance is transient, while essence is enduring. Appearance is of the present, while essence is, definitively, of the past and the future. In this relation, the present – which, according to Performance Studies' orthodoxy, is the place of birth, life and eternal rest for performance events[1] – is illusory and apt to dissemble, while the past and future provide an apparently more secure foundation for meaning. Or, in other words, *mere* appearance is little more than a cipher for *true* essence. Yet, despite this bias, training as a human technology of time may ultimately trouble this relation and invert this time-honoured hierarchy of social theory positing *now* as the primary and most credible tense of our understanding.

The idea that values have tangible and more or less permanent reality bound up with the actions of, and enacting of, social institutions is a central tenet of the cultural materialist perspective which predicated

Base and Superstructure as the 'real' foundation of societies and which more recently has rooted itself in discourse analysis, for which values, in their interpersonal form as power relations, provide the basis for social intercourse.[2] Sheltered in the encompassing shadow of discourse analysis, late twentieth-century performance scholars have tended to see training as the name given to various institutions explicitly concerned with the transference of knowledge. The 'turn'[3] towards embodiment in theatre and performance scholarships has tended to proceed from the assumption that, as Simon Shepherd put it, 'theatre is, and always has been, a place which exhibits what a human body is, what it does and what it is capable of'[4] or, as Benjamin Spatz has more succinctly stated, 'what a body can do'.[5] Here the display of bodies through various practices, and chiefly performative ones, becomes the code for bodies, or the Body as such, and analyses of these displays seek to describe and define knowledge about bodies via acts of display. Appearance, analytically speaking, is germane to this discourse insofar as it is a gateway to depth and to an analysis of *what is really going on* with bodies. In this epistemological view, knowledge is seen as a thing abstruse which may be studied in and of itself and for which bodies provide a material retainer and conduit, even if knowledge remains indivisible from this fleshy envelope. The function of knowledge transfer across generations is seen as a process that *uses* bodies and one which can be witnessed, theorized, celebrated or denigrated, via bodies and the study of bodies.[6]

Knowledge, in the form of ideological premises, can be seen to reproduce across generations by means of the social intercourse of training institutions. As discussed in STIMULATION, Colin Counsell has described this reproduction occurring in the 'style-without-style' misconception of late twentieth-century actor training.[7] Of course, knowledge in the form of ideological premises can evidently be seen to reproduce across generations by means of *all* forms of social intercourse, via the workplace, the family, etc., by virtue of their being social intercourses. Given the propensity for scholars to feed training through the pitiless meat grinder of epistemology in pursuit of better understanding of its intrinsic knowledge, one may be forgiven for seeing training as one of many more or less identical institutions for the propagation of ideological values and the promulgation of power by one group over another. This scholarly effort across multiple disciplines has foregrounded ideology in our understanding of all aspects of training, from selection and initiation to pedagogy, interpersonality and community. For example, the psychiatrists Johannes Cremerius[8] and Arthur Kleinman[9] have meditated upon the ideals expounded through the application of selection criteria to the training experience while the psychoanalysts Marguerite Valentine[10] and Robert Hinshelwood[11] have tracked the relationship between such criteria and the 'fragmented community' of training institutions where 'schools' assert ideological ascendancy in opposition to others. However, training generally and actor training very specifically operate via a model of knowledge transfer that is quintessential to and definitive of its own institutions and their practices. While it may be the case that imitation plays a role in all social institutions, training offers a particularly conscious and explicit intensification of imitation as a fundamental pedagogic principle to an extent that has even set it apart historically from its close relative, education.[12]

Reproduction, in the form of imitation – the form of demonstration and emulation – is a more or less irreducible tenet of training practices. Even in forms of practice which may purport to have no formal technique to be demonstrated, such as Butoh dance,[13] there remain expert practitioners, such as Katsura Kan, Marie-Gabrielle Rotie and Francis Barbe, who teach the form through a highly recognizable pedagogy of the practising of demonstration-based exercises and tasks.[14] Where we find training we shall also find imitative instruction; we shall find experts purporting models of practice and students emulating the practice modelled by experts. This function is formally inscribed in multiple training practices, such as swimming, weightlifting, acrobatics, gymnastics, track and field athletics, musicianship, singing, surgery, bushcraft and, to take a particularly ubiquitous example, the fitness class. Throughout the boom in the so-called 'fitness industry' – an adjunct to the 'leisure industry', one of the developed world's key markets and chief exports to developing economies – the format of the 'group class' led by an 'instructor' has prevailed.[15] The 'fitness boom' insofar as this is an economic phenomenon of capitalism is usually dated to the late twentieth century and to archetypal exercise 'fads' of the 1970s and 1980s, such as the actress Jane Fonda's 'workout' video and various iconic devices of the shopping channels, such as 'ab rollers' and the 'Thighmaster'. Although the lineages of aerobics videos and home exercise machinery owe something quite directly to Francis Lowndes's late eighteenth-century invention, the Gymnasticon[16] – a domestic, solo exercise machine of pulleys and flywheels – they may also be seen in the context of one history of training dating back to antiquity throughout which instruction by imitation has been a key motif.

Ancient Greek and Roman military instruction gradually permeated throughout these respective societies, giving rise to a physical culture of sporting competition and athletic display.[17] The precedents of the Roman Gymnasia and the Greek Olympic Games notwithstanding, it was during the Renaissance that an interest in the body, health and physical education became more widespread across European societies. In 1420, the Italian Vittorino da Feltre opened a school where alongside humanist subjects students practised 'physical education' and by 1553, *El Libro del Ejercicio Corporal y Sus Provechos*, by Cristobal Mendez, was published – seemingly the first book to study the physical benefits of exercise exclusively.[18] The book classified exercises, games and sports and analysed the medicinal effects and ramifications of each, as well as offering guidance on injury prevention and recovery. In 1569, the Italian physician Mercurialis published *De Arte Gymnastica*,[19] which compiled information on the ancient Greek and Roman approaches to exercise as well as diet and hygiene while also detailing principles of physical therapy. It is sometimes considered the foundational text of sports medicine, and it influenced the wave of physical education and training regimes and institutions emerging in Europe two centuries later: in 1774, Johann Bernard Basedow opened the Philanthropinum in Germany providing education through physical exercise and games including wrestling, running, riding, fencing, vaulting and dancing.[20] Techniques were taught by an instructor in a manner very familiar to users of leisure centres and fitness clubs today; so ubiquitous is the practice of physical instruction of groups of people by imitation of one individual that we may tend to think of this pedagogic model as *a priori* of physical training rather than as a dynamic development in practice emergent across Europe in the eighteenth century and identifiable in the numerous institutions modelled on the Philanthropinum, such as the Hauptschule (1786) and the Schnepfenthal Institution (1784).

Before the end of the eighteenth century, the famous Guts Muths, another German teacher and educator, developed the basic principles of 'artistic gymnastics'. His *Gymnastik für die Jugend* (*Gymnastics for the Youth*) was the first systematic textbook in gymnastics (1800), undoubtedly influential over Friedrich Jahn, a German gymnastics educator and fervent nationalist seemingly motivated to train the populace so as to arm against another Napoleonic invasion.[21] In 1811, Jahn opened the first Turnplatz, or open-air gymnasium, in Berlin. His gymnastics movement (pun unavoidable), 'Turnverein', spread rapidly throughout the country and five years later he published *Die Deutsche Turnkunst* (*The German Gymnastics*), detailing fully his gymnastics system. Jahn was the inventor of the pommel horse and horizontal and parallel bars and a proponent of gymnastic rings. He sponsored festivals of gymnastics and physical activity attracting tens of thousands of attendees; the popular focus of these athletic jamborees was nationalism and critics and biographers of Jahn have debated his *völkischness* and influence on Nazism.[22] Jahn was, of course, the prototypical Turnverein instructor – Turnvater Jahn, or 'Father of Gymnastics, Jahn', as his followers knew him – and himself a powerful and self-conscious symbol of the merits of his physical training.

Pehr Henrik Ling, a Swedish physical educator, developed Jahn's gymnastic principles integrating bodily development with ideals of physical beauty. By contrast with the German system, this Swedish approach employed few apparatuses and although Ling invented wall bars he probably can't be held accountable for the Thighmaster. Ling categorized four areas of his system of gymnastics: pedagogic, military, medical and aesthetic. Definitively, all movements had to be performed correctly and collectively under a leader's direction.

Emulation as an instructional model was fully formalized within this physical culture movement and spread as a key pedagogic principle of physical training throughout Europe in the nineteenth century. In Spain, Francisco Amoros founded a military gymnastics school in Madrid and then the Normal Gymnastic Civil and Military School in 1819, publishing *A Guide to Physical, Gymnastic and Moral Education* in 1830. In 1847, the French strongman Hippolyte Triat founded a huge gymnasium in Paris and in the 1870s, following the loss of Alsace-Lorraine, physical education blossomed in French schools. In Scotland, the Highland Games began during the 1830s and a Czech 'Sokol' movement was founded in 1862, inspired by the German Turnverein, wherein ultimately training extended to all economic classes and to women.

This expansive wave across Europe took some time to wash up on American shores, perhaps because, owing to the United States' relative isolation, the motivation for the militarized nationalism underlying and motivating the physical curriculum provided by Jahn, Amoros and Triat was comparatively minimal. By the mid-eighteenth century, Catharine Beecher had developed a programme of calisthenics performed to music and taught at her Hartford Female Seminary from 1823. Many 'Turners' (devotees of Jahn's gymnastic system) emigrated to the United States and in 1824 Charles Beck opened an outdoor gymnasium in Massachusetts, modelled on the Turnplatz. Dudley Allen Sargent was director of the Hemenway Gymnasium at Harvard University at the turn of the twentieth century. There he taught the German and Swedish system and famously challenged the Victorian view of females as feeble and prone to fainting, and encouraged freedom of dress and vigorous activity for girls and women.[23]

In economic terms, we can see this part of the historical narrative as the exposition to the climax of the twentieth-century fitness boom and today's dénouement of a well-organized, global marketplace and industry. Before the end of the twentieth century two fitness entrepreneurs, Georges Hebert and Professor Edmond Desbonnet, had made physical exercise and strength training truly fashionable and truly marketable through the publication of fitness journals and by opening exercise clubs.[24] Frequented only by the wealthy, the First World War undermined this social hierarchy and by the middle of the twentieth century the working classes also started to gain access to this physical culture 'movement' by consuming its various products.

Bernarr Macfadden, a publisher of a fitness journal, staged the first physique contest in America, in 1903, and subsequent competitions in 1921 and 1922 launched one of the fitness industry's greatest ever icons, Charles Atlas. Atlas's '13 Lesson' course was purchased by millions of consumers in the 1920s all buying into the promise of fitness and physical beauty *in just 15 minutes*.[25] Indeed, the late twentieth and twenty-first centuries made fitness ever more marketable as it became ever more consumable, ever more bite-size and accessible and attainable within 'today's busy lifestyle'.

Key to the marketability of exercise regimes and products now, just as it was central to the development of the physical culture 'movement', is instruction by demonstration and education by emulation. Throughout the history of physical culture in Anglo-European societies, we can see this model of instruction by imitation coming in various forms the most recognizable and widespread being the 'group class'. One-to-one or personal instruction, the exercise 'home video' and YouTube tutorial and the quasi-auto-didacticism of the automated exercise machine used both in the gym and in the living room are various different modes for the imitation of physical forms. Emulation has increasingly also included not only an imitation of physical action as a core pedagogic principle but also the imitation of appearance as a quintessential goal of training. This pivot, from *doing like me* to *looking like me*, would appear to have been achieved by Ling and to have reached its apotheosis in Charles Atas, whom every subsequent fitness icon has in some way imitated.

Without wishing to generate yet another linear, Euro-centric history of ideas, the seeds of the principle of training by imitation could be traced right back to Greece and Rome and perhaps further to the military cultures of Assyria, Babylon, Egypt and Persia via some key nodal points in pedagogy. In the early sixteenth century, Desiderius Erasmus (1466–1536) took up Aristotle's interest in imitation as an educational technique and published two books, *The Right Method of Instruction* and *The Liberal Education of Boys*, that each proposed, according to historian of education Edward J. Power, 'sound advice on the use of imitation in teaching the classics'.[26] While it may have been Isocrates (436–338 BC) who properly founded the principle of imitation and emulation in the tradition of teaching oratory, which historically speaking appears to have occupied a space between education and training, he would appear to have borrowed the two principles of 'care' and 'imitation' from writings[27] on physical instruction produced by the 'paidotribes'. Paidotribes were early (*c*. 800–400 BC) Greek proto-PE teachers who, according to extant sources, 'teach students the techniques which have been discovered for [proto-sporting, or physical] competition'.[28] In his glossary of terms of the ancient sporting world, Waldo Sweet defines the paidotribe as an 'athletic trainer'.[29]

Cicero's (106–43 BC) educational code recommended imitation in the teaching of oratorical skill – a practice blurring the already loose distinctions between education and training as a combination of intellect and practical performance[30] – and Quintilian (35–100 AD) also appears to have recognized imitation as both a teaching practice and a human skill.[31] In this tradition, Edward Power describes Chyrsoloras's (1355–1415) entire education code, founded upon 'repetition', as a 'theory of imitation' and one that was 'based on the proposition that what is experienced and assimilated will in the end' have an improving effect.[32]

Foucault's writings on the subject of 'discipline' suggest that theorists should also see this physical culture movement, originating in Greece and Rome and rooting itself in societies from the Middle Ages onwards, as connected to the increasing enmeshment of religion and the institutions of the state. By the dusk of the Middle Ages, imitative training pedagogy was becoming increasingly relevant to both religious education and social conduct. Thomas à Kempis's *The Imitation of Christ* (*c*. 1418–1427) is an important touchstone to this shift, and the medieval guilds in England took this theological premise and applied it throughout the conduct and training of their workforces, deepening the cultural inscription of imitation as sine qua non training within European societies throughout the Middle Ages.[33] The spiritual practice of the imitation of Christ predates à Kempis's seminal work and can be dated to the Pauline Epistles and the monastic practice of the Desert Fathers – the first monastic communities who emulated the life of Christ by a withdrawal from society and into the wilderness of the Scetes desert of Egypt in the third century. This tradition mixes the predicate of training by imitation resurgent in the emerging physical culture of the fifteenth century with the spiritual prerequisite of becoming 'good' by 'doing good', which goes right back to Aristotle, who posited that good virtue was a disposition inculcated by habit[34] and which, as David Torevell has explained, remains a core and highly performative aspect of Christian liturgy today.[35]

As the fitness industry has spread throughout Europe and America, it has participated in the globalizing of commerce along rather familiar lines, appropriating various 'indigenous' physical practices before ultimately marketing these back to their own populations. Neo-Rousseauian fantasies about barefoot running[36] and single-breath swimming[37] influential within contemporary jogging and freediving sports can be situated alongside the Orientalist discourse of martial arts in the West as exemplars of dubious intercultural exchanges in the global conversation conducted in the so-called international language of sport. In this context, one practice, yoga, has perhaps outstripped all these other examples and assumed a place as the most effectively globally distributed fitness practice.

Bhikhu Paarek, in the essay 'Globalisation for a Multicultural World', describes yoga as a quintessential part of a 'thin global culture', 'familiar to all societies'.[38] Paarek places yoga alongside 'Karate, Judo, alternative medicine ... Coca-Cola, McDonalds ... Nike, Adidas ... Rolex, Channel and Levi-Strauss jeans' as 'almost universal' products all of which although not 'equally cherished or even respected by all societies and groups within them, are nonetheless, 'intellectually accessible and intelligible to them all'.[39] The special place and role of yoga in the discourse of globalization has been noted by many scholars, including Jeremy Carrette and Richard King, who have remarked upon the rise of 'yoga entrepreneurs'[40] in the international marketplace for *Selling Spirituality* (the title of their co-authored book on the subject). Others, such as Simon Coleman,[41] have also noted the diffusion of yoga across other globalized religious, quasi-religious and secular practices including in the international spread of 'charismatic Christianity', while Judith Coney has described Sahaja Yoga as a 'global religion' in which the 'somatic experience of ritual provides members with an intimate feeling of belonging to an "international collective"'.[42] The teaching of postural yoga, whether as a fitness practice or as a fundamental religious ritual, is predicated upon the imitation by students of physical forms or postures practised by a yoga teacher. The posture forms of Ashtanga, for example, provide a clear example of the pedagogic role of imitation in physical training: the practising of Ashtanga requires both that students imitate teachers and that teachers imitate fixed forms as they copy, for both their own practice and their teaching, a repertoire of postures.

I asked my colleague at Plymouth Conservatoire, Lee Miller, a qualified Ashtanga Yoga teacher, about how his teaching as a yoga instructor and as a university lecturer compare. 'When I teach trikonasana (triangle pose)', he said,

> I start by standing at the front of the class and doing the posture. Then I use various linguistic strategies to explain what I've done – finding the space between big two and little toe; opening the hips and chest to the ceiling, for example, and then I move about the studio looking at people practicing and laying my hands on them to offer physical corrections to get them closer to the posture form.[43]

'That's not an approach I would take when teaching in a university context', he explains. He finds that there is something troubling about the revelation of yoga teaching's imitative nature and especially in the notion that his students are copying him and that he may therefore provide some form of idealized role model: 'I bridled a bit at that but, of course, that is a fair and accurate description of yoga teaching.'[44] 'For me', he explained, 'it's interesting because I'm also a teacher and I am a very different person when I teach students [of theatre] than I am when I teach yoga'.[45] He ventured that something very interesting happens for him whenever one of his university students attends one of his yoga classes: 'In the yoga studio I might seem both harder and softer', he explained; 'the two [forms of teaching] are each differently "bodied", and also there is a different relationship apparent between the teacher and the thing that they are teaching'.[46] 'I think there is a kind of role-modelling in each', he proffered, 'where the teacher is standing as a kind of ideal, it's just that he or she stands for a different set of ideals in each'.[47]

Seeking to define the difference between education and training can often lead to the imposition of an illusory conflict and, in the history of Western philosophy, this conflict runs as a fault-line through pedagogic theory. Emeritus Professor of Philosophy Peter Rickman, writing in *Philosophy Now*, makes this opposition stark in the title of an article, 'Education versus Training'.[48] Following the familiar narrative, Rickman juxtaposes education where 'people learn to think, make judgements, appreciate the beautiful and the good' with training, which is an acritical practising of 'skills and information'.[49] While there is a ring of validity to this well-worn description of two related but differentiated categories, there is also the palling toll of tautology; the differentiation relies largely upon the self-referential definitions of education and training which inscribe, rather than isolate, this difference. Ultimately, as Rickman acknowledges, the categories cannot be mutually exclusive – there remains 'overlap'[50] – and this sub-irreducibility calls the taxonomical enterprise into doubt.

Most definitions of education and training, and even those offered by emeritus professors of philosophy, tend to derive from the seemingly self-evident facts of day-to-day social conventions rather than being derived by a scrupulous analytical scepticism about categories. Putting forth a rather orthodox view of the differentiation, Rickman associates training with manual tasks – 'we can hardly do without farmers, engineers, doctors, dentists, teachers, builders and so on' – and with 'elementary education' that requires, he suggests, a level of rote learning.[51] Although Rickman concludes his opine to the teaching of philosophy in higher education with a warning that 'to replace education by training is to threaten the human future', he strikes a positive if condescending tone regarding training, observing that 'it is rightly argued that the prosperity of a country, indeed its survival and the quality of life of its citizens, depends on extensive and efficient training in a whole range of skills'.[52]

At a rigorous philosophical level, Rickman's arguments are representative, stereotypical perhaps, of the abiding attitudes towards education and training that have been cultivated within Western philosophy from the germ of Aristotle's *Nicomachean Ethics*, which put forth the case repeatedly that the philosophical life is superior to the political one. Aristotle's central thesis regards human 'happiness' (*eudaimon*) and about and in relation to which he asks what the 'function' (*ergon*) of human beings is. He argues that the function of human beings is to act rationally in accordance with virtue and thereby achieve happiness. In the matter of acting rationally the philosophical life, associated with education, is exemplary.[53] In the opening few lines of his *Ethics*, Aristotle states that the 'good' is that at which all things aim and, in a complexification of the contradistinction between thought and action, education and training, he appears to suggest that all living things exist to imitate the contemplative activity of god.[54] This is, for Aristotle, definitively human: plants and animals, he claims, reproduce themselves only so as to participate in a perpetual series, and this is the closest they can get to the ceaseless thinking of the 'unmoved mover' (in Greek, *ho ou kinoúmenos kineî* and in Latin, *primum movens*). He makes this point throughout his works[55] contending that the happiest human life resembles a divine one and that god is a being of a 'single and simple pleasure [of thought]',[56] whereas humans, because of their complex worldliness, grow weary of what they do.

Hannah Arendt upended this tradition with her three classifications of human work in *The Human Condition* (1958). Of the three she posits 'action', which is essentially the political enterprise of being together and talking about things, as the most superior and, in partial disagreement with Rickman, as the basis of humankind's salvation from itself.[57] While Arendt carries on devoutly Aristotle's commitment to the human and humanizing force of reflective thought she is overtly critical of Western philosophy's tendency to reify thinkers and glorify their thoughts.[58] When transposing Arendt's theorization of the temporal effects of human thinking on the practices of training, it appears that these activities are no less prone to thoughtfulness than is abstract contemplation. This is, in part, because it becomes necessary to recognize the co-dependence of abstract knowledge and phenomenological facts and that even if one activity (education) may be seen to reside more fulsomely in the domain of the former while the other has its home in the latter, as Rickman nonchalantly acknowledges, 'practice may require some theory and education may require some skills'.[59] As Theatre and Performance Studies have more latterly accepted, most distinctions drawn between practice and theory, mind and body, thinking and doing, have been fairly unedifying to both theory and practice as well as to the disciplines of education and training.[60] A more productive and substantive distinction may be drawn, however, in relation to the modes of instruction proposed by the various activities that assemble under the categories of education and training given that, despite the co-mingling of the terms and practices over several thousand years of Western history, generally speaking, all forms of activity that tend to be described as training entail the kind of imitative model of instruction described by Lee Miller, whereas educational teaching may or may not.

What is being taught is less definitive as a distinction than *how* it is being taught and the modes appropriate to the different contexts of training and education. As Miller points out with reference to his roles as both instructor and teacher, the shift between modes accomplished across these two activities is palpable. Presumably his bridling at the suggestion that yoga teaching is instructive by imitation results, at least in part, from his awareness as a university lecturer of the potential limitations and dangers of copying as a process that can impute doing without understanding or doing merely because it must be done. Perhaps it also results from the deep-seated bias in Western practices of thought against political life within the world and in favour of a philosophical one abstracted from it.

In the ambivalent context of higher education, actor training (which occupies status as both formal education and professional training) imitation as a pedagogic technique poses some further complexities. In my own training practice at the Conservatoire, I am reluctant to even demonstrate completely the 'correct' practising of an exercise because of my sense that much of the instructional value contained within exercises comes from the exercise itself and not from being told or shown how to address the challenges that the exercise poses. This is quite a different mode to the one described by Miller. Perhaps my own modes result from my own education in the UK, which balances uneasily or the twin fulcrums of the Socratic method of deductive reasoning – the cornerstone of Western higher education – and Aristotelian imitation – the fundamental pedagogic principle of training. Imitation in training is profoundly complex given that it is a matter of both copying actions and copying people performing those actions. When trainees emulate their trainers, they do so in at least two senses: emulating a specific task or exercise and also giving a more expansive imitation of the trainer as a person or, as James Davies has put it, as the 'embodied answer'[61] to problems posed by training. This, presumably, is another aspect of Miller's discomfort.

The anthropologist Anthony Wallace was among the first to describe education as a very material matter of personal transformation back in 1961. His study of 'ritual learning' showed how stressful situations elicited by education could bring about extensive and permanent cognitive and emotional changes, and this phenomenon has only recently been definitively tracked in the stressful 'restructuring of behaviour'[62] students undergo when training: for example, in training to become nuclear physicists, psychiatrists[63] medical doctors[64] and psychotherapists.[65] In his study of the institutional character of the training of psychotherapists, James Davies has noted an 'understandable anxiety' about progressing through training, which tends to predispose students towards emulating and reflecting tutors' values simply because 'of the … economic and personal losses that any extension of training would entail'.[66] Davies traces this predisposition towards conformity with institutional values as they are expressed in the person of tutors as a form of 'evaluative apprehension',[67] a specific fear that one will be judged unsuitable for a profession.

Describing the particular institutional conditions of actor training in the UK, Mark Seton has rendered some 'psycholinguistic' observations about the prevalence of 'imagery … attendant upon loss of innocence, [and] a need for penetration' and the recurrence of themes of 'vulnerability and seduction'[68] in actor training. The psycholinguistic trope of subjection or, as discourse analysis might say, asymmetrical power relations between trainers and trainees within these institutions may also suggest another cause for 'evaluative apprehension' and one which may suggest emulation to students as a cogent strategy for ameliorating this anxiety.

In yet another field, the training of medical doctors, Becker, Geer, Hughes and Strauss have argued that the social organization of training assembles institutional expectations which students must 'read' and 'respond to' in order to succeed,[69] mirroring both the explicit practices and the implicit values of institutional superiors. As James Davies, in his paper on the training of psychotherapists notes, in training, 'conflict avoidance often guides students' behaviour by communicating far more clearly than overt pedagogical demands in what direction as novices they [students] are to strive to succeed'.[70]

While tutors might assert implicitly the worth of the craft of acting, for example, through training the simple fact that they are themselves actors and that they act may also function as what Davies has called the 'embodied answer' to the question 'What do trainers want?'.[71] Irrespective of a tutor's ability or propensity to demonstrate 'correct' practice, the simple fact of their professional status may provide an 'embodied answer', which, through reflection by a student, can act as 'a palliative for "evaluative apprehension" and its associated fears'.[72]

It is well known that approval is crucial to educational progress not only because of its motivational effect but also because without it, as Davies puts it, 'self-belief might be experienced as illegitimate'.[73] However, as Davies shows, students 'quickly learn that they are judged on something more intangible, less quantifiable than "examination performance"', namely on what can be 'experienced as a vaguer kind of "suitability" as defined by those socially positioned as responsible for adjudication'.[74] As Davies writes, what constitutes such 'aptness' – the student's 'traits' or 'behaviours' as distinct from their academic results – 'might remain a mystery to many trainees until they are informed about how they are perceived by their seniors'.[75]

If a facility to perceive and intuit institutional values insofar as they are expressed in persons holding institutional roles is integral to the experience of learning across all social institutions, then this basic pedagogic fact accrues new and more complex significance in actor training where the specific craft being taught is inherently bound to the practice of imitating others. This is not to reduce the craft of realist traditions of acting to 'mere' imitation. Following Stanislavski's denunciation of the superficial acting style of his day, eschewing simplistic and superficial mimicry is in practically every subsequent approach or 'system' or realist actor training, a prerequisite of both rhetoric and practice about acting. Stanislavski reserves his most excoriating criticism for acts of self-flagellation, setting a tone for future discourse. He writes of 'powerful old ingrained [bad] habits' acquired by 'many years of amateur acting'; despite warm audience response as a child, he bemoans, 'I was applauded because schoolgirls cannot tell the difference between the actor and the part' and 'like a fool', he regrets, 'I forged ahead making all my old mistakes'.[76] Stanislavski's tendency, in the guise of Tortsov, to contrast the 'superficial resemblance, the outside of a character', with the 'very *soul*' of the 'character itself'[77] no doubt gave a practical precedent to a deeply rooted internal–external opposition in acting theory and practice created by Diderot and which many subsequent theorists and practitioners reiterated. As Dick McCaw notes, Grotowski (to name but one) employed 'metaphors [concerned with] rejection of the superficial in favour of the internal': his image of the mask, with an 'outside … associated with insincerity and affection' and the 'truth' found 'under the skin'.[78]

Imitation has, for some time, been seen by actor trainers in the realist tradition as both an imperfect definition of 'proper acting' and an apt description of acting styles and performances, both amateur and professional, that differ from the 'style without style' orthodoxy. Nonetheless, in a specific and more limited sense, imitation is key to success in actor training. Imitation, or rather mimesis, is of course central to a UK drama school training in general, which is largely modelled around acting theories associated with a theatre of realist verisimilitude that developed in the latter part of the twentieth century but which can (and frequently do) trace (and assert) a lineage back to the dramatic forms of ancient Greece and Aristotle's foundational work on staged drama and mimesis, *Poetics*. Precisely what is entailed by mimesis – whether it is 'imitative' or 'productive'[79] – is a complex issue but, as Jerome and Julia Frank have indicated, imitation in a common-usage sense might be central to the experience of learning itself. They argue that a trainee's dependency on a supervisor's guidance and approval disposes them towards 'imitating' tutors' values, perspectives and judgements.[80] Such imitation, or 'modelling' as they call it, has been shown to be a powerful didactic mechanism in learning, especially of children.[81] In this belief, the Franks are decidedly Aristotelian – imitation would appear to be, as Aristotle wrote, a fundamental human trait. Aristotle contends that *mimêsis* is *natural* in the sense that it is indivisible from our human nature and that from an early age we begin to learn by aping adults. Indeed, we learn and grow precisely because we imitate and learning is both natural and a delight.[82] Following from this, in a certain sense, we can see imitation operating across all social institutions.

Training is a little different, however, to the extent that imitation is an explicit and indivisible part of its processes and practice. What in other contexts may be a *natural* proclivity is in training redoubled and recapitulated as an artificial or explicitly fabricated exercise and in the specific case of actor training this significance is compounded further still. Herein we encounter the complexity of imitation, and the different strands thereof, that so trouble Aristotle's teacher, Plato. Plato used *mimêsis* to refer to the process of making a copy – the act of the trainee imitating or emulating the practice of a more expert performer – and *mimêma* to refer to the outcome – to the copy itself and not the act of copying. It may help these definitions to observe that the social reproduction occurring across generations that so fascinates epistemology is principally a matter of *mimêma*, whereas the reproduction occurring during training practices, where trainees model their conduct on experts, is a case of *mimesis*.[83]

Plato also makes a three-way distinction between *forms*, *things* and *copies of things*, with the latter being the most troublesome: forms exist on a divine plane (in Plato, the concept of a table, for example), while things made on earth by humans are imperfect realizations of divine form (a table made by a carpenter).[84] Despite their imperfection these efforts are, as it were, honest[85] because they produce a true opinion[86] of form in which their own imperfection is entailed. Copies of things (in Plato, a painting by an artist of a table made by a carpenter), however, intensify this weakness present in things (made by humans) and fail twice or doubly precisely because they offer an 'imitation of appearance' that is apt to deceive or mislead about its own inherent inadequacy.

While Plato is relatively sanguine about imitation in Book 3 of *The Republic*, as is well known, by Book 10 he has lost his cool and resorted to banishing theatre and other forms of art from the Republic's perfect society largely because of the threatening potential of the 'imitation of appearance',[87] even if he does so in rather salutary terms: 'If a man were to arrive in the city whose wisdom [*sophia*] empowered him to become everything and to mimic all things', writes Plato, 'we would worship him as someone holy [*hieron*] and wonderful and pleasant', but, nonetheless, the good citizens would have to 'tell him there is no man like him in our city, nor by our traditional law [*themis*] can come to be here' and so they 'would send him off to another city' but not before 'pouring myrrh on his head and crowning him with wool'.[88] Most actors would find this to be a rather mixed message. It seems to me this proto-Kafkaesque scene is the foundational basis of the post-dramatic diorama which, as Nic Ridout has explained, in practice and in theory, has taken 'theatricality' to be a 'key' and 'negative term'.[89]

In English, reproduction is perhaps more often used to denote the copy rather than the copying – the *mimêma* rather than the *mimêsis* – and imitation is linked to reproduction and reproducing because all three entail the appearance of something as well as the disappearance of that same thing. This is a somewhat complex proposition whose complexity derives from the mutual exclusivity of appearance and disappearance and to the extent that the appearance of the copy must necessarily make the original disappear we may get a sense of one of the root causes of Plato's fear about mimesis. While it was worrying enough, for Plato, that imitating a villain may cultivate villainous traits – the argument being that the republic can do without the presentation of rogues, fly-by-nights, Johnny-come-latelys and all manner of shoddy characters, because acting such parts cultivates the behaviours that are characteristic of the personalities being impersonated[90] – it is no less and perhaps more worrying that imitating a hero may displace heroism altogether.

It is tempting for the contemporary reader to see this proposition – the simultaneous appearance and disappearance of the *thing* in the process of imitation – through the lens of Baudrillard's concept of the simulacrum[91] which inverts the juxtaposition between 'real' and 'unreal' by a troubling of the visible and invisible and of appearance and disappearance as grounds for truth.[92] However, for Plato the problem with mimêsis is the foundational existence of the original (the *form*). The mutual exclusivity of appearance and disappearance of the *thing*, which we may think of in terms of form, albeit not necessarily divine form, should not be confused with Rebecca Schneider's juxtaposition of 'vanishment' and 'remains'[93] in the theatre form. Rather these categories – appearance and disappearance – pertain to what is made present and imitation has a fundamental relationship to that which is made present both in the sense of what is presented to our senses and in the sense of what is occurring now. 'Being and appearing coincide',[94] writes Hannah Arendt in *The Life of the Mind*. This does not mean that disappearing is synonymous with non-Being but rather that 'to be alive means to live in a world that preceded one's arrival and that will survive one's own departure'.[95] The world into which we are born 'contains many things, natural and artificial, living and dead, transient and sempiternal, all of which have in common that they *appear*'.[96] As Arendt goes on to explain, because of this simple fact, 'the word "appearance" would make no sense if recipients of appearance did not exist';[97] this is the world's 'phenomenal nature'.[98] Disappearance is an end to appearance or to what Arendt more properly describes as appearingness (the phenomenal fact of the world) and not an alternative relationship to what Immanuel Kant might call 'the grounds' of appearance:[99] the transcendent forms cherished by Plato. In contrast to Kant who, following Plato's logic, asserted that 'appearances must have grounds which are not appearances',[100] Merleau-Ponty argued that 'I can flee being only into being', and since being and appearance coincide, as Arendt wrote, this means that 'I can flee appearance only into appearance'.[101] 'Living things', writes Arendt, 'make their appearance, like actors, on a stage set made for them'[102] and so 'to be alive means to be possessed of an urge towards self-display which answers the fact of one's own appearingness'.[103] This self-display is not the narcissism of Shakespeare's Sonnet I but a necessary adjunct to the phenomenal nature of the world. The metaphysical fallacy[104] of the two-world theory – the transcendent realm of forms and their appearance and non-appearance in our own worldly realm – has persisted because it 'so plausibly corresponded to some basic experiences'[105] of our sense of the difference between 'true' Being and our apprehension of appearances.[106] The fallacy pertains to theory also where the superficial appearance of things, such as performance events, has been subordinated to their 'deep' meaning – where, as Shepherd and Spatz contend, the superficiality of practice can be penetrated to yield deep information about embodiment.[107] In my own earlier writings in this field, although I have tended to posit training as a category above disciplines – a meta-disciplinary category – rather than a set of values operating beneath the surface of disciplines, exposing the dichotomy of *mere* appearance and *true* significance has, I suspect, motivated some of my enquiries. This metaphysical fallacy, as Arendt calls it, and the associated hierarchy of surface and depth, is at least as old as Plato's allegory of the shadows on the cave wall and certainly as well rooted in theory. However, more recently and at least since the 1970s, this hierarchy has come under challenge in a number of fields of practice: the Swiss zoologist Adolf Portmann contested the foundational assumption of biology that reproduction is a means by which animals die and species survive by the elementary observation that 'the simplistic functional hypothesis that holds that appearances in living beings serve merely the twofold purpose of self-preservation and preservation of the species'[108] is flawed because 'it looks as though, on the contrary, the inner non-appearing organs exist only in order to bring forth and maintain the appearance'.[109] Arendt herself has applied this same observation to the philosophical foundations of the surface–depth fallacy asking, 'could it be that appearances are not there for the sake of the life process but, on the contrary, the life process is there for the sake of appearances?'[110] Since we 'live in an *appearing* world is it not much more plausible that the relevant and the meaningful in this world of ours should be located precisely on the surface?', she enquired.[111]

'There is no *Schein* without an *Erscheinung*, every *Schein* is the counterpart of an *Erschenung*', wrote Merleau-Ponty, provoking Arendt to suggest that it 'is to say the least, highly doubtful' that 'modern science in its relentless search for *the* truth behind *mere* appearances will ever be able to resolve this predicament'.[112] The cultural-materialist assumptions about social reproduction via training institutions, and the epistemological perspectives that chart the 'knowledge' that transfer across epistemes, find themselves in this same predicament and perhaps unconsciously fall back on the ancient metaphysical fallacy that depth is somehow more meaningful than surface, a hypothesis which, as Portmann and Arendt have shown, has no phenomenological basis and which since ancient times has been challenged by mimesis itself.

However, at the 'sheer level of being alive, appearance and disappearance, as they follow upon each, are the primordial events, which as such mark out time'.[113] The finite lifespan determines 'not merely life expectancy' but also 'time experience'. It is, as Arendt writes, 'the secret prototype for all time measures'.

Imitation, as a matter of appearance and disappearance, provides the basic structure for the human artefact of time and indeed for time itself as a physical proposition and thus the foundational basis for our categories of past and present and future – what no longer appears, what is appearing and what has not yet appeared. Imitation, in the pedagogic context of training activities, is not a form of appearing given to transcendent *forms* in the Platonic sense but rather the iterative reappearing of decidedly worldly forms whose very *appearingness* is itself the foundation of meaning and significance rather than the outer skin of these. The urge towards self-display that corresponds to the phenomenal nature of the world has been particularly harnessed by training and reconceived as a technology for development in individuals and across generations and throughout recorded history. Reproduction may be understood, therefore, as encompassing more than the recitation of ideological values across generations by training. Doing again activities (practice) that were done before is not merely a means for the social continuity of knowledge but for the very premise of knowledge itself. Imitation, insofar as it represents a calculated response to the urge towards self-display, entailed by the appearingness of our world predicates 'again' as a phenomenologically valid experience of *now*, thereby emptying *now* of some of its seeming phenomenal significance and filling this evacuated space with meaning from the *before* and also from the *yet to be*. Reproduction, which in training entails imitation and the emulation of both practice and practitioners, thus posits time as a continuum and lays down what Arendt called the 'secret prototype' for all measures of time.

As simple and profound a fact as it is, training is predicated upon imitation and as a result training has asserted itself throughout the recorded history of Western societies as a means by which humans and humanity has inserted itself within the world and subjected that world, which is otherwise a mass of sheer change, to the predicate of time.

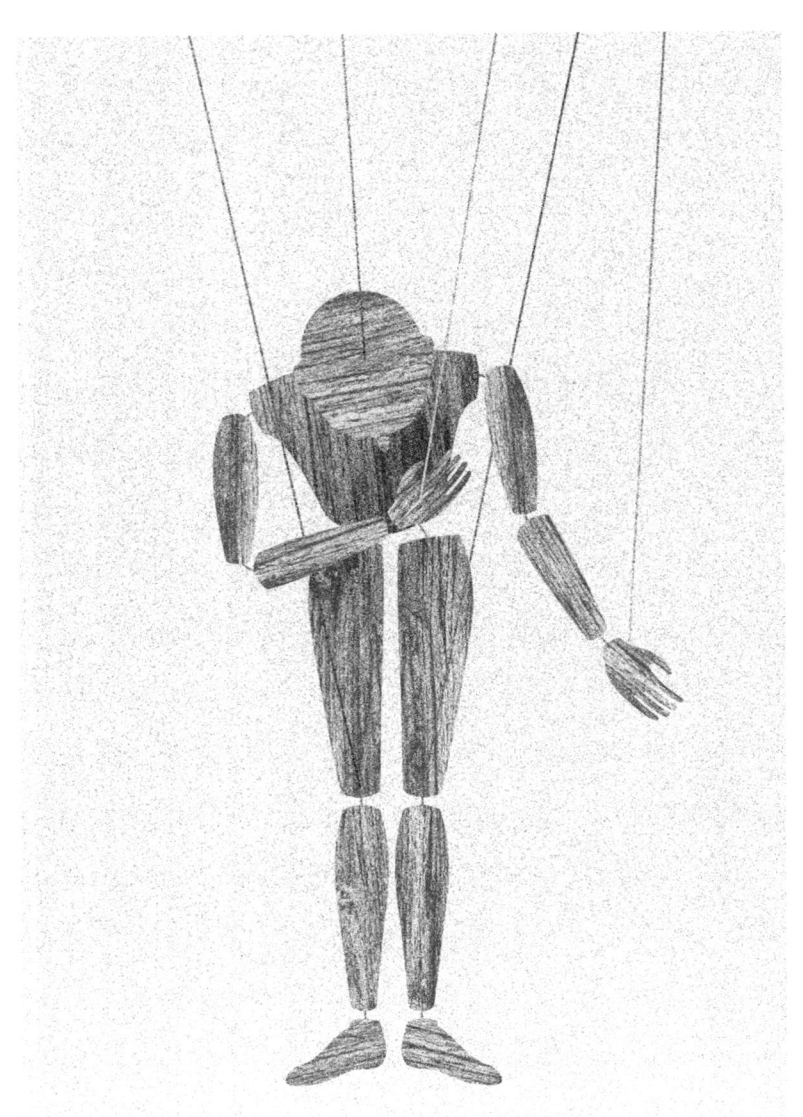

7
HERITABILITY

Heritability is a matter concerning all three tense-concepts of time – past, present and future – in the Life of a species, as well as in the lives of individual members of a species. In this final chapter, these three concepts, as they have emerged within the previous six chapters in varying relationships to the category of training, adhere to one another, suturing training's temporal experiences into a time continuum that provides continuity to human lives and to the Life of the human species. Reflecting, as this book does, on the relationship between training and time suggests fresh ways of thinking on the ontic qualities of training. Meditating on these ontic qualities in relation to human beings and human Being also proposes some new ways of thinking about performance ontology – new opportunities to rethink the relationship between performance and training on the basis of the ontic supremacy of the latter over the former.

This rethinking is a provocation to scholarship and an inversion of the assumed causal relation between performance and training. Or perhaps not an inversion but a reconfiguration of the linear temporal relationship posited between the two, a provocation to the sense of causality – which is, of course, temporal, tout court – in this relationship also and a hypothesis that there may be something useful to theory and practice in beginning to think of performance as a brief phenomenal interruption in the continuous and contiguous ontic category of training.

With respect to its relationship to our human Being, training may be seen as *the thing* and performance as a brief and superficial exemplification of its cultural value. Through retuning the ontological interests within the discipline, performance events may be seen as demonstrations rather than reifications of the ontic nature of human Being and thereby enable a recalibration of the theoretical claims of and for performance in light of training's correlation to time.

In this book, thinking through the association between training and time has meant thinking outside of the research paradigm which has situated training firmly within history. History, counter-intuitively, does not have very much to do with the category of time; it is only concerned by it insofar as it is representative of some of the content of the past tense. Nonetheless, history has established one readily accessible narrative account of training disciplines providing continuity for the human species via the transference of skills and expertise or knowledge-as-technique, as Ben Spatz has described it, across generations. Scholars of theatre training practices have recorded the transmission of particular training exercises across geographical space and time, and tracing these nexuses of technique has also been a research focus within the field of Theatre and Performance Studies.[1] As I have explored in the previous six chapters of this book, describing training's relationship with time requires thinking philosophically about training in ways that do not reduce it to merely existing within the past. Understanding the kind of knowledge summoned and mobilized in and by training requires addressing it in terms that do not constrain that knowledge to the present, either. Training, much like thinking, gives to humans a means to produce themselves by giving rise to the tense-concepts of past, present and future and making of these a habitat for human action.

Training allows human beings to produce themselves not only in the sense of the social construction of identity but in the foundational sense of species-identity, which provides the basis for all identity constructs and construction. As anthropology has so compellingly shown, and as performance scholarship has so emphatically reiterated, identity constructions are spatio-temporally specific and their apparent integrity relies upon their performed-ness, which is to say it relies upon their phenomenal presence. Being decisively phenomenal in nature, they are quintessentially of the present, albeit with mythic (in the Barthesian sense) relation to the near and sometimes distant past. The relationship of identity constructs to the future is, at best, precarious, especially in the context of a post-structuralist world wherein the analytical lens of 'play' has revivified our phenomenological perspectives on performativity and self-identity. Yet, training, even in this contemporary context, continues to play a role in salvaging some degree of fixedness for our self-constructs and permits and predicts a degree of surety in an otherwise instable future. In point of fact, training, even more so than thinking, has, can and does hold out the promise of influence, and perhaps even near-perfect influence, within the most elusive of all three tenses – the future.

Rather than focus on the 'product' of training practices – 'technique' – and its appearance in time, which has been the concern of history and epistemology, my approach in this book has been to attend to the processes of training and how these have and can offer to individuals and to generations the means to individuate the human species by producing for it temporal concepts and contexts for action. In this labour, I have been able to follow Hannah Arendt, who has made a very similar claim for thinking and who differentiated the process of thinking from the outcomes of thought, grounding her enquiry in the domain of philosophy and ontology rather than methodologies of history and epistemology.

As the preceding six chapters explain, training, much like thinking, may be providing for individuals and for the species the basis for the tense-concepts that predicate time. Training, much like thinking, generates time by necessity, time being the human response to the indifference of the flow of sheer change that constitutes the phenomenal nature of the world. Training, much like thinking, is a mechanism by which human agency and its associated categories of identity, responsibility and ethics, insert themselves into a powerful, unpredictable and contingent reality.

The Life of Training has sought to connect my theorization of training with Arendt's theorization of thinking in *The Life of the Mind* and to develop my claims in interlocution with her own. It seems fitting to start this final chapter where she left off. In the final meditation of her first volume, *Thinking*, Arendt writes:

each new generation, every new human being, as he becomes conscious of being inserted between an infinite past and an infinite future, must discover and ploddingly pave anew the path of thought. And it is after all possible, and seems to me likely, that the strange survival of great works, their relative permanence throughout thousands of years, is due to their having been born in the small, inconspicuous track of non-time which their authors' thought they had beaten between an infinite past and an infinite future by accepting past and future as directed, aimed, as it were, at themselves, their predecessors and successors, their past and their future, thus establishing a present for themselves, a kind of timeless time in which men are able to create timeless works with which to transcend their own finiteness.[2]

With characteristic optimism and bathos, Arendt indicates the monumental achievement of human thinking simultaneously with the un-remediated limitation of human thought. The 'relative permanence' of human works would seem to be a childlike imitation of the infiniteness of past and future: an imprint, with half-life decay, caused by the daring and ineffectual assertion, by humans, of *the now* as a category holding out the potential to overthrow the very tense-concepts by which time becomes itself.

The various temporal experiences that humankind has created for itself, and their thematization into the three tenses of past, present and future, are fully realized only when in relation to each other. Time predicates continuity, even more so than any sense of its cyclicality or linearity, time proposes sequentially, which is the basis of causality, responsibility, sense-perception, intuition, intellect and any other human property that one may care to imagine and also the context for human action as such.

As a human activity, training is more perfect even than thinking in its attention to the predicated sequentiality of time. Where thinking may, and does, occur in what Arendt called a 'time out of time', training, precisely because of its embodied everyday-ness and the quotidian commitment it requires of humans, places our experiences of selfhood into an unbroken series whose resilience is both an envelope for and an expression of our agency and of what Arendt called our human condition.[3]

Scholars have rather expertly described the appearance of training within various epistemological contexts[4] and have shown conscientious attention to the history and historicity of training exercises, techniques, regimens, systems, rituals, institutions and practitioners, in the field of Theatre and Performance Studies[5] and more generally. History, historicity, epistemology as well as the various quasi-methodologies of the 'archive' and the 'repertoire'[6] have enabled Performance Studies to occupy the past as a research domain and, to an extent, allowed it to have regard for the present. In this closing chapter, I wish to meditate on heritability – that characteristic of human life that allows us to recognize it as such: as the life of a *species*. To reflect on that aspect of training by which it accrues a sense of temporal continuity to human Life and to human lives and that may permit Performance Studies to address the future with credibility.

While the metaphor of social reproduction has given much impetus to scholars[7] and allowed them to chart the ideological values arising with n and transferring between social institutions and, to some extent, among individuals too, heritability, as a transaction between generations, has been somewhat taken for granted in the hectic flurry of all this historical description. Heritability is not the characteristic instance of the emergence in another future context of a fact or value or practice identifiable in a different past context but is rather the philosophical proposition that this coincidence is itself a characteristic of Life.

Sociology has, throughout the twentieth century, impelled us to accept that social institutions take on some of the traits of the human lives lived within them and also that the human lives lived within them can perpetuate institutional values and practices as a corollary to their own biological reproduction. While knowledge, in the form of techniques or exercises or conventions of practice and codes of institutional conduct, may, evidently, be reproduced socially by training we may also see each characteristic associated with the life of training and described in the chapters of this book as a heritable trait of the onto-historical category of training. The transference of knowledge in its various forms provides scope for historical or epistemological research and for theorization, while the heritability of the characteristics of training that permit knowledge generation gives scope for an ontological account of the activity of training which, in being ontological, is associated with Being and Time as well as with beings and our temporal experiences.

As I suggested in the opening chapter, HOMEOSTASIS, it is, paradoxically, the persistent sameness of training practices across history that allows us to study each as discrete and distinct variations of the genus. This persistent sameness is in contradistinction to the insistent flux of the phenomenal nature of the world and integrally linked to the unity and persistence of a thing called human Being within it and also of human beings' sense of self-identity as such.

Sameness provides a form of resistance against the indifference and unpredictability of 'sheer change', which is the phenomenal basis of the world. Out of this indifferent drift of sheer change, training, much like the activity of thinking, provides a means for generating human experience as sensible, factual and broadly predictable and controllable out of the phenomenal nature of existence.

Perhaps we may not tend to see GROWTH as a heritable trait but rather as a biological prerequisite. Yet, in the continuum of human temporal experience, the ongoing project of progress relies upon the accretion over generations of incremental extensions to human potential staked out and made credible by the evidence of human performance. Furthermore, our sense of self-identity requires our coordination with past and future generations, and in the activities of training the concept of talent has provided a coordinate for this triangulation.

Individuals grow and the abilities of individuals grow and develop towards the epiphany described by Arendt, and with these developments in human lives human Life plumbs deeper what Aristotle called the abyss of its potential. History has recorded how the surpassing of seemingly unattainable milestones of athletic performance that have often for generations appeared to be the very bottom depth of the abyss – the four-minute mile, the ten-second 100-metre dash – has invariably been followed hastily by the consolidation of new norms and expectations. The most radical shifts in the paradigm of theatrical performance – Garrick's 'dazzling' appearance on the Parisian scene in 1767[8] or the confusion, outrage or bewilderment heralding the opening productions of *Ubu Roi* (1896), *En Attendent Godot* (1953), *The Playboy of the Western World* (1907) and *Blasted* (1995) – have swiftly been recuperated to that paradigm as the expected baseline of present and future performance. Talent has emerged across all disciplines of performance as a concept denoting the atypicality of individual abilities in relation to these baselines and norms and to the perpetual promise of further human achievement and the expansion of our potential as individuals and collectively in the future.

Training works with our given human nature, or 'condition', as Arendt would say, and delivers into human hands the capacity to self-direct and to a large extent to control our own potential, which, with regard to the caprice of contingency and the indifference of the phenomenal world, will never properly belong to us. Nonetheless, training offers to human subjects a level of agency and also what Isaiah Berlin would cal 'positive freedom'[9] and gives to humankind a future that is, if not fully, subject to human will at least within the remit of our aspirations. In this offering, training is akin to and not second to thinking as an activity enabling individual self-realization and also an albeit temporary cessation of the flux of sheer and unpredictable change threatening the integrity of selfhood.

Human potential remains abysmal, in the Aristotelian sense, but the dark and expanse of the abyss is illuminated and filled by the actualization of potential attained by successive generations, and this bi-faceted character of GROWTH – that individuals develop and that collective potential develops also – is contained and self-consciously exploited by training.

Amid the persistent sameness of training, the presentness of *now*, which I described in STIMULATION, provides the context wherein the 'I' finds both stability and capability despite the torsion between the cyclical and rectilinear time concepts by which we live our lives today.

Actors in the realist genre are emblematic of the paradox of human acting in a broader sense, expected as they are to premeditate at length their actions as well as to execute actions spontaneously and thus 'authentically' while bearing responsibility for both intended and unintended consequences.[10] While the ability to respond to external stimulation is an innate and characteristic element of Life, humans' apparent capacity to develop new abilities and to take 'better' action, both as individuals and as a species, is definitive of what Arendt called our human condition. While all living creatures appear to be able to get better at doing things, human creatures appear to possess both a capacity for and a disposition towards getting better at doing anything, even if these things may ultimately be detrimental to human survival.[11]

As discussed in STIMULATION, 'now', the present, is profoundly linked to uncertainty and to newness: the twin pillars of ignorance and innovation that motivate and frame human action. The condition of uncertainty is sine qua non the condition of the present and attuned to the phenomenal nature of the world even if the present is an invention of the rectilinear metaphor and its spatial conceptualization of time. The human concept of the present, its utter imminence and seeming immanence, is a profound illustration of what Arendt repeatedly calls the 'fighting presence' of humankind in the context of the phenomenal world of flux. For Arendt, thinking is a means to produce and elongate the present as a region of 'time-out-of-time'. Training has also taken on the constituting of an 'enduring present', which is the 'habitual, normal, banal act of our intellect', and given it both a quotidian and an 'extra-daily'[12] feel. Time experienced in training is rarefied everywhere as a *special time*, a time with sociocultural, economic, aesthetic and even ethical and moral value, even while the feeling it gives in the presentness of now may be one of boredom and pain.

In its gloriously unapologetic tediousness, training actors, just as with training in general, is predicated upon repetition and the cyclical time metaphor whereby developmental experiences are linked to the very materials of biological life. The developmental potential of repetitive and iterative action is a central ideological conceit of training just as is the supposition that such repetitive action provides for cessation of everydayness and an immersion in presentness.

The act of will required to submit to, enjoy or to be fulfilled or satisfied by such tedious conduct is a paramount example of the 'fighting presence' and the human tenacity required to carve time out from the mass of sheer change that constitutes the world. Training, in its many disciplines and guises, valorizes this act of will and situates a hard-won presentness at the fulcrum of past inabilities and future possibility. It is a horrifyingly potent illustration of the ambition and obstinacy of the ideology of human fruition.

Training's relationship to fruition and its fixation on this imperative can be seen in its characteristic organization whereby, in the modern age, we see what Arendt described as 'the emergence of the Future to the rank formerly occupied by the Present or the Past'.[13] As training has, in the modern age at least, developed as an increasingly rigorously organized phenomenon and become, in many fields, increasingly granular in its organization and its objectives, so too has scholarly discourse on training become ever more organized and scientific. We find in training, and in scholarly discourses on training, a strong sense of continuity achieved 'step by step through contributions of generations of explorers building upon and gradually amending the findings of their predecessors'.[14] This statement, which Arendt made of the enterprise of thinking, is the foundational assumption of historians and epistemologists of practice: namely, that training remains, by the continuity of the knowledge expressed within and by it over generations, essentially *productive*.

Describing this thing – training – rather than its appearance has been my project since my first book. In *Training for Performance*, my task was to seek to describe, philosophically, 'what is called training'[15] rather than to analyse this training or that training. Clearly the concept and the term – 'training' – had huge currency within theatre and performance scholarship and also more broadly in multiple domains of human life. In the same way that 'discipline' emerged throughout twentieth-century philosophy[16] as a distinct category, training appeared ready to be similarly described and also to be differentiated from discipline with which it was repeatedly conflated or confused.

Describing the processes innate within this category made it forcefully apparent that these processes, and thus the category, were reliant upon the category of 'human', and so my second book set about describing how we train because we are human and how we become human because we train. *Anatomy of Performance Training* examines the co-reliance of the category of training and the human condition, taking account of the necessarily embodied-ness of training and the necessarily trained-ness of having and being a body.

Describing the category of training in relation to the category of human and in the context of our understanding of embodiment made clear the necessity to understand and describe training and human Being ontologically, given that each category predicated the other and both were, evidently, coeval in philosophical terms. This gave a temporal context by which to start theorizing the relationship between training and human Being and has given rise to accounts of training and time in this book. Again, as in my previous two books, Hannah Arendt has been my guide, preoccupied in her thinking, as she was, by the nature of action, its appearance and non-appearance and the responsibilities that we, as humans, bear for it.

For all philosophers, there is a primal value to thinking which is corrective to our misperceptions and a deep conscientizing imperative to thought that undoes misunderstanding. For Arendt, thought was less useful to the human species than thinking and, generally speaking products less helpful than processes. Knowledge, according to Arendt, was of relatively little use to 'men in the singular';[17] its application to successive generations and to humankind as a whole was its chief ideological premise. In the context of technique, which Spatz has described as a particular form of knowledge,[18] there may be, as Mark

Seton[19] and Kathy Leahy[20] have shown, considerable professional advantage associated with its acquisition. In the history of practice, craftsmen and craftswomen used the method of trial and error and, as Arendt noted, found by this approach 'certain improvements in their crafts'.[21] As a measure of the historical reach of the concept of development, which, in the form of progress, became rampant in the modern age, we find that, even within the medieval guilds, there was attention to 'continuity' even if not 'the progress of craftsmanship'.[22]

As well as serving as protectionist cartels for goods made within the city and as quasi-autonomous organizations for religious control,[23] the guilds functioned as institutional mechanisms for the transmission of technique. As I have described in 'What Is a Workshop?', guilds thrived from the twelfth to the mid-fifteenth century because of their proficiency in ensuring the ongoing capacity among citizens to produce goods, which was achieved by a formalized process of knowledge transfer across the generations. Indeed, it is from the late medieval guilds that we get our contemporary understanding of apprenticeship and although it would be rather ahistorical to view the guilds as organs providing social mobility for skilled individuals, they did provide a limited upward mobility to apprentices albeit as a by-product of their commercial activities as opposed to as the result of their core business.

While most historians have tended to view the guilds from a cultural-materialistic perspective,[24] we may also see these institutions as prototypical for the schools, academies, conservatoires and training facilities of today which represent sites for the communication of expertise downwards, across generations, and the animation of a continuum of what Spatz has defined as 'technique'. In the generation of knowledge in the form of technique, training is characterized as that process that deconstructs the complex phenomena of performance into units – exercises, drills, tasks, games, etc. – and which sequences and re-sequences units – of information, action, activity, etc. – into flexible and complex systems for the transfer, maintenance and generation of knowledge – this knowledge being frequently understood as a kind of performance potential, subject to talent and contingency and yet overwhelmingly cultivatable.

Amid the rigorous scholarly study of the complexity of technique, we may have come to take for granted the need for training, just as Arendt suggested that we have typically taken 'for granted man's need to think'.[25] Perhaps the ubiquity of training across more and more domains since the 'modern age' has caused it to be taken for granted. Or, perhaps the modern fixation with progress has made so urgent the need to act, and to act better, that training has inserted and asserted itself in more and more places. What scholars such as Alison Hodge have described as the emergence of actor training in the Western world in the modern age is perhaps better conceived as the predominance of a hyper-rationalized and hyper-rationalizing form of training – training forms that are actively goal-directed and insistently attentive to progress.

While training of all sorts may be reliant upon an ideology of the 'unending perfectability of the human species' – an ideology that achieved supremacy in the eighteenth-century Enlightenment[26] – actor training, at least from Stanislavski until now, has represented a means both to contend with the restrictions to our agency caused by our fallible and imperfect human abilities and to increase our agency, and our liberty, by the correction and perfection of these abilities. In this way, training has been able to fulfil, even if only partially, the futurological ideology of progress integral to science by grounding it in the lives of individual humans and thereby admitting progress into the personal realm and the human lifespan.

With regard to the lifespan of humans, training plays a role in both the likelihood of our annihilation and the prospect of deliverance from increasingly serious environmental threats, which we humans have ourselves created. What Arendt described as the ethical indifference of *animal laborans* to the consequences of progress may not ultimately be constrainable by the sociality of *homo faber* and, working with both our animal and ethical nature, training has, throughout history, given itself as the means by which humans have taken control of their biological propensity for adaptation. This hard-won control has, as Arendt bemoans, not always driven adaptations in the direction of ethical perfection but rather by the bearings of our expectations and desires.

Despite its increasing goal-orientation, training has asserted itself strongly in the present moment in many forms wherein it acts as a self-supporting and self-justifying ideology of human betterment. The useless 'cult', as Lingis describes it, of bodybuilding has pushed itself into a cultural mainstream and expanded virulently through a burgeoning and diversifying gym and fitness industry wherein the appeal of the 'end in itself' account of human action has taken on a grotesque form.

Human betterment, blossoming as an ideology in what Possamai, Heelas and others have described as 'Perrenism' and the 'human potential ethic',[27] has vigorously assaulted the phenomenal world in diverse ways, fighting a wide-ranging conflict in the form of the global project of human self-determination. The world has, thus far, maintained a seemingly perpetual stalemate in which the principle of contingency has left humans doggedly boxing a shadow.

Time is integral to the principle of contingency seeing as the cancellation of this principle would entail handing over all human potential to time given that, in this case, the individual could, as Pierre-Michel Menger puts it, 'express the totality of his potentialities provided that he has enough time to actualize them'.[28] Individual 'failure or incompletion would exist only for lack of time'[29] rather than because of a change in the weather, a slump in the markets, a pothole in the road or a sore thumb. Indeed, the principle of contingency which rules the natural world has inveigled itself into the very biological nature of the human condition; as George Orwell phrased it, this is the 'uselessness' and 'treachery of the human body which freezes into inertia at the exact moment when a special effort is needed' because in 'moments of crisis' one is always 'fighting against one's own body', which swells 'up until it fills the universe' making life, despite its pretensions and aspirations, a 'moment-to-moment struggle against hunger or cold or sleeplessness, against a sour stomach or an aching tooth'.[30]

Performance anxiety, in its specific form as stage fright, gave impetus to the entire history of European and American actor training since the emergence of the seeds of realism in the nineteenth century. Indeed, one may choose, as Nic Ridout has, to read Stanislavski's oeuvre as principally concerned with the stage-frightened 'predicament of the actor'[31] or, as Rose Whyman has, to see these works in the context of the (two) 'problems of acting': 'how the actor can overcome stage fright' and how 'he or she can truly *experience* a role'.[32] Since this time in the theatre a dominant discourse has been running in which training proposes a response to this anxiety and an affront to the principle of contingency.

Despite this attractive promise, training has occupied a second-order position in relation to performance and the chapter ORGANIZATION suggested some ways in which the characterization of training as adjunct and subservient to performance, because of its seemingly deconstructive relation to it and its apparent generation of the knowledge required for it, has become ubiquitous across multiple domains of practice and scholarship. The knowledge purportedly generated through training is executed in performance, knowledge understood as a kind of performance potential which, although beholden to talent and contingency, remains cultivatable. However, if we regard the fact that training has an ontic integrity which pertains across all tense-concepts, by contrast with performance, which, as Phelan famously suggested, has no 'life' outside the present,[33] it would seem rather aberrant to regard performance as the basis for training's ontic status. It would be rather more logical to assume the inverse.

The ontology of performance is no longer the hot topic that it was in the time of Phelan's seminal publication, *Unmarked: The Politics of Performance* (1993). This fervour has cooled somewhat, although the key assertions made then still emit a comfortable glow today and a source of energy that some have found problematic. As I wrote in STIMULATION, Phelan's still-much-cited claim that 'performance's only life is in the present … [it] becomes itself through disappearance'[34] and Herbert Blau's evocation of theatre at a 'vanishing point',[35] enthral to its own disappearance, have assumed a near-foundational status in the discipline. Rebecca Schneider has taken issue with this premise, which, she writes, has 'gathered added steam over the last 40 years',[36] on the basis that they have limited the discipline to one particularly enculturated understanding of the performance event, an understanding that suits an archival doctrine.[37]

Another and even more encompassing problem with this premise twenty years on from Schneider's redress is that it has introduced into the discipline a philosophical fault which has corralled scholarship and theory down an ever-narrowing path. The 'ontology of performance', as proposed in Phelan's *Unmarked: The Politics of Performance*, though self-avowedly concerned with 'live'[38] bodies, took the phenomenological conditions of performance to be identical with the ontic nature of performance. The self-substantiating claim that performance 'cannot be saved, recorded, documented, or otherwise participate in the circulation of representations *of* representations: once it does so it becomes something other than performance',[39] misled – no event can undergo such a transformation and still be said to be the same thing. There is nothing special about performance in this respect, just as merely being ephemeral does not constitute anything ontic about performance; many things are ephemeral and, in fact, this is only constitutive of performance insofar as it is an 'event'. Rather than being strictly of the ontic being of performance, Phelan's ontology is a study of performance phenomena and their phenomenological basis in appearance.

Appearance has an obvious fascination for Performance Studies and especially so during a time when representation, and its study via semiology, had established itself as a core research methodology and pedagogical mainstay in the discipline. In this historical context, wherein play and display became the chief interests of the discipline, performance events renewed their value to scholarship by the proclaimed exceptionality of their ontic status and by the potential claimed for them as a result of this status. Yet, in the broader context of the ontology of art, Performance Studies was, seemingly as ever, reinventing the wheel and in so doing rolling over some well-worn terrain: the ontological question what is a work of art? had already stimulated numerous competing responses in philosophy, most of which did not make their way, explicitly, into performance scholarship. These may provide some useful and well-attuned departure points from the properly ontological question, what kind of thing is performance?, which is, strictly, a question about existence rather than appearance.

Many twentieth-century philosophers approached the question on the ontology of art via the assertion that minds and their activities have something to do with the existence of works of art, and yet they were often emphatic in stating that this does not mean that works of art are somehow less real than natural physical entities. Benedetto Croce, who has exerted considerable influence over the philosophical debate about the ontic status of art, wrote that artworks cannot be physical entities (and thus should not be reduced to their phenomenological status) precisely because they are 'supremely real', whereas the phenomenal world is 'unreal'.[40]

Two powerful pre-twentieth-century philosophical perspectives in the debate on the ontological status of art come from figures related intimately to Arendt's own thesis about the ontology of thinking: Thomas Aquinas and Immanuel Kant. The perspectives of Kant and Aquinas emphasize the role of the human faculties of will and knowledge in the production of artworks and thereby ground the ontic status of art in the ontological Being of humans. In *Summa Theologica* Aquinas writes, 'ars est recta ratio factibilium',[41] which is usually understood to mean that art is the right reason of things to be made, or even more starkly, art is knowing how to make things. Kant also identified a work, or *opus*, as the product of a doing; *opus* stands in contrast to the activities of nature, which are not products in the sense that they are not the outcomes of the exercise of a capacity to choose.[42] The exercise of choice – the will, in Arendt's terms – *is* art in Kant's writings.[43]

Developing these themes, C.E.M. Joad in his still-cited *Guide to Philosophy* (1936) gifted (implicitly) to Performance Studies many of its positions vis-à-vis the status of the performance event, arguing that ideas forming in the minds of spectators could not be identified, in a work such as *Hamlet*, with a script, a production and even the title 'Hamlet'. Instead, Joad suggested performative works of art were archetypal of what he called *subsistent* objects, which are universal and constituent of Being itself rather than mental or material properties. In this way, these *subsistent objects* are not ephemeral even if ideas forming about them may be.

Radical as this perspective may seem it is not atypical in ontological philosophy. Étienne Gilson classified works of art as substances in the Aristotelian sense[44] and also claimed that art works have aesthetic, artistic as well as substantial (or material) modes of existence. With particular relevance to performance, Gilson suggested that a work exists artistically qua product of the artist's activity and that it exists aesthetically when and because it is the object of someone else's contemplation.[45] We may find in this theorization a basis for the 'relational aesthetics'[46] that were popularized throughout Performance Studies discourses from the 1990s to the present day. Performance Studies in the twentieth century was rather more captivated by existential and post-structuralist perspectives on art, and Phelan and Blau's interest in the ephemerality of the performance event were simpatico with these perspectives.

Part-time dramatist Jean-Paul Sartre is often associated with the contention that artworks are illusory in their nature in the sense that their derivation is a form of error about their own mode of existence: Beethoven's Seventh Symphony, for example, as being 'irreal ... nowhere ... not there ... entirely outside the real'.[47] Sartre also made the somewhat pedantic point that what one hears when one listens to the Seventh is not the Seventh at all in any credible ontological way but rather what we hear is a composition in our own imaginations.

Sartre's position was influenced by Nicolai Hartmann, who was professor of theoretical philosophy in Berlin during the time that Sartre was at the city's Institut Français (1933–1934). Hartmann contrasted psychological and ontological approaches to aesthetics and championed the latter, his central thesis being that works of art are fictions dependent upon perceptual and imaginative activities conducted by both artists and audiences.[48] An artwork, according to Hartmann, is an 'observer-relative' appearance experienced as such. An appearance experienced *as appearance* and not to be confused with illusion. Illusion possesses no activity of self-reflexive awareness whereby it is known that something is being imagined as opposed to being believed. Hartmann deployed a decidedly performative illustrative example: children's play which, for the adult, 'remains fiction'.[49]

Around the same time, Margolis[50] contributes the supporting, self-evident observation that without the right kind of attention, the work of art ceases to exist as such even though its physical system remains. This current in philosophy led towards Roland Barthes's[51] assertion about the repressive ideology of the concept of artworks and his claim for the liberating conception of 'textuality' as that sphere of indeterminate possibilities which would sweep away fixed meaning and with it authorship, ownership and other mechanisms of repression. It is this developing trend in philosophy that exerts greatest influence over Performance Studies throughout the latter part of the twentieth century, and with that influence comes tacitly a very particular understanding of the category of performance.

Several philosophers endorse the idea that all works of art should be classified as actions or performances as opposed to the objects seemingly resulting from these activities. Following Croce, Collingwood and Dewey,[52] Jeffrey Maitland proposed that works of art are 'doings' and argued that an artwork is a 'performative presence' while three years later Dennis Dutton contended that 'as performances, works of art represent the ways in which artists solve problems, overcome obstacles, make do with available materials',[53] adding that 'the work of art has a human origin, and must be understood as such'.[54]

Currie put artworks in the category of 'action types', claiming that artworks are types of events, and events, according to Currie, form a 'natural ontological category'.[55] Currie even proposes a formula: an agent, A, discovers a structure, s, via a heuristic path, H, and a time, t. Thus, according to Currie, the artwork is something the artist 'performs' in doing; the artist does not create or discover the work.

These perspectives simultaneously revalue and depreciate the performance event as the anchor for the loci of the artwork. The sociocultural frameworks delineating artworks as artworks give out under philosophical analysis and the pressure caused as they are made to hold the weight of the ontological. Liveness is a useful structure to understand what performance is only insofar as it can describe the sociocultural expectations about a specific form of event. With regard to the ontic qualities of performance – if, indeed, it can even be said to have any that are divisible from sociocultural habits – performance is no more, and no more definitively live, than anything else that happens in the present moment. The various philosophical attempts to elevate art to the level of ontology must all make recourse to some form of object which predates and survives the artwork itself: an enduring category, path (Currie), doing (Maitland), attentiveness (Margolis), activity (Hartmann), substance (Gilson) or mode (Sartre).

Following the rigour of this philosophical thought, performance may be understood as a mode of training rather than training as a mode of performance. Performance events can be conceived of as exemplary – as exemplifications of the human 'fighting presence', as Arendt calls it – and this exemplary-ness is qualified by the extent to which it resists contingency and the incoherence of the phenomenal world, thereby emblematizing human presence as an agency attaining near-perfect control over itself. Even in performance events characterized by the aesthetic resistance to mastery, there still pertains mastery presenting itself through a different aesthetic formula – what Kear calls a 'tightly orchestrated mise-en-scène'[56] organizing the apparent unboundedness of amateurs in certain contemporary performance works.

Untangling the phenomenal from the ontic in the status of performance events makes space to comprehend the ontological nature of training. The phenomenological is that which appears to our senses while the ontological is that which relates to Being as such; ontic 'things' have, or relate to, Being that surpasses their sense-appearance and which can be derived by logical proposition substantiated by evidence from the senses, but whose proof is not reducible to or reliant upon sense apprehension alone. Performance, as an event of appearance as such, may constitute a particular phenomenal occurrence, socially and culturally coded, of the life of training, which pertains within the *now* of this event and also beyond it into the infinite past and infinite future. Rather than an adjunct to performance – a more or less inessential preparatory act – training may be the fundamental ontological ground of performance and performance a comparative phenomenal flash-in-the-pan.

This view proposes an inversion of our traditional hierarchy within the field of Theatre and Performance Studies whereby the cultural event of performance maintains supremacy over all other objects of study. Rebecca Schneider's criticisms notwithstanding, this is in one sense quite fitting – what else should be the primary focus of Theatre and Performance Studies if not the theatrical or performative event. What is less necessary for the fields and what may in fact be limiting of them is a myopic focus on these ephemeral phenomena as the sole or even primary basis of the ontic status of artworks. Performance cannot have ontic status as such except perhaps within the 'natural ontological category' of events precisely because it cannot exist in the same form with continuity in all three tenses of past, present and future. Ontology requires that we see the phenomenon with total temporal continuity and if the discipline of Performance Studies is to properly accept this prerequisite, performance may become in our understanding a phase or state within the continuity of training – an intensification of certain of its dynamics rather than training being a sublimation of the dynamics of performance as theory has traditionally supposed.[57]

Things that do not have permanence cannot by definition be thought of as ontological or rather cannot occupy the same ontic category as things which are permanent. Appearance and disappearance have relatively little to do with ontology which is defined by permanence and impermanence and continuity throughout time. In staging the question about performance's ontological nature on the grounds of its appearance and disappearance, Performance Studies has overvalued the event of performance which, really, has no special ontic significance even if it may occupy a self-consciously valuable place in society and culture.

Performance events may be to thought what training experiences may be to thinking. Events, like thought, may be coherent and boundaried and may even attain a sense of relative permanence, despite their ephemerality, on the basis of the irreducibility of their contents. Experiences without temporal boundaries, as with mental processes that do not complete themselves in conclusions, may achieve a different kind of permanence that resides not in outcomes but in the consistency with which they are involved in the *same thing*. This is what I have sought to describe as HOMEOSTASIS in the context of training, as that which finds its analogy in the fluctuating and unending, and yet self-identical, process of thinking. The imperative of truth may be the preserve of the transient event of performance – truth attained by the verifiability, veracity, invariance and irrefutability or things which appear to the senses – just as thought, in its crystallization as knowledge, represents truth in the form of facts that push out from the sheer flow of change and accrue relative stability in the continuum of time. The imperative of meaning, which bears a relationship to truth, remains in constant relation to the flow of change; meaning is active and not fixed, processual, contingent, adaptive, organized, developmental and yet, despite its variance, it attains great integrity insofar as it continues in loci about the same point or, to put it colloquially, stays on topic. Meaning is about some-thing whereas truth is a thing. As history has shown, meaning is bound to human Life as indivisibly as breathing is a part of human existence; truth, which achieves itself differently in each apparent fact established at any given point in time, is, by comparison, a hiccup. According to Arendt, both things – meaning and truth – issue from reason, which is, as philosophy from Kant onwards has established, a profound and perhaps foundational imperative. 'The need of reason is not inspired by the quest for truth', Arendt writes, 'but by the quest for meaning', and the 'basic fallacy, taking precedence over all specific metaphysical fallacies, is to interpret meaning on the model of truth'.[58] Perhaps the disciplines of theatre and performance, in both scholarship and practice, have succumbed to a specific version of this fallacy whereby the value of training has been secured by its relationship to performance events. Conversely, when one thinks ontologically about performance and training one cannot but help to see the former as the less credible claimant on ontic status, and so perhaps the ontic value of transient performance events is to be found not in their fugacity but in their occurrence within and because of enduring processes of training; their sense of truth may be anchored only by its connection to the persistent meaning of the activity, secured by our human efforts to do it, and indeed to do everything, better. Performance events, in their perfect temporal circumscription, are both the subject matter for and the justification of theatre history and performance epistemology, and for theory that has produced itself out of these archival remains. Rather than being of the present, as Phelan and Blau so persuasively suggested, performance is of the past because its sense of being performance as such comes only into being as it ceases to be as such. Training, either in the specific example of theatre-related activities or more broadly as the meta-disciplinary category that I have hitherto defined,[59] encompasses all three tenses, of past, present and future, with performance events being only one expression of its perpetuity in human lives and in human Life.

The life of training, as with the life of the mind, is productive of time and envelopes our human experiences of it. Training, like thinking, is a means by which humans can insert themselves into the world having made that world for themselves out of the inchoate materials given to them by the biological fact of their existence. Training, like thinking, is a means for humans to attain imperfect control over that world and to, within the remit of contingency predicated by the biological fact of their existence, perfect that control. Training, like thinking, is the means for humans to pass on to other humans the means for this control, and for its perfection, thereby defining what human means beyond the narrow scope of the biological fact of their existence. Training, like thinking, despite its ability to do all this, contains no safeguards against failure or mistakes and indeed contains within itself the latent and potent potential to expose humans to their utter subjection to the biological fact of their existence rather than to insulate against it. In this way, training, like thinking, models for time an unbreakable connection between the lives of individuals and the life of the species and makes sense of the fact that lives will begin and end but that time is infinite, even if human existence within it may be limited. Training and thinking are not opposites, and what is more, in relation to the stability of individual and species identities, the growth and development of people and of the human race, the human emersion in an environment, and our capacity to adapt to that environment, and to reproduce both ourselves and our achievements, their roles may be identical.

NOTES

Introduction

1 Letter to Ulrike, May 1799, in High, J.L., & Clark, S. (eds), *Heinrich von Kleist: Artistic and Political Legacies*, Amsterdam, Netherlands: Rodopi, 2013, 171.

2 See Sadie Stein's article 'The Final Chapter', in *The Parise Review*, 16 October 2014.

3 Read, A., *Theatre, Intimacy and Engagement: The Last Human Venue*, Houndsmills, Basingstoke & New York: Palgrave Macmillan, 2008, 283.

4 Ibid.

5 Arendt, H., *The Life of the Mind*, San Diego, New York, London: Harcourt Inc., 1978, 210.

6 Ibid.

7 Ibid., 15.

Chapter 1

1 Gillett, J., *Acting Stanislavksi*, London & New York: Methuen Drama (Bloomsbury), 2014, 83.

2 Ibid., 83.

3 Stanislavski, K., *An Actor Prepares*, London: Routledge, 2003 [1936], 97–98.

4 Ibid., 98.

5 This is a tradition that I have analysed and discussed in greater detail in the chapter 'Automatisation' in my first book *Training for Performance*, London: Methuen Drama (Bloomsbury), 2011.

6 Benjamin Spatz, for example, situates his own via Mauss, Foucault and Samuel Taylor Coleridge, Nicholas Crossly and Randy Martin (Spatz, B.,

What a Body Can Do, London & New York: Routledge, 2015, 26–36). In parallel to this secular tradition, the Christian lineage, from writers such as Thomas Merton, leads back, via Thomas Aquinas, to the same Aristotelian start point.

7 *Nicomachean Ethics* Book VI.

8 See Spatz (*What a Body Can Do*), whose project is primarily concerned with the conflation of these propositions and who identifies a trend in performance scholarship, influenced by J.J. Gibson and the phenomenological approach to perception towards their imbrication (42–44).

9 The two terms date back to the writings of Xenophon, who, in point of fact, does not differentiate but rather deploys them as near synonyms (Xenophon, *Memorabilia and Oeconomicus*, translated by E.C. Marchant, Loeb Classical Library, Cambridge: Harvard University Press, 1979). Plato too uses the terms almost interchangeably in his dialogues; Plato, *Complete Works*, John M. Cooper (ed.), Indianapolis: Hackett Publishing Co., 1997. Aristotle is the first to put some space between the terms that his forbears seemed intent on co-mingling.

10 For a fuller explication, see *Anatomy of Performance Training*, London & New York: Methuen Drama (Bloomsbury), 2014, 15–17.

11 *Metaphysics*, Book I.

12 Marx somewhat inverted this relation by arguing that the 'contemplative life' was a superstructure of the fundamental processes of life in society, and Arendt remarks on the fact that he uses 'praxis' to refer simply to 'what man does' in opposition to what man thinks (Arendt, *The Life of the Mind*, San Diego, New York & London: Harcourt Inc., 1978, 7).

13 Arendt, *The Life of the Mind*, 90.

14 Ibid., 93.

15 For a fuller explication, see the chapter 'The Wholly Actor', in my first book *Training for Performance*.

16 Schechner, R., *Performance Theory*, London; New York: Routledge, 2003, 30.

17 Arendt, *The Life of the Mind*, 205.

18 Ibid.

19 *The Imperative*, Bloomington, IN: University of Indiana Press, 1998, 179.

20 Ibid.

21 These are selected findings from my first two books, *Training for Performance* and *Anatomy of Performance Training*.

22 Read, *Theatre, Intimacy and Engagement*.

23 In a handwritten journal entry dated July 1953, she likened Heidegger to a fox attempting to lure potential victims into a trap that none of them can enter because the fox is itself trapped within it.

24 Arendt, *The Life of the Mind*, 5.

25 Ibid., 4.

26 For a fuller explication of the role of training in the context of twentieth- and twenty-first-century globalization, see *Anatomy of Performance Training*, 65–67.

27 For a fuller discussion, see *Training for Performance*, 14–15, and throughout chapter 2 (40–65).

28 Ibid.

29 Patterson, S., & Crane, T., *History of the Mind–Body Problem*, London; New York, NY: Routledge, 2000, 79.

30 Ibid.

31 Arendt, *The Life of the Mind*, 5.

32 Ibid., 8.

33 See *Training for Performance*, 14–15, chapter 2 (40–65) and chapter 7 (205–219).

34 See *Training for Performance*, 37–38, 76–78, 90–117, 123–126.

35 Arendt, *The Life of the Mind*, 205.

36 The Latin phrase meaning, literally, 'man as maker' was probably adopted by Arendt from the philosopher Henri Bergson (1859–1941).

37 Sennett, R., *The Craftsman*, New Haven & London: Yale University Press, 2008, 7.

38 The Renaissance philosopher Pico della Mirandola in his work, *Oration on the Dignity of Man* (1486), adds the 'my own maker' slant to the 'man as maker' definition of *homo faber*, and Sennett is convinced that Pico is an unacknowledged source for Arendt (Sennett, *The Craftsman*, 72).

39 Ibid., 8.

40 See *Anatomy of Performance Training*, 123–144.

41 'Factical Dasein exists as born; and, as born, it is already dying, in the sense of Being-towards-death ... birth and death are "connected" in a manner characteristic of Dasein. As care, Dasein is the "between"'. *Being and Time*, translated by J. Macquarrie and E. Robinson, Oxford: Basil Blackwell, 1962 (first published in 1927), 73.

42 Ibid., 63. Readers may note here a formal similarity to Aristotle's writings on the imperative, which so heavily influence Heidegger.

43 For example, Biskowski, L.J., 'Politics vs Aesthetics: Arendt's Critiques of Nietzsche and Heidegger', *The Review of Politics*, 57 (1) (Winter, 1995), 59–89.

44 See Section 1, 'Appearance', in Arendt, *The Life of the Mind*, 19–68.

45 *The Human Condition*, Chicago: University of Chicago Press, 1958, 220.

46 Ibid., 237. It may only appear this way to me but I can't help but read 'in the darkness of Martin's lonely heart' here, but this is perhaps more as a result of my fascination with the psychodrama of human relations than the rigour of philosophy.

47 Ibid., 8–9.

48 Ibid., 199.

49 Arendt, *The Life of the Mind*, 34.

50 Ibid., 34.

51 Ibid.

52 While the idea of 'natural' things has fallen rather out of fashion in performance theory, the description seems quintessential here. Indeed, while Irving Goffman and Judith Butler, and their numerous disciples, have emphasized the performative aspects of social roles, and of identity most specifically, the ontological nature of human life itself has received rather less attention in Performance Studies. In point of fact, the strictures of performing self and the immediate requirement to do so can and should be seen in the context of the human project of training.

53 Arendt, *The Life of the Mind*, 20.

54 Ibid.

55 Ibid., 21.

56 Ibid., 22.

57 Spatz, *What a Body Can Do*, 1.

58 Ibid.

59 Ibid., 23–72.

60 Ibid., 120.

61 Ibid.

62 Ibid., 56.

63 See 'Foot' in *Anatomy of Performance Training,* 54–75.

64 This is a basic principle of comparative analysis. A scholar may compare two plays so as to analyse each and is only able to do so, and to derive knowledge about each, precisely because each is *a play*. Comparing a play with a chair or aeroplane engine, for example, will not afford a comparative analysis (even if it may be the basis for a metaphor) and cannot generate knowledge about plays, as such.

65 Spatz, *What a Body Can Do*, 120.

66 I did not, and do not, contend that these processes are the only meta-disciplinary processes of training.

67 See *Training for Performance*.

68 See *Anatomy of Performance Training*.

69 See *Training for Performance*.

70 Smith, C.U.M., *The Problem of Life: An Essay in the Origins of Biological Thought*, New York: Wiley, 1976, 72.

71 Arendt, *The Life of the Mind*, 20–21.

72 In Agamben, G., *Potentialities*, Stanford, CA: Stanford University Press, 1990, 182.

73 See Peggy Phelan's *Unmarked: The Politics of Performance* (New York & London: Routledge, 1993) for the archetypal example, as well as Hebert Blau's *Take Up the Bodies: Theatre at the Vanishing Point* (Urbana: University of Illinois Press, 1982).

Chapter 2

1 In Agamben, *Potentialities*, 182.

2 Arendt, *The Life of the Mind*, 34.

3 Anatomically speaking, the inner surfaces of the lungs and of the digestive track are also, technically, outer surfaces because they come into direct physical contact with non-bodily agents. However, I am using 'surface' in a more commonplace way here to refer to the outer, and visible, anatomical parts of the human body.

4 *Four Essays on Liberty*, Oxford: Oxford University Press, 1969, 19.

5 Kumpulainen, Seppo, 'From Sweat and Tears towards Sweat and Harmony', *Theatre, Dance and Performance Training*, 3 (2), 2012, 4.

6 For example, ranking each student, publicly, in front of an audience of hundreds of people (ibid., 7).

7 Ibid., 5.

8 Ibid., 9.

9 Kumpulainen, 'From Sweat and Tears towards Sweat and Harmony', 10.

10 'Power and Presence in the Actor-Training Institution Audition', *Australasian Drama Studies*, 50, April 1996, 139.

11 Seton, M., 'Recognising and Mis-Recognising the "x" Factor: The Audition Selection Process in Actor-training Institutions Revisited', *Australasian Drama Studies*, 50, 2007, 170. In acting, as in many other contexts of performance – such as sport or dance – talent's irreducibility to any concept other than itself is indicative: she's got 'it', one may assert, and at the same time affirm that what 'it' is cannot be described in any terms other than its *it-ness.* In English-language usage, 'it' features as the nominative of an impersonal verb – *so it goes* – or as transitive to an intransitive verb – *that's it; there it is; that's just the way it goes* – and so accordingly, 'it' serves as a very effective placeholder for the perceived ipseity or 'giveness' of talent. Mark Seton has observed that assumptions about the giveness, illustrated through its near synonym gifted, tend to avow a sense of talent as an object, or a 'having', as Aristotle would have it. Seton suggests that we err to see talent as an object or attribute of a person and that we may be better served to see talent as a 'becoming-in-between', a 'transactional agency' rather than 'a self-sufficient giveness', and indeed the training concept itself is anchored to the idea that irrespective of a person's 'gifts', these will need to be cultivated with and by others in order to attain their epiphany.

12 The essay 'Uber das Marionetten Theater' was first published in four installments in the daily *Berliner Abendblatter* from 12 to 15 December 1810. Kleist was editor of the newspaper. See *The Drama Review: TDR*, 16 (3), September 1972, 22–26.

13 Seton, 'Recognising and Mis-Recognising the "x" Factor', 170.

14 Murray, S., 'Keywords in Performer Training', *Theatre, Dance and Performance Training*, 6 (1), 2015, 46–58.

15 Murray writes, 'My plea, as it were, is that as performer trainers, or as writers about performer training, we exercise considerably more self-reflexivity – and awareness of context – as we utter or write these words' (ibid.).

16 Aujla, Imogen J., Sanna M. Nordin-Bates, Emma Redding and Veronica Jobbins, 'Developing Talent Among Young Dancers: Findings from the UK Centres for Advanced Training', *Theatre, Dance and Performance Training*, 5 (1), 2014, 16.

17 Ibid.

18 Ibid., 15.

19 Ibid.

20 This selection is exclusively male, largely because these discussions focus on the role of Hamlet, which is typically played by a man.

21 Quoted in Turner, Camilla, 'Working with Michael Gambon was "Hair Raising," says Dame Maggie Smith', *The Telegraph*, 1 March, 2015.

22 Quoted in Iqbaal, Noshen, 'Michael Gambon Bows Out of Alan Bennet's *The Habit of Art*', *The Guardian*, 2 October, 2009.

23 Quoted in Harrison, David, 'Unscripted end to Gambon's Career on Stage', *The Sunday Times*, 8 February 2015.

24 Quoted in Heighton, Luke, 'Sir Michael Gambon Forced to Quit Theatre due to "Frightening" Memory Loss', *The Telegraph*, 8 February 2015.

25 *The National Theatre Story*, London: Oberon Books, 2013, 66.

26 Ibid., 66–67.

27 Ibid., 67.

28 Ridout, N., *Stage Fright: Animals and Other Theatrical Problems*, Cambridge: Cambridge University Press, 2006, 9.

29   Cited in Ellis, Samantha, 'Hamlet. National Theatre. October 1963' *The Guardian*, 12 March 2003.

30   Ibid.

31   In Sellers, Robert, *Don't Let the Bastards Grind You Down: How One Generation of British Actors Changed the World*, Vauxhall, London: Arrow Books, 2012, 400.

32   Ibid.

33   In Raine, Kathleen, *Yeats the Initiate: On Certain Themes in the Writings of WB Yeats*, Savage, MD: Barnes & Noble, 1990, 320.

34   Fielding, Henry, *The History of Tom Jones: A Foundling Volume 2*, London: Baines & Son, 1825, 308.

35   Reynolds, Frederick, *The Life and Times of Frederick Reynolds*, London: Henry Colburn, 1826, 88.

36   Aggerholm, Kenneth, *Talent Development, Existential Philosophy and Sport: On Becoming an Elite Athlete*, London and New York: Routledge, 2015.

37   Ibid., 27.

38   Ibid., 31.

39   Ibid., 29–31.

40   Sartre, J.-P., *Being and Nothingness: An Essay on Phenomenological Ontology*, trans. H.E., Barnes, London and New York: Routledge, 2013, 124.

41   Aggerholm, *Talent Development, Existential Philosophy and Sport*, 31.

42   Ibid.

43   Ibid.

44   Ibid., 32.

45   Ibid., 29.

46   Ibid., 30.

47   Ibid.

48   Ibid.

49   Ibid.

50   See Arendt, H., 'What Is Existential Philosophy?', in *Essays on Understanding: 1930–1954*, New York: Schoken Books, 2005.

51   Agamben, *Potentialities*, 177.

52   Ibid.

53   Even if these are the partial and subjectively established aims of art as opposed to science.

54   Trans. Agamben, *Potentialities*, 183.

55   Ibid., 182.

56   Ibid.

57 Italics in original, Agamben, *Potentialities*, 182.

58 For a fuller discussion, see 'Suffering Alteration', in *Training for Performance*, London and New York: Methuen Drama (Bloomsbury), 2011, 19–20.

59 Italics in original, Agamben, *Potentialities*, 183.

60 Ibid., 184.

Chapter 3

1 Roach, J., *The Player's Passion: Studies in the Science of Acting*, London and Toronto: Associated Universities Press, 1985, 56.

2 Ibid.

3 Joseph Roach's book, *The Player's Passion*, traces this history with reference to the co-emergence of ideas and ideals in science and art. Benedetti, J., *The Art of the Actor: The Essential History of Acting, From Classical Times to the Present Day*, London: Methuen Drama, 2005, also describes this historical shift, within the specific realm of aesthetics.

4 The former referring to our given, biological being and the latter referring to our human activities throughout (Western) history, as discussed in Arendt's work of the same name.

5 *Poetics*, 4, 1448b 4–9 (quoted in Somville, P., *Essai sur la Poétique d'Aristote et sur quelques aspects de son posterité*, Paris: J. Vrin, 1975, 44).

6 Book I, chapter IX.

7 Strasberg, in Cohen, L. (ed.), *The Lee Strasberg Notes*, London and New York: Routledge, 2010, 1.

8 The counter-argument would, of course, be that human activities with no apparent survival advantage (such as, for example, art-making) may have indirect advantages to this end, for example, vis-à-vis social solidarity or tribal identity. This argument seems to me tenuous at least and not falsifiable at best, and therefore to be considered more an ideological premise than a research finding.

9 Trans. Hapgood, E., *An Actor Prepares*, New York: Theatre Arts Inc., 1936, 20, 43, 72, 68, 140, 307.

10 Ibid., 76, 84.

11 Ibid., 56, 274, 122, 277, 149, 275.

12 Trans. Hapgood, E., *Building a Character*, New York: Theatre Arts Inc., 1949, 216.

13 Ibid., 241.

14 Ibid.

15 Trans. Hapgood, E., *Creating a Role*, New York: Theatre Arts Inc., 1961, 22–23.

16 Arendt, H., *The Life of the Mind*, San Diego, New York and London: Harvest Inc., 1978, 211.

17 Benedetti suggest the enlightenment and the key texts as pivotal in an historical shift from declamation to acting (*Art of the Actor,* 40–85).

18 In Benedetti, *The Art of the Actor*, 79.

19 See ibid., 57, and also Roach, *The Player's Passion*, 56–57.

20 List some of Csikszentmihalyi books.

21 It is generally agreed that Csikszentmihalyi first recorded the psychological state of 'flow', giving it its name and provoking a sub-field of research, *Flow: The Psychology of Optimal Experience*, New York: Harper & Row, 1990.

22 Csikszentmihalyi, M., and Jackson, S.A., *Flow in Sport*, Champaign, L: Human Kinetics, 1999, 5–6.

23 Ibid., 6.

24 Ibid.

25 For fuller explication of 'now' and 'nows' in Aristotle, see Sarah Waterlow's article, 'Aristotle's Now', *Philosophical Quarterly*, 34 (135), 1984, 104–128.

26 *Finding Flow: The Psychology of Everyday Life*, New York: Basic Books, 1997, 8.

27 Csikszentmihalyi, *Flow: The Psychology of Optimal Experience*, 66–67.

28 Csikszentmihalyi, *Flow in Sport*, 73.

29 Ibid., 74.

30 Essays I. ii. 24.

31 In *The Critique of Judgement* (trans. Werner S. Pluhar, Indianapolis: Hackett Publishing, 1987), Kant writes that art 'is a way of presenting that is purposive on its own and that furthers, even though without a purpose, the culture of our mental powers to [facilitate] social communication' and 'it must have the look of nature even though we are conscious of it as art' (173–174).

32 Csikszentmihalyi, *Flow: The Psychology of Optimal Experience*, 213.

33 Seton, 'Recognising and Mis-Recognising the "x" Factor', 171.

34 Murray, S., *12 Keywords in Performer Training,* published online: 26 January 2015, 46–58.

35 See chapter 2 of *Training for Performance* for full discussion.

36 Grotowski, via negativa, Lang Primal Scream plus chapter 2 of *Training for Performance*.

37 See 'The Wholly Actor', in *Training for Performance*, London and New York: Methuen Drama (Bloomsbury), 2011, 40–66 and also 'FOOT', in *Anatomy of Performance Training*, London and New York: Methuen Drama (Bloomsbury), 2014, 53–76.

38 For a fuller discussion see 'Automatisation', in *Training for Performance*, London and New York: Methuen Drama (Bloomsbury), 2011, 173–204.

39 Although well-discussed by numerous authors, the variations in Stanislavski's approach throughout his own life, and the various impacts of these variations, are especially well-captured in Rose Whyman's scholarly work, *The Stanislavsky System: Legacy and Influence in Modern Performance*, Cambridge: Cambridge University Press, 2008.

40 Benedetti, J., *Stanislavski: His Life and Art*, revised edn, London: Methuen, 1999 [1988], 325 and 360 and *The Art of the Actor*, 121. Also in Roach, J., *The Player's Passion: Studies in the Science of Acting*, Ann Arbor: University of Michigan Press, 1985, 197–198, 205, 211–215. Benedetti indicates that Stanislavski's earliest explorations of this approach date back to 1916, but he did not test these practically until the early 1930s (*Stanislavski: His Life and Art*, 356 and 358). Robert Gordon has contested that the shift towards this approach occurred earlier, during the 1920s (*The Purpose of Playing: Modern Acting Theories in Perspective*, Ann Arbor: University of Michigan Press, 2006, 49–55).

41 Benedetti, *Stanislavski: His Life and Art*, 326. Also in Magarshack's, *Stanislavsky: A Life*, London and Boston: Faber, 1986 [1950], 372–373.

42 Benedetti, *Stanislavski: His Life and Art*, 70 and 355–356. Also in Leach's *Makers of Modern Theatre: An Introduction*, London: Routledge, 2004, 29, and Magarshack, *Stanislavsky: A Life*, 373–375.

43 Benedetti, *Stanislavski: His Life and Art*, 355 and Magarshack, *Stanislavsky: A Life*, 375. Also in Whyman's *The Stanislavsky System of Acting: Legacy and Influence in Modern Performance*, Cambridge: Cambridge University Press, 2008, 242.

44 See previous chapter, and also Kumpulainen, Seppo, 'From Sweat and Tears to Sweat and Harmony', *Theatre, Dance and Performance Training*, published online: 25 June 2012, 229–241.

45 Csikszentmihalyi, Mihaly, *Creativity: Flow and the Psychology of Discovery and Invention*, New York: Harper Collins, 1996, 113.

46 Phelan, *Unmarked*, 146.

47 Blau, *Take Up the Bodies*, 28.

48 Ibid., 94.

49 Schneider, Rebecca, 'Performance Remains', *Performance Research*, 6 (2), 2001, 101.

50 Ibid., 100.

51 Ibid.

52 Arendt, *The Life of the Mind*, 17.

53 Deutshcer, Max, *Judgement after Arendt*, London and New York: Routledge, 2016, 82.

54 See *Anatomy of Performance Training*, 77–108.

55 Arendt, *The Life of the Mind*, 205–206.

56 Ibid., 206.

57 Ibid., 210.

58 Ibid., 13.

59 Ibid.

60 Ibid., 207.

61 Ibid.

62 Ibid.

63 Ibid., 209.

64 Ibid., 12.

65 Ibid.

66 A real-world example of this interplay can be found in the chapter 'HEART', in *Anatomy of Performance Training*, London and New York: Methuen Drama (Bloomsbury), 2014, 109–130.

67 The thinking ego – the 'I' – is not the same thing as the 'incarnation' of body and mind.

68 Arendt, *The Life of the Mind*, 206.

69 Ibid.

70 One of Stanislavski's actor's, Vasili Toporkov, gives a fairly detailed account of this approach from Stanislavski's own rehearsals in his *Stanislavski in Rehearsal: The Final Years*, trans. Jean Benedetti, London: Methuen, 1987.

71 *An Actor's Work on a Role*, London and New York: Routledge, 2010, 55.

72 Ibid.

73 *The Stanislavsky System of Acting*, 67–70.

74 Gillett, *Acting Stanislavksi*, 81 (emphasis in original).

75 *Signs of Performance: An Introduction to Twentieth Century Theatre* London and New York: Routledge, 1996, 24.

76 Ibid., 25.

77 Cooper-Albright, Ann, *Choreographing Difference: The Body and Identity in Contemporary Dance*, Middletown, CT: Wesleyan University Press, 1997, xii.

78 Ibid., 84–85.

79 Personal correspondence with the author, 27 April 2017.

80 Ibid.

81 I have written about this practice at greater length in 'What Is a Workshop?', *Theatre, Dance and Performance Training*, 3 (3), 2012, 349–361.

82 Personal correspondence with the author, 27 April 2017.

83 Personal correspondence with the author, 28 April 2017.

84 Personal correspondence with the author, 27 April 2017.

85 Personal correspondence with the author, 28 April 2017.

86 Personal correspondence with the author, 27 April 2017.

87 Arendt, *The Life of the Mind*, 43.

Chapter 4

1 Arendt, *The Life of the Mind*, 7.

2 Ibid., 114.

3 Ibid.

4 Ibid.

5 Ibid., 120.

6 Ibid., 153.

7 Ibid., 151.

8 Ibid., 152.

9 Ibid.

10 Ibid.

11 Ibid.

12 Ibid.

13 Ibid.

14 Ibid. See also my article 'What Is a Workshop?', 349–361.

15 Ibid., 153.

16 Ibid.

17 Ibid.

18 Ibid.

19 In Arendt, *The Life of the Mind*, 118.

20 Ibid., 153.

21 Some might say, with recognizing the phallocentric rhetoric of progress or of its ideals.

22 A small range of examples of the 'training packages' that I have accessed through my employer this year alone.

23 This is exemplified in the philosophy of Alfred North Whitehead and his idea of the 'rhythms' of learning, expressed in his *Aims of Education*, New York: The Free Press, 1929.

24 See *Training for Performance*, 67–103.

25 Matthews, *Training for Performance*, 71, and also Cochran, Larry, *The Sense of Vocation: A Study of Career and Life Development*, Albany, NY: SUNY Press, 1990.

26 Matthews, *Anatomy of Performance Training*, 141.

27 Personal correspondence with the author, 28 July 2017.

28 Ibid.

29 Subtitle of the book: 'The essential history of acting from classical times to the present day'.

30 See *The Player's Passion*, 23–47.

31 Hall, J., 'Cicero and Quintilian on the Oratorical Use of Hand Gestures', *The Classical Quarterly*, 2, 54 (1), May 2004, 143.

32 John Hall makes the point that we have frustratingly 'little evidence' from Cicero about his own 'practices of oratorical delivery' (ibid.).

33 See Caplan's introduction to *Rhetorica ad Herennium*, Massachusetts: Harvard University Press, 1954.

34 Book XII, 'Introduction'.

35 Quintilian, *Instutio Oratoria*, Book 12.4.

36 Ibid.

37 Ibid., Book 11.3.1.

38 Ibid., Book 10.2.1.

39 Ibid., Book 11.2.

40 See Roach, *The Player's Passion*, 33.

41 Ibid., 29.

42 Quintilian, *Institutio Oratoria*, Book 11.3.88–89.

43 Trans. Hapgood, *Building a Character*, 77.

44 Ibid., 183.

45 Hodge, Alison (ed.), *Twentieth Century Actor Training*, London and New York: Routledge, 2000, 2.

46 Arendt, *The Life of the Mind*, 26.

47 Ibid., 4.

48 See Jones, Michael T., 'Heidegger the Fox: Hannah Arendt's Hidden Dialogue', *New German Critique* No. 73, Special Issue on Heiner Muller, Winter 1998, 164–192.

49 Heidegger, Martin, *What Is Called Thinking?*, trans. J. Glen Gray, New York: Harper & Row, 1968, 121.

50 In 1928–1929, Levinas travelled to Freiburg to study with Edmund Husserl and attended Heidegger's seminars in these years. In the 1930s he published writings on the philosophy of his two teachers, including 'Martin Heidegger and Ontology' ('Martin Heidegger et l'ontologie' first appeared in *Revue philosophique*, in 1932. It was reprinted in abridged form in Levinas, *En découvrant l'existence avec Husserl et Heidegger*, Paris: Vrin, 1949 [1967], 53–76) and 'The Work of Edmund Husserl' (first published in the *Revue Philosophique*, January–February 1940; reprinted in *En découvrant l'existence avec Husserl et Heidegger*, 53–76).

51 Heidegger, *What Is Called Thinking?*, 3.

52 Ibid.

53 An almost interchangeable position with Levinas's translator, Alphonso Lingis, regarding the 'imperative': see Lingis, *The Imperative*, 1.

54 Heidegger, *What Is Called Thinking?*, 14.

55 Ibid.

56 *Anatomy of Performance Training*, 4.

57 Heidegger, *What Is Called Thinking?*, 14–15.

58 See *Meditations of First Philosophy* (first published 1641), especially Meditations II and VI.

59 See *An Essay concerning Human Understanding* (first published 1689), especially Book II, chapter 27, Sections 15 & 16.

60 See *A Treatise concerning the Principles of Human Knowledge* (first published 1710).

61 See *A Treatise of Human Nature* (first published 1738).

62 See *Leviathan* (1651), but also more pertinently in this context, *De Cive* (1642), in English as, *On the Citizen* (1651), as a part of the trilogy, including *De Corpore* (1655) and *De Homine* (1658), concerning human knowledge.

63 See Kim, J., *Philosophy of Mind*, 3rd edn, Boulder, CO: Westview Press, 2010.

64 Ibid., 3.

65 Heidegger, 1951, in Farrell Krell, D. (ed.), *Heidegger: Basic Writings*, 2nd edn, London: Routledge & Kegan Paul, 1993, 369.

66 Ibid., 374.

67 Arendt writes that according to traditions of Christian time, when philosophy had become the handmaiden of theology, thinking became meditation and meditation again ended in contemplation, a kind of blessed state of the soul where the mind was no longer stretching out to know the truth but, in anticipation of a future state, received it temporarily in intuition.

68 Arendt, *The Life of the Mind*, 7.

69 Ibid., 129.

70 Ibid.

71 Ibid., 121.

72 Ibid.

73 Arendt, *The Life of the Mind*, 129.

74 Ibid., 131.

75 Ibid.

76 Ibid., 153.

77 Ibid.

78 Ibid., 154.

79 Ibid.

80 Hodge, *Twentieth Century Actor Training*, 1.

81 bid.

82 bid., 1–2.

83 bid., 2.

84 Ibid.

85 Ibid.

86 Ibid., 3.

87 Arendt, *The Life of the Mind*, 24.

88 Ibid.

89 Ibid.

90 Ibid., 26.

91 Ibid., 21.

92 *The New Age Movement*, Oxford: Blackwell Publishing, 1996, 169.

93 *Religion in the Modern World: From Cathedrals to Cults*, Oxford: Oxford University Press, 1996, 197.

94 See Andrew Ross's *Strange Weather: Culture, Science and Technology in the Age of Limits*, London and New York: Verso, 1991, 21, and Wendy Parkin's 'Oprah Winfrey's Change Your Life TV and the Spiritual Everyday', *Journal of Media and Cultural Studies*, 15 (2), 2001, 145–157.

95 Heelas, P., 'The New Age in Cultural Context: The Premodern, the Modern and the Postmodern', *Religion*, 23, 1993, 103–116, and Heelas, P.L.F., 'Prosperity and the New Age Movement. The Efficacy of Spiritual Economics', in B. Wilson and J. Cressell (eds), *New Religious Movements: Challenges and Response*, London: Routledge, 1999, 49–77.

96 'Power and Empowerment: New Age Managers and the Dialectics of Modernity/Postmodernity', *Religion Today*, 9 (3), 1994, 3–13.

97 'L'emergence d'un "marche spirituel" religieux', *Social Compass*, 46 (2), 1999, 161–172.

98 *In Search of New Age Spiritualities*, Hampshire: Ashgate, 2005, notably 131–133.

99 *Anatomy of Performance Training*, 69–73.

100 Ibid., 54.

101 Reportedly, Boardman's exact words were 'shite when it mattered' in James Witts, *The Science of the Tour De France*, London: Bloomsbury, 2016, 110.

102 Ibid.

103 'British Cycling Appoints New Head of Secret Squirrel Club', *BBC*, posted online, 14 May, 2013, accessible at http://www.bbc.co.uk/sport/cycling/22525004.

104 June edition, 2017.

105 Ibid.

106 Arendt, *The Life of the Mind*, 54.

107 Ibid.

108 *Stanislavski: An Introduction*, 4th edn, London and New York: Bloomsbury, 2015, 'Introduction'.

109 Trans. Hapgood, *An Actor Prepares*, New York and London: Routledge, 1989 [1936], 8.

110 Trans. Hapgood, *Creating a Role*, New York and London: Methuen Drama (Bloomsbury), 2013 [1981], 220.

111 Trans. Hapgood, *An Actor Prepares*, 15.

112 Ibid.

113 Ibid.

114 Ibid., 16.

115 Trans. Hapgood, *Creating a Role*, 220.

116 Ibid.

117 Benedetti, J., *Stanislavski and the Actor*, London: Random House (Methuen), 1998, ix.

118 *Towards a Poor Theatre*, New York: Theatre Arts Book, 2012 [1968], 35.

119 *The Empty Space*, New York: Touchstone, 1996 [1968], 28.

120 *The Actor and the Target*, London: Nick Hern Book, 2002, 6.

121 *A Challenge for the Actor*, New York: Scribner, 1991, 42.

122 *Stanislavski: An Introduction*, New York and London: Methuen Drama (Bloomsbury), 2008 [1982], ix.

123 In Stanislavski, K., *An Actor's Work*, trans. J. Benedetti, New York and Oxon: Routledge Classics, 2017, xv.

124 Ibid., xviii.

125 Ibid.

126 Ibid.

127 Ibid.

128 Ibid.

129 Ibid., xix.

130 Ibid.

131 Ibid., x.

132 Arendt, *The Life of the Mind*, 55.

133 Ibid., 57.

134 Ibid., 59.

135 Ibid., 62.

136 See ibid., 64–65.

137 Barba, E., 'An Amulet Made of Memory', in P.B. Zarrilli (ed.), *Acting (re) Considered: A Theoretical and Practical Guide*, London and New York: Routledge, 2002, 101.

138 For a fuller discussion, see *Anatomy of Performance Training*, 21–23.

139 'Recognising and Mis-Recognising the "x" factor', 170–182.

140 'Power and Presence in the Actor-Training Institution Audition', 139.

141 Ibid.

Chapter 5

1 Mark, Eric, *Business Darwinism: Evolve or Dissolve, Adaptive Strategies for the Information Age*, New York: John Wiley & Sons, 2002.

2 Symon, Alex, *Mel Brooks in the Cultural Industries: Survival and Prolonged Adaptation*, Edinburgh: Edinburgh University, 2012.

3 Newitz, Annalee, *Scatter, Adapt and Remember: How Humans Will Survive a Mass Extinction*, New York, London, Toronto, Sydney, Auckland: Doubleday [Random House], 2013.

4 New House, M. and Mesaline, P., *The Actors Survival Kit*, 5th edn, Toronto and Oxford: Simon & Pierre, 2010.

5 Flanagan, M., *An Actor's Survival Guide*, Boulder, CO: Sentient Publishing, 2008.

6 Tucker, P. and Ozanne, C., *The Actors Survival Handbook*, New York and London: Routledge, 2005.

7 Menger, Pierre-Michel, *The Economics of Creativity*, Cambridge, MA and London: Harvard University Press, 2014, 1.

8 Ibid., 2.

9 Ibid.

10 Ibid.

11 Arendt, *The Life of the Mind*, 7.

12 Arendt, *The Human Condition*, 151.

13 *The Hidden Philosophy of Hannah Arendt*, London and New York: Routledge Curzon, 2002, 256.

14 Feenberg, A. and Barney, D.D., *Community in the Digital Age: Philosophy and Practice*, Boulder, CO: Rowman and Littlefield Publishers Inc., 2004, 41.

15 Arendt, *The Human Condition*, 320–321.

16 Soles, Clyde, *Climbing: Training for Peak Performance*, 2nd edn, Seattle, WA: The Mountaineers Books, 2008, 131, and also in Chiras, Daniel D., *Human Biology*, 5th edn, Burlington, MA: Jones & Bartlett Publishers, 2005, 229.

17 *The Science of Training*, Abingdon, Oxon and New York: Routledge, 2007, 2.

18 Ibid.

19 Personal correspondence with the author, 21 November 2017.

20 Usain Bolt, the multi-Olympic gold medallist and World Champion sprinter, made the same statement about 'vomiting daily' during intensive training in the 2016 documentary film *I am Bolt* (directed by Gabe & Benjamin Turner, London: Fulwell 73).

21 Lingis, A., *Foreign Bodies*, London and New York: Routledge, 1994, 41.

22 Fuchs, Wolfgang W., 'Seeing the Named. Naming the Seen', in A.E. Hooke and W.W. Fuchs (eds), *Encounters with Alphonso Lingis*, Lanham, Boulder, New York, Oxford: Lexington Books, 2003, 27.

23 See Arendt, *The Human Condition*, 150–153.

24 Arendt, *The Life of the Mind*, 15.

25 Ibid., 27.

26 Fuchs, *Encounters with Alphonso Lingis*, 26.

27 Ibid., 23.

28 Ibid.

29 Ibid.

30 Ibid., 26–27.

31 Trueman, Matt, 'Drama Schools Are a Waste of Money Says National Youth Theatre Director', *The Guardian,* 24 October 2013, and Merrifield, Nicola, 'Three-Year Drama Training Not Needed by "Majority of Actors"', *The Stage*, 24 October 2013.

32 In Trueman, 'Drama Schools Are a Waste of Money Says National Youth Theatre Director'.

33 Ibid.

34 Ridout, N., *Stage Fright and Other Theatrical Problems*, Cambridge: Cambridge University Press, 2006, 41.

35 Ibid.

36 Ibid., 97.

37 Ibid.

38 Ibid.

39 See 'Part 1: Ancient', in Ridout, N., *Theatre & Ethics*, Basingstoke, Hampshire: Palgrave Macmillan, 2009.

40 *Training for Performance*, 37.

41 Ibid., and for a fuller discussion, see pages 35–37.

42 Sewell, A., *Black Beauty: Autobiography of a Horse*, Woodbridge, Suffolk: Jarrold & Sons, 1877, 62.

43 Arendt, *The Life of the Mind*, 123.

44 Ibid.

45 Ibid.

46 Ibid.

47 Ibid., 203–205.

48 Sohmer, S., *Shakespeare's Mystery Play: The Opening of the Globe Theatre 1599*, Manchester and New York: Manchester University Press, 1999, 204.

49 Arendt, *The Life of the Mind*, 123–124.

50 In Berger-Helmschen (ed.), *The Economics of Creativity*, London and New York: Routledge, 2013, 99.

51 See 'HEART', in *Anatomy of Performance Training*, 109–130.

52 Menger, in Berger-Helmschen, *The Economics of Creativity*, 99.

53 Ibid.

54 Ibid.

55 Ibid.

56 Ibid.

57 See 'ORGANIZATION' page 96.

58 Menger, in Berger-Helmschen, *The Economics of Creativity*.

59 Ibid.

60 Ibid., 100.

61 Ibid.

62 Ibid.

63 Ibid.

64 Arendt, *The Life of the Mind*, 74.

65 See Hodge, *Twentieth Century Actor Training*.

66 *Gardzienice: Polish Theatre in Transition*, Amsterdam B.V.: Harwood Academic Publisher, 1997, 105.

67 *The Art of Stillness*, New York: Palgrave Macmillan, 2003, 132.

68 Ibid., 7.

69 Ibid., 97.

70 Ibid., 126.

71 See Matthews, J., 'Acting Freely', *Performance Research*, 14 (2), 2009, 103–112.

72 Berlin, I., 'Two Concepts of Liberty', in *Four Essays on Liberty*, Oxford: Oxford University Press, 1969 [1958], 122.

73 Ibid., 131.

74 This is an argument within my article 'Acting Freely', 103–112.

75 See Matthews, J. and Ladron deGuevara, V., 'Auditions and Stress', *Stanislavski Studies*, 5 (2), 2017, 217–231.

76 Artaud, A., *Antonin Artaud: Selected Writing*, ed. S. Sontag, Berkeley: University of California Press, 1988, 260.

77 Ibid., xxxii.

78 Wolford, L. and Schechner, R. (eds.), *The Grotowski Sourcebook*, London and New York: Routledge, 1997, 10.

79 Grotowski, J., *Towards a Poor Theatre*, London: Methuen, 1991 [1968], 17.

80 *The Actor and the Target*, 2.

81 Ibid.

82 *Anatomy of Performance Training*, 40–41.

83 *Training for Performance*, 40–66.

84 Slowiak, J. and Cuesta, J., *Jerzy Grotowski*, Abingdon, Oxon: Routledge, 2007, 73.

85 In *New Theatre Quarterly*, 8 (31), August 1992, 252.

86 Trans. Camilleri, Frank, *On Training and Performance: Traces of an Odin Teatret Actress*, Abingdon, Oxon and New York: Routledge, 2014, 58.

87 According to Frank Camilleri, 'Odin Teatret Performers Learnt [exercises] Directly from Ryzard Cieslak in the 1960s', in Camilleri, *Odin Teatret,* 26–27.

88 Ibid., 58.

89 Ibid.

90 Ibid., 59.

91 Ibid.

92 See Roach, J., *The Player's Passion: Studies in the Science of Acting*, Ann Arbor: University of Michigan, 1993 [1985], 39–42.

93 Benedetti, *The Art of the Actor*, 20.

94 See Hodge, *Twentieth Century Actor Training*.

95 https://www.theguardian.com/stage/2003/jul/26/theatre.artsfeatures.

96 Roudané, Matthew Charles, *Conversations with Arthur Miller*, Jackscn and London: University Press of Mississippi, 1987, 76.

97 Counsell, C., *Sign of Performance: An Introduction to Twentieth Cenīury Theatre*, London and New York: Routledge, 1996, 56.

98 Ibid.

99 Hirsch, F., *A Method to Their Madness: A History of the Actors' Studīo New York*, New York: W.W. Norton, 1984, 75.

100 'Recognising and Mis-Recognising the "x" Factor', 170–182.

101 'Power and Presence in the Actor-Training Institution Audition', 139.

102 See Seton, M., with Maxwell, I. and Szabó, M., 'The Australian Actors' Wellbeing Study: A Preliminary Report', *About Performance: The Lives of Actors*, 13, 2015, 69–113; Seton, M., with Prior, R., Maxwell, I. and Szabó, M., 'Responsible Care in Actor Training: Effective Support for Occupational Health Training in Drama Schools', *Theatre, Dance and Performance Training*, 6 (1), 2013, 59–71; and Seton, M., 'Traumas of Acting Physical and Psychological Violence: How Fact and Fiction Shape Bodies for Better or Worse', *Performing Ethos*, 4 (1), 2010. 25–40.

103 In Fraleigh, S. (ed.), *Somatic Transformations through Dance, Yoga, end Touch*, Urbana, Chicago: University of Illinois Press, 2015, 136.

104 Ibid., 142.

105 Arendt, *The Life of the Mind*, 22.

106 Ibid.

107 Personal correspondence with the author, 17 October 2017.

108 See Spatz, *What a Body Can Do*.

Chapter 6

1 See Phelan's *Unmarked* for the archetypal example, as well as Blau's *Take Up the Bodies*.

2 Examples of this narrative in the development of cultural theory are numerous. For an example, see Cavallaro's meta-analysis in *Critical end Cultural Theory*, London and New Brunswick, NJ: The Athlone Press, 2001.

3 As Benjamin Spatz has stated, 'the growing interdisciplinary interest in embodied practice' (*What a Body Can Do*, 2) goes beyond theatre and performance scholarship and may be seen as part of the broader 'practice turn' in theory and philosophy, described in Schatzki, Cetin and von Savigny, E. (eds), *The Practice Turn in Contemporary Theory*, Lonndon and New York: Routledge, 2001.

4 *Theatre, Body and Pleasure*, London and New York: Routledge, 2006, 1.

5 *What a Body Can Do*.

6 This is the objective of Benjamin Spatz's book *What a Body Can Do*, which aims to 'propose' an epistemology of practice (*What a Body Can Do*, 10) that in turn proposes 'technique as knowledge' (23).

7 See Chapter 4, 'ORGANIZATION', page 70.

8 Cremerius, J., 'Training Analysis and Power', *Free Associations*, 20, 1990, 114–138.

9 Kleinman, A., *Rethinking Psychiatry*, New York: Free Press, 1991 [1988].

10 Valentine, M., 'The Abuse of Power in the Analytical Setting', *British Journal of Psychotherapy*, 19 (2), 1996, 174–181.

11 Hinshelwood, R.D., 'Questions of Training', *Free Associations*, 2, 1985, 7–18.

12 James Davies has explained this in his paper 'The Transformative Conditions of Psychotherapeutic Training: An Anthropological Perspective': studies of the 1960s, notably by Frank and Frank, 'have illustrated that trainees' dependency on supervisors' guidance and approval inclines them to 'imitate' seniors' values and ways. While such imitation or 'modelling' has been shown to be one of the most powerful mechanisms of learning, especially in children, in psychotherapy this mechanism is activated by conditions unique to the training context: while supervisors impart valuable knowledge to trainees, as well as assert the worth of the craft trainees are to master, they also stand as the 'embodied answer' to the question 'what do trainers want?' Imitation, then, not only provides sources of learning, of 'self-belief' and of conviction in the system but a palliative for 'evaluation apprehension' and its associated fears (i.e. fear of failing, of negative judgement [and what this means], etc.), *British Journal of Psychotherapy*, 24 (1), February 2008, 60.

13 One well-known Western scholar of Butoh dance is Sondra Fraleigh, who has differentiated Butoh from other 'postmodern dance forms' on the basis that despite its 'intense physicality' and its rootedness in Kabuki and Noh, in its training practices there is no clearly defined practice for the 'development of technique'. *Butoh: Metamorphic Dance and Global Alchemy*, Champaign: University of Illinois Press, 2010, 3.

14 I offer these teachers as exemplars because I have trained with them, personally, and can comment from the perspective of a student on their pedagogic style.

15 Throughout this chapter, I will take my narrative of the history of the 'fitness industry' from various sources but principally from Karen A.E. Volkwein's edited collection, *Fitness as Cultural Phenomenon*, New York, München and Berlin: Waxmann, 1998.

16 Good, J.M., Gregory, O. and Bosworth, N., *Pantologia. A New (Cabinet) Cyclopaedia*, London: Oxford University Library holding, 1819.

17 A second key reference, alongside Volkwein, for the narrative of physical culture in this chapter is Donald G. Kyle's *Sport and Spectacle in the Ancient World*, 2nd edn, Maldon, MA and Oxford: Wiley Blackwell, 2015.

18 See William Harrison Woodwood's *Vittorino da Feltre and Other Humanist Educators*, Toronto, Buffalo and London: University of Toronto Press, 1996.

19 See McIntosh, P.C., 'Hieronymus Mercurialis "De Arte Gymnastica": Classification and Dogma in Physical Education in the Sixteenth Century', *The International Journal of the History of Sport*, 1 (1), 1984.

20 See Power, Edward J., *A Legacy of Learning: A History of Western Education*, Albany: State University of New York Press, 1991.

21 See Leonard, Fred Eugene, 'Friedrich Ludwig Jahn and the Development of Popular Gymnastics (vereinsturnen) in Germany', *American Physical Education Review*, 10 (1), 1905.

22 Peter Viereck famously described Jahn as something like the spiritual founder of National Socialism (Viereck, Peter, *Metapolitics: The Roots of the Nazi Mind*, New York: Capricorn Books, 1961) but other scholars, notably Jacques Martin Barzun, have been more ambivalent about Viereck's role and critical of Viereck's 'cariacture'.

23 See Bennett, Bruce Lanyon, *The Life of Dudley Allen Sargent, M.D., and His Contributions to Physical Education*, Ann Arbor: University of Michigan Press, 1947.

24 See Chapman, David L., *Sandow the Magnificent: Eugene Sandow and the Beginnings of Bodybuilding*, Urbana and Chicago: University of Ilinois Press, 1994.

25 See Frank Hoffman and William Bailey's *Sport and Recreation Fads*, New York, London and Sydney: Halworth Press, 1991.

26 Power, *A Legacy of Learning*, 179.

27 According to Power, these principles were written down and contained in 'books' used by the paidotribes (ibid., 42).

28 Sweet, Waldo E., *Sport and Recreation in Ancient Greece*, New York and Oxford: Oxford University Press, 1987, 114; 116; 219.

29 Ibid., 279.

30 Power, *A Legacy of Learning*, 85.

31 Ibid., 90.

32 Ibid., 168.

33 For a fuller discussion, see my article 'What Is a Workshop?', 103–112.

34 *Nicomachean Ethics*, 1105, lines 25–26.

35 See 'Performing Life, Living Performance', in J. Matthews and D. Torevell (eds), *A Life of Ethics and Performance*, 2nd edn, Newcastle Upon Tyne: Cambridge Scholars, 2013, 19–35.

36 See 'FOOT' in my book *Anatomy of Performance Training*, 53–77.

37 See 'HEART', in *Anatomy of Performance Training*, 109–131.

38 In Horton, K. and Patapan, H. (eds), *Globalisation and Equality*, London and New York: Routledge, 2004, 133.

39 Ibid.

40 Carrette, J. and King, R., *Selling Spirituality: The Silent Takeover of Religion*, New York and London: Routledge, 2005, 8.

41 *The Globalisation of Charismatic Christianity*, Cambridge: Cambridge University Press, 2000.

42 '"Belonging to a Global Religion": The Sociological Dimensions of International Elements in Sahaja Yoga', *Journal of Contemporary Religion*, 10 (2), 1995, 111.

43 Personal correspondence with the author, January 2018.

44 Ibid.

45 Personal correspondence with the author, February 2018.

46 Ibid.

47 Ibid.

48 *Philosophy Now*, Edition 47, 2004, 31.

49 Ibid.

50 Ibid.

51 Ibid.

52 Ibid.

53 *Nicomachean Ethics* 1097, line 22–1098, line 20.

54 1153, lines 31–32.

55 See, for example, *De Anima* 415, lines 23–27.

56 *Nicomachean Ethics* 1154, line 26.

57 'Action, the only activity that goes on directly between men without the intermediary of things or matter, corresponds to the human condition of plurality ... this plurality is specifically the condition – not only the *conditio sine qua non*, but the *conditio per quam* – of all political life' (*The Human Condition*, 7).

58 Arendt is disparaging about what Kant calls 'professional thinkers' throughout *The Life of the Mind* and assertively (and perhaps somewhat disingenuously) contests that she has 'neither claim not ambition' to be a philosopher (*The Life of the Mind*, 3).

59 *The Life of the Mind*, 31.

60 This is the central argument of the chapter 'The Wholly Actor: What Comes after Body-Mind Discourse Is What Comes First', in my first book *Training for Performance*, 40–67.

61 Davies, J., 'The Transformative Conditions of Psychotherapeutic Training: An Anthropological Perspective', *British Journal of Psychotherapy*, 24, 2008, 60.

62 Gusterson, H., *Nuclear Rites: A Weapons Laboratory at the End of the Cold War*, Berkeley: University of California Press, 1996.

63 Luhrman, T., *Of Two Minds*, New York: Borzoi Books, 2001.

64 Sinclair, S., *Making Doctors: An Institutional Apprenticeship*, Oxford: Oxford University Press, 1997.

65 Davies, 'The Transformative Conditions of Psychotherapeutic Training'.

66 Ibid., 54.

67 Ibid., 23.

68 Seton, M., 'The Ethics of Embodiment: Actor Training and Habitual Vulnerability', *Performing Ethos*, 1 (1), 2010, 5–6.

69 Becker, H.S., Geer, B., Hughes, E.C. and Strauss, A.L., *Boys in White: Student Culture in Medical School*, London: Transaction Publishers, [1997] 2002, 441.

70 Davies, 'The Transformative Conditions of Psychotherapeutic Training', 50.

71 Ibid., 60.

72 Ibid.

73 Ibid.

74 Ibid., 54.

75 Ibid.

76 McCaw, D., *Bakhtin and Theatre: Dialogues with Stanislavsky, Meyerhold and Grotowski*, London and New York: Routledge, 2016, 112.

77 Ibid., 114.

78 Ibid., 226.

79 This is the central question posed by Adrian Kear in 'Troublesome Amateurs: Theatre, Ethics and the Labour of Mimesis', in J. Matthews and D. Torevell (eds), *A Life of Ethics and Performance*, Newcastle Upon Tyne: Cambridge Scholars, 2013 [2011].

80 Frank, D. and Frank, J.B., *Persuasion and Healing*, Baltimore, MD: Johns Hopkins Press, 1993 [1961], 195.

81 Bandura, A., *Social Learning Theory*, Englewood Cliffs, NJ: Prentice-Hall, 1977.

82 See *Poetics*, 1148, 4–24.

83 Benjamin Spatz has negotiated more nimbly than many between the epistemic concerns of *mimêma* and the practical experience of *mimêsis* in training contexts throughout his book *What a Body Can Do* (2015) Spatz associates Foucault's 'discipline', Bourdieu's 'habitus' and Butler's 'performativity' with the understanding of 'the limits of agency and consciousness in the face of social norms and ideologies'. His reading of these three theorists 'suggests two entirely different kinds of training': 'conscious imitation', which 'may be an act of individual agency' and 'unconscious mimesis that reproduces habitus'. Spatz counterpoints Bourdieu, whom assumed that what is 'learned by body is not something that one has, like knowledge that can be brandished, but something that one is', assuming the opposite, 'namely, that epistemic practice involves a continuous and mutually constituting transformation, back and forth, between the two categories of conscious and unconscious knowledge'. Or, putting it more simply, training entails a reciprocation between 'what one has (knowledge) and what one is (identity)' (*What a Body Can Do?*, 51). Spatz's approach is aligned with my own, expressed in *Training for Performance*, 201–203, and developed further in *Anatomy of Performance*, 123–144, although both Spatz and I come to this argument rather later than our colleagues in theology, who have been examining this proposition since at least the nineties (e.g. see Olivelle, P., in Wimbush, V.L. and Valantasis, R. (eds), *Asceticism*, Oxford: Oxford University Press, 1995, 188).

84 See *Republic*, 595a–608b.

85 Ibid., 596b.

86 Ibid., 601e.

87 This is, of course, a more complex proposition that I have been able to render here. Accounts of the disparity and reconciliation of the concepts in Book 3 and Book 10 are numerous, and just a handful of examples include Belfiore, Elizabeth, 'A Theory of Imitation in Plato's *Republic*', *Transactions of the American Philological Association*, 114, 1984, 121–146; Halliwell, *Plato Republic Book 10: With Introduction, Translation, and Commentary*, Oxford: Aris & Phillips, 1988; Nehamas, 'Plato on Imitation and Poetry in *Republic* 10', in J. Moravcsik and P. Temko (eds), *Plato on Beauty, Wisdom, and the Arts*, Totowa, NJ: Rowman & Littlefield, 1982, 47–78; Naddaff, *Exiling the Poets: The Production of Censorship in Plato's Republic*, Chicago: University of Chicago Press, 2002; and Lear, 'Mimesis and Psychological Change in *Republic* III', in P. Destree and F.G. Herrmann (eds), *Plato and the Poets*, Leiden and Boston: Brill, 2011, 195–216.

88 *Republic*, 398a.

89 Ridout, *Stage Fright*, 5.

90 *Republic*, 395c–397e.

91 First published in French as *Simulacres et Simulation* (1981).

92 See Jean Baudrillard, *Selected Writings*, ed. Mark Poster, Stanford: Stanford University Press, 1988, 166–184.

93 Schneider, R., 'Performance Remains', *Performance Research*, 6 (2), 2001, 100.

94 Arendt, *The Life of the Mind*, 19.

95 Ibid., 20.

96 Ibid., emphasis in original, 19.

97 Ibid.

98 Ibid.

99 Kant insists, repeatedly, that appearances are appearances of something that is not itself an appearance, and there are numerous passages in which Kant describes *things in themselves* as more fundamental, ontologically, than appearances or, indeed, describes *things in themselves* as the *grounds* of appearances (e.g. *Critique of Pure Reason* (1st edn, 1781) 251–252, (2nd edn, 1787) xxvi–xxvii, 306, 307, and see Königlichen Preußischen (later Deutschen) Akademie der Wissenschaften (ed.), *Kants gesammelte Schriften*, Berlin: Georg Reimer (later Walter De Gruyter), 1900–, 4: 314–315).

100 n Arendt, *The Life of the Mind*, 24.

101 bid., 23.

102 bid., 21.

103 bid.

104 bid., 22.

105 Ibid., 22–23.

106 Ibid., 22–24.

107 See Shepherd, *Theatre, Body and Pleasure*, and Spatz, *What a Body Can Do*.

108 Ibid., 27.

109 Ibid.

110 Ibid.

111 Ibid.

112 Ibid., 28.

113 Ibid., 21.

Chapter 7

1 Much work has been done in this regard with reference to the transference across Europe and America of Stanislavski's ideas and techniques. As one example of a node within this tradition, both Colin Counsell (*Signs of Performance*) and Sharon-Marie Carnicke (*Stanislavsky in Focus*, New York: Routledge, 1998) reference Foster Hirsch's study of the appearance of Stanislavskian ideas in Actor's Studio in America (*A Method to Their Madness*, Cambridge, MA: De Capo Press, 2001 [1984]).

Similar epistemological academic discourses exist around the transfer of Grotowski's ideas and ideals for theatre, and Ben Spatz's *What a Body Can Do* (2015) represents a recent meta-analysis of such networks and trends.

2   Arendt, *The Life of the Mind*, 210–211.

3   This is a central argument in *A Life of Performance Training*.

4   See Spatz, *What a Body Can Do*.

5   For an example, see Hodge, *Twentieth Century Actor Training*.

6   See Taylor, D., *The Archive and the Repertoire: Performing Cultural Memory in the Americas*, Durham and London: Duke University Press, 2003.

7   This concept appears to originate in Marx's *Das Kapital* (1867) and was developed by Pierre Bourdieu, notably in *Reproduction in Education, Society and Culture* (1970). The concept appears in diverse works across multiple disciplines today, including, as a prototypical Performance Studies example, Spatz's *What a Body Can Do* (2015).

8   Roach, *The Player's Passion,* 127.

9   See *Four Essays on Liberty*, Oxford: Oxford Paperbacks, 1969.

10   Joseph Roach's book, *The Player's Passion* (1985), traces this history with reference to the co-emergence of ideas and ideals in science and art. Benedetti's *The Art of the Actor* (2005) also describes this historical shift within the specific realm of aesthetics.

11   This observation vexes Arendt's works on the subject of Adolf Eichmann and motivates her philosophy of *animal laborans* and *homo faber.*

12   See Ian Watson's writings on Eugenio Barba, notably, *Towards a Third Theatre: Eugenio Barba and the Odin Teatret*, London and New York: Routledge, 2003 [1993], 32–34.

13   Ibid., 152.

14   Ibid.

15   This was the title of my PhD thesis and, clearly, in reference to Heidegger's *What Is Called Thinking?*

16   See Foucault, *Discipline and Punish: The Birth of the Prison* (Surveiller et punir : Naissance de la prison), and for a meta-analysis, see Jon McKenzie's *Perform or Else: From Discipline to Performance*, London and New York: Routledge, 2002.

17   Ibid.

18   Spatz, *What a Body Can Do*.

19   'Recognising and Mis-Recognising the "x" Factor'.

20   'Power and Presence in the Actor-Training Institution Audition', 139.

21   Arendt, *The Life of the Mind*, 152.

22   Ibid. See also my article 'What Is a Workshop?', 349–361.

23 Matthews, 'What Is a Workshop?', 357.

24 Ibid.

25 Arendt, *The Life of the Mind*, 129.

26 Ibid., 55.

27 For a fuller discussion, see *Anatomy of Performance Training*, 70–75.

28 *The Economics of Creativity*, Cambridge, MA, and London: Harvard University Press, 2014, 99.

29 Ibid.

30 *1984*, New York: Harcourt Inc., 1949, 96.

31 *Stage Fright: Animals and Other Theatrical Problems*, Cambridge: Cambridge University Press, 2006, 35.

32 *Stanislavski: The Basics*, London and New York: Routledge, 2015, 17.

33 'Performance's only life is in the present', says Phelan (*Unmarked: The Politics of Performance*, Abingdon, Oxon and New York: Routledge, 1993, 146.)

34 Ibid.

35 *Take Up the Bodies*, 28.

36 Schneider, Rebecca, 'Performance Remains', *Performance Research*, 6 (2), 2001, 101.

37 Ibid., 100.

38 Phelan, *Unmarked: The Politics of Performance*, 29.

39 Ibid., 146.

40 *Breviario di estetica*, Bari: G. Laterza e figli, 1965 [1913]; Romanell, Patrick (trans.), *Guide to Aesthetics*, Indianapolis: Bobbs-Merrill, 1965 [1913], 9–10.

41 I-II, 57, 4c.

42 See Guyer, Paul, 'From Jupiter's Eagle to Warhol's Boxes: The Concept of Art from Kant to Danto', *Philosophical Studies*, 25 (1), 1997, 83–116.

43 Kant, Immanuel, *Kritik der Urteilskraft. Kants gesammelte Schriften*, vol. 5, Berlin: Walter De Gruyter, 1902 [1790]; see Guyer, Paul, *Critique of the Power of Judgment*, P. Guyer (ed.), E. Matthews (trans.), Cambridge: Cambridge University Press, 2000.

44 Mellon lectures presented at the National Gallery in Washington in 1955, published as Gilson, É., *Painting and Reality*, Princeton: Princeton University Press, 1957.

45 Étienne Souriau also posited plural modes for the ontic nature of art works – thing-like (*chosale*), aesthetic and transcendent. See Souriau, É., *Les différents modes d'existence*, Paris: Presses Universitaires de France, 1953, and *La correspondance des arts: éléments d'esthétique comparée*, Paris: Flammarion, 1947.

46   Bourriard, N., *Relational Aesthetics*, Dijon: Les Presses Du Reel, 2002.

47   *The Imaginary: A Phenomenological Psychology of the Imagination*,
London and New York: Routledge, 2004. First published in French as
L'Imaginaire: Psychologie phénoménologique de l'imagination, Paris:
Gallimard, 1940. See page 371 in the original work.

48   Hartmann's central thesis on the ontology of art is that works are
dependent on perceptual and imaginative activities, both of artists and
of audiences for artworks. In Hartmann, the work has two 'strata': the
perceptible foreground, for example colours on a surface or audible
sounds, and the aesthetic experience of the 'background', which
is imaginative and, in his view, 'higher'. The work itself is caused by
the relation between these 'heterogeneous' strata and, because the
work is dependent upon imagination, the work cannot be said to have
independent being, which Hartmann calls '*Ansichsein*'. See Hartmann, N.,
'Über die Stellung der ästhetischen Werte im Reich der Werte überhaupt',
in Edgar Sheffield Brightman (ed.), *Proceedings of the Sixth International
Congress of Philosophy*, New York: Longmans, Green, and Co., 1927,
428–436.

49   Hartmann, N., *Ästhetik*, Berlin: De Gruyter, 1953, 53. Stephen C. Pepper
is also interested in the imagination and its role in creating the 'aesthetic
work of art' from 'out of a physical work of art'. See Pepper, S.C.,
Aesthetic Quality: A Contextualist Theory of Beauty, New York: Charles
Scribner and Sons, 1937, 231.

50   'The Mode of Existence of a Work of Art', *Review of Metaphysics*, 12 (1),
1958, 26–34.

51   'De l'œuvre au texte', *La Revue d'esthétique*, 3, 1971, 225–232;
trans. Josué V. Harari (ed.), 'From Work to Text', in *Textual Strategies:
Perspectives in Post-Structuralist Criticism*, Ithaca, NY: Cornell University
Press, 1979, 73–81.

52   Croce, Collingwood and Dewey are key and influential figures in this area
of philosophy. In his 'On the Aesthetics of Dewey', Croce lists familiar
ideas in Dewey's work, and among these is the notion (which Croce
claims to have arrived at first) that 'there are not artistic "things", but only
an artistic doing, an artistic producing' ('On the Aesthetics of Dewey', *The
Journal of Aesthetics and Art Criticism*, 6 (3), 1948, 205).

53   Dutton, D., 'Artistic Crimes', *The British Journal of Aesthetics*, 19 (4),
1979, 305.

54   Ibid.

55   See Currie, G., *An Ontology of Art*, London: Macmillan, 1989.

56   In Matthews, J. and Torevell, D. (eds), *A Life of Ethics and Performance*,
Newcastle Upon Tyne: Cambridge Scholars, 2012 [2011], 89.

57 This does not exclude the 'everyday'; as I have shown through my examples, the everyday is the foundational basis for more exclusive forms of training. Neither does it exclude the 'found performance' concept – the semiotic proposition that we may frame any event as performance provided that we choose to see it as such – for this itself is a consequence of the training of the spectator: his or her habituation towards this act of witnessing.

58 Arendt, *The Life of the Mind*, 15.

59 First proposed in *Training for Performance* (2011).

BIBLIOGRAPHY

Agamben, G., *Potentialities: Collected Essays in Philosophy*, Stanford, CA: Stanford University Press, 1999.

Aggerholm, K., *Talent Development, Existential Philosophy and Sport: On Becoming an Elite Athlete*, London and New York: Routledge, 2015.

Allain, P., *The Art of Stillness*, New York: Palgrave Macmillan, 2003.

Allain, P., *Gardzienice: Polish Theatre in Transition*, Amsterdam B.V.: Harwood Academic Publisher, 1997.

Arendt, H., *The Human Condition*, Chicago: The University of Chicago Press, 1958.

Arendt, H., *The Life of the Mind*, San Diego, New York and London: Harcourt Inc., 1978 [1971].

Arendt, H., 'What Is Existential Philosophy?', in *Essays on Understanding: 1930–1954*, New York: Schocken Books, 2005.

Artaud, A. and Sontag, S. (eds), *Antonin Artaud: Selected Writing*, Berkeley: University of California Press, 1988.

Aujla, I.J., Nordin-Bates, S.M., Redding, E. and Jobbins, V., 'Developing Talent among Young Dancers: Findings from the UK Centres for Advanced Training', *Theatre, Dance and Performance Training*, 5 (1), 2014.

Bandura, A., *Social Learning Theory*, Englewood Cliffs, NJ: Prentice-Hall, 1977.

Barba, E., 'An Amulet Made of Memory', in P.B. Zarrilli (ed.), *Acting (re) Considered: A Theoretical and Practical Guide*, London and New York: Routledge, 2002.

Baudrillard, J. *Selected Writings*, Stanford, CA: Stanford University Press, 1988.

Becker, H.S., Geer, B., Hughes, E.C. and Strauss, A.L., *Boys in White: Student Culture in Medical School*, London: Transaction Publishers, 2002 [1997].

Benedetti, J., *The Art of the Actor: The Essential History of Acting, From Classical Times to the Present Day*, London: Methuen, 2005.

Benedetti, J., *Stanislavski: His Life and Art*, London: Methuen, 1999 [1988].

Bennett, B.L., *The Life of Dudley Allen Sargent, M.D., and His Contributions to Physical Education*, Ann Arbor: University of Michigan Press, 1947.

Berger-Helmschen, T. (ed.), *The Economics of Creativity*, London and New York: Routledge, 2013.

Berlin, I., *Four Essays on Liberty*, Oxford: Oxford University Press, 1969.

Betz Hull, M., *The Hidden Philosophy of Hannah Arendt*, London and New York: RoutledgeCurzon, 2002.

Biskowski, L.J., *Politics vs Aesthetics: Arendt's Critiques of Nietzsche and Heidegger*, The Review of Politics, 57 (1), Winter 1995.

Blau, H., *Take Up the Bodies: Theater at the Vanishing Point*, Urbana: University of Illinois Press, 1982.

Bourriard, N., *Relational Aesthetics*, Dijon: Les Presses Du Reel, 2002.

Brightman (ed.), *Proceedings of the Sixth International Congress of Philosophy*, New York: Longmans, Green, and Co, 1927.

Brook, P., *The Empty Space*, New York: Touchstone, 1996 [1968].

Bruce, S., *Religion in the Modern World: From Cathedrals to Cults*, Oxford: Oxford University Press, 1996.

Camilleri, F., *On Training and Performance: Traces of an Odin Teatret Actress*, Abingdon, Oxon, and New York: Routledge, 2014.

Carnicke, S.-M., *Stanislavsky in Focus*, New York: Routledge, 1998.

Carrette, J. and King, R., *Selling Spirituality: The Silent Takeover of Religion*, New York and London: Routledge, 2005.

Cavallaro, D., *Critical and Cultural Theory*, London and New Brunswick, NJ: The Athlone Press, 2001.

Chapman, D.L., *Sandow the Magnificent: Eugene Sandow and the Beginnings of Bodybuilding*, Urbana and Chicago: University of Illinois Press, 1994.

Charles Roudané, M., *Conversations with Arthur Miller*, Jackson and London: University Press of Mississippi, 1987.

Cohen, L. (ed.), *The Lee Strasberg Notes*, London and New York: Routledge, 2010.

Coleman, S., *The Globalisation of Charismatic Christianity*, Cambridge: Cambridge University Press, 2000.

Cooper-Albright, A., *Choreographing Difference: The Body and Identity in Contemporary Dance*, Middletown, CT: Wesleyan University Press, 1997.

Counsell, C., *Signs of Performance: An Introduction to Twentieth Century Theatre*, London and New York: Routledge, 1996.

Cremerius, J., 'Training Analysis and Power', *Free Associations*, 20, 1990, 114–138.

Croce, B., 'On the Aesthetics of Dewey', *The Journal of Aesthetics and Art Criticism*, 6 (3), 1948.

Csikszentmihalyi, M., *Creativity: Flow and the Psychology of Discovery and Invention*, New York: Harper Collins, 1996.

Csikszentmihalyi, M., *Finding Flow: The Psychology of Everyday Life*, New York: Basic Books, 1997.

Csikszentmihalyi, M. and Jackson, S.A., *Flow in Sport*, Champaign, IL: Human Kinetics, 1999.

Currie, G., *An Ontology of Art*, London: Macmillan, 1989.

Davies, J., 'The Transformative Conditions of Psychotherapeutic Training: An Anthropological Perspective', *British Journal of Psychotherapy*, 24 (1), 2008.

Deutshcer, M., *Judgement after Arendt*, London and New York: Routledge, 2016.

Donnellan, D., *The Actor and the Target*, London: Nick Hern Book, 2002.

Dutton, D., 'Artistic Crimes', *The British Journal of Aesthetics*, 19 (4), 1979, 305.

Ellis, Samantha, 'Hamlet: National Theatre, 1963', *The Guardian*, 12 March 2003.

Farrell Krell, D. (ed.), *Heidegger: Basic Writings*, 2nd edn, London: Routledge & Kegan Paul, 1993.

Feenberg, A. and Barney, D.D., *Community in the Digital Age: Philosophy and Practice*, Boulder, CO: Rowman and Littlefield Publishers Inc., 2004.

Fielding, H., *The History of Tom Jones: A Foundling Volume 2*, London: Baines & Son, 1825.

Foucault, M., *Discipline and Punish: The Birth of the Prison Surveiller et punir: Naissance de la prison*, Paris: Gallimard, 1975.

Fraleigh, S., *Butoh: Metamorphic Dance and Global Alchemy*, Champaign: University of Illinois Press, 2010.

Fraleigh, S. (ed.), *Somatic Transformations through Dance, Yoga, and Touch*, Urbana and Chicago: University of Illinois Press, 2015.

Frank, D. and Frank, J.B., *Persuasion and Healing*, Baltimore, MD: Johns Hopkins Press, 1993 [1961].

Fuchs, W.W., 'Seeing the Named. Naming the Seen', in A.E. Hooke and W.W. Fuchs (eds), *Encounters with Alphonso Lingis*, Lanham, Boulder, New York, Oxford: Lexington, 2003.

Gillett, J., *Acting Stanislavksi*, London: Methuen Drama (Bloomsbury), 2014.

Gilson, É., *Painting and Reality*, Princeton, NJ: Princeton University Press, 1957.

Gordon, R., *The Purpose of Playing: Modern Acting Theories in Perspective*, Ann Arbor: University of Michigan Press, 2006.

Grotowski, J., *Towards a Poor Theatre*, New York: Theatre Arts Book, 2012 [1968].

Gusterson, H., *Nuclear Rites: A Weapons Laboratory at the End of the Cold War*, Berkeley: University of California Press, 1996.

Guyer, P., 'From Jupiter's Eagle to Warhol's Boxes: The Concept of Art from Kant to Danto', *Philosophical Studies*, 25 (1), 1997.

Guyer, P., *Critique of the Power of Judgment*, P. Guyer (ed.), E. Matthews (trans.), Cambridge: Cambridge University Press, 2000.

Hagen, U., *A Challenge for the Actor*, New York: Scribner, 1991.

Hall, J., 'Cicero and Quintilian on the Oratorical Use of Hand Gestures', *The Classical Quarterly*, 2, 54 (1), May 2004.

Hannah, A., *The Life of the Mind*, San Diego, New York and London: Harcourt Inc., 1978 [1971].

Harrison, D., 'Unscripted End to Gambon's Career on Stage', *The Sunday Times*, 8 February 2015.

Hartmann, N., *Ästhetik*, Berlin: De Gruyter, 1953.

Hartmann, N., *Proceedings of the Sixth International Congress of Philosoohy*, New York: Edgar Sheffield.

Heeas, P., 'The New Age in Cultural Context: The Premodern, the Modern and the Postmodern', *Religion*, 23, 1993, 103–116.

Heeias, P., *The New Age Movement*, Oxford: Blackwell Publishing, 1996.

Heelas, P., 'Prosperity and the New Age Movement: The Efficacy of Spiritual Economics', in B. Wilson and J. Cressell (eds), *New Religious Movements: Challenges and Response*, London: Routledge, 1999.

Heidegger, M., *Being and Time*, trans. J. Macquarrie and E. Robinson, Oxford: Basil Blackwell, 1962 [1927].

Heidegger, M., *What Is Called Thinking?*, trans. J. Glen Gray, New York: Harper and Row, 1968.

Heighton, Luke, 'Sir Michael Gambon Forced to Quit Theatre due to "Frightening" Memory Loss', *The Telegraph*, 8 February 2015.

Hirsch, F., *A Method to Their Madness*, Cambridge, MA: De Capo Press, 2001 [1984].

Hirsch, F., *A Method to Their Madness: A History of the Actors' Studio New York*, New York: W.W. Norton, 1984.

Hodge, A. (ed.), *Twentieth Century Actor Training*, London and New York: Routledge, 2010 [1999].

Hodge, A. (ed.), *Twentieth Century Actor Training*, London and New York: Routledge, 2000.

Hoffman, F. and Bailey, W., *Sport and Recreation Fads*, New York, London and Sydney: Halworth Press, 1991.

Horton, K. and Patapan, H. (eds), *Globalisation and Equality*, London and New York: Routledge, 2004.

Iqbaal, Nosheen, 'Michael Gambon Bows Out of Alan Bennet's *The Habit of Art*', *The Guardian*, 2 October 2009.

Kant, I., *Critique of the Power of Judgment*, trans. Guyer and Matthews, Cambridge: Cambridge University Press, 2000.

Kant, I., *Kritik der Urteilskraft. Kants gesammelte Schriften*, vol. 5, Berlin: Walter De Gruyter, 1902 [1790].

Kim, J., *Philosophy of Mind*, 3rd edn, Boulder, CO: Westview Press, 2010.

Kleinman, A., *Rethinking Psychiatry*, New York: Free Press, 1991.

Kumpulainen, S., 'From Sweat and Tears towards Sweat and Harmony', *Theatre, Dance and Performance Training*, 3 (2), 2012.

Kyle, D.G., *Sport and Spectacle in the Ancient World*, Maldon, MA, and Oxford: Wiley Blackwell, 2015.

Leach, R., *Makers of Modern Theatre: An Introduction*, London: Routledge, 2004.

Leahy, K., 'Power and Presence in the Actor-Training Institution Audition', *Australasian Drama Studies*, No. 28, April 1996, 139.

Leonard, F.E., 'Friedrich Ludwig Jahn and the Development of Popular Gymnastics (vereinsturnen) in Germany', *American Physical Education Review*, 10 (1), 1905.

Lingis, A., *Foreign Bodies*, London and New York: Routledge, 1994.

Lingis, A., *The Imperative*, Bloomington: University of Indiana Press, 1998.

Luhrman, T., *Of Two Minds*, New York: Borzoi Books, 2001.

Magarshack, D., *Stanislavsky: A Life*, London and Boston: Faber, 1986 [1950].

Matthews, J., *Anatomy of Performance Training*, London and New York: Methuen Drama (Bloomsbury), 2014.

Matthews, J., 'What Is a Workshop?', *Theatre, Dance and Performance Training*, 3 (3), 2012, 349–361.

Matthews, J. and Torevell, D. (eds), *A Life of Ethics and Performance*, Newcastle Upon Tyne: Cambridge Scholars, 2012 [2011].

McCaw, D., *Bakhtin and Theatre: Dialogues with Stanislavsky, Meyerhold and Grotowski*, London and New York: Routledge, 2016.

McIntosh, P.C., 'Hieronymus Mercurialis "De Arte Gymnastica": Classification and Dogma in Physical Education in the Sixteenth Century', *The International Journal of the History of Sport*, 1 (1), 1984.

McKenzie, J., *Perform or Else: From Discipline to Performance*, London and New York: Routledge, 2002.

Menger, P.-M., *The Economics of Creativity*, Cambridge, MA, and London: Harvard University Press, 2014.

Michael, T., 'Heidegger the Fox: Hannah Arendt's Hidden Dialogue', *New German Critique* No. 73, Special Issue on Heiner Muller, Winter 1998.

Murray, S., 'Keywords in Performer Training', *Theatre, Dance and Performance Training*, 6 (1), 2015, 46–58.

Parkins, W., 'Oprah Winfrey's Change Your Life TV and the Spiritual Everyday', *Journal of Media and Cultural Studies*, 15 (2), 2001, 145–157.

Patterson, S. and Crane, T., *History of the Mind–Body Problem*, London and New York: Routledge, 2000.

Pepper, S.C., *Aesthetic Quality: A Contextualist Theory of Beauty*, New York: Charles Scribner and Sons, 1937.

Phelan, P., *Unmarked: The Politics of Performance*, Abingdon, Oxon, and New York: Routledge, 1993.

Possamai, A., *In Search of New Age Spiritualities*, Hampshire: Ashgate, 2005.

Power, E.J., *A legacy of Learning: A History of Western Education*, Albany: State University of New York Press, 1991.

Raine, K., *Yeats the Initiate: On Certain Themes in the Writings of WB Yeats*, Savage, MD: Barnes & Noble, 1990.

Read, A., *Theatre, Intimacy and Engagement: The Last Human Venue*, Houndsmills, Basingstoke, Hampshire: Palgrave Macmillan, 2008.

Reilly, T., *The Science of Training*, Abingdon, Oxon, and New York: Routledge, 2007.

Reynolds, F., *The Life and Times of Frederick Reynolds*, London: Henry Colburn, 1826.

Ridout, N., *Stage Fright: Animals and Other Theatrical Problems*, Cambridge: Cambridge University Press, 2006.

Ridout, N., *Theatre & Ethics*, Basingstoke, Hampshire: Palgrave Macmillan, 2009.

Roach, J., *The Player's Passion: Studies in the Science of Acting*, Ann Arbor: University of Michigan Press, 2002 [1985].

Ross, A., *Strange Weather: Culture, Science and Technology in the Age of Limits*, London and New York: Verso, 1991.

Sartre, J.-P., *Being and Nothingness: An Essay on Phenomenological Ontology*, trans. H.E. Barnes, London and New York, Routledge, 2003.

Sartre, J.-P., *The Imaginary: A Phenomenological Psychology of the Imagination*, London and New York: Routledge, 2004.

Schatzki, C. and von Savigny, E. (eds), *The Practice Turn in Contemporary Theory*, London and New York: Routledge, 2001.

Schneider, R., 'Performance Remains', *Performance Research*, 6 (2), 2001, 101.

Sellers, R., *Don't Let the Bastards Grind You Down: How One Generation of British Actors Changed the World*, Vauxhall, London: Arrow Books, 2012.

Sennett, R., *The Craftsman*, New Haven and London: Yale University Press, 2008.

Seton, M., 'The Ethics of Embodiment: Actor Training and Habitual Vulnerability', *Performing Ethos*, 1 (1), 2010, 5–6.

Seton, M., 'Recognising and Mis-Recognising the "x" Factor: The Audition Selection Process in Actor-Training Institutions Revisited', *Australasian Drama Studies*, 50, 2007.

Sewell, A., *Black Beauty: Autobiography of a Horse*, Woodbridge, Suffolk: Jarrold & Sons, 1877.

Shepherd, S., *Theatre, Body and Pleasure*, London and New York: Routledge, 2006.

Sinclair, S., *Making Doctors: An Institutional Apprenticeship*, Oxford: Oxford University Press, 1997.

Slowiak, J. and Cuesta, J., *Jerzy Grotowski*, Abingdon, Oxon: Routledge, 2007.

Smith, C.U.M., *The Problem of Life: An Essay in the Origins of Biological Thought*, New York: Wiley, 1976.

Sohmer, S., *Shakespeare's Mystery Play: The Opening of the Globe Theatre 1599*, Manchester and New York: Manchester University Press, 1999.

Sourau, É., *La correspondance des arts: éléments d'esthétique comparée*, Paris: Flammarion, 1947.

Sourau, É., *Les différents modes d'existence*, Paris: Presses Universitaires de France, 1953.

Spatz, B., *What a Body Can Do: Technique as Knowledge, Practice as Research*, New York and London: Routledge, 2015.

Sweet, Waldo E., *Sport and Recreation in Ancient Greece*, New York and Oxford: Oxford University Press, 1987.

Taylor, D., *The Archive and the Repertoire: Performing Cultural Memory in the Americas*, Durham and London: Duke University Press, 2003.

Turner, Camilla, 'Working with Michael Gambon Was "Hair Raising" Says Dame Maggie Smith', *The Telegraph*, 1 March 2015.

Valentine, M., 'The Abuse of Power in the Analytical Setting', *British Journal of Psychotherapy*, 19 (2), 1996.

Volkwein, K.A.E. (ed.), *Fitness as Cultural Phenomenon*, New York, München and Berlin: Waxmann, 1998.

Waterlow, S., 'Aristotle's Now', *Philosophical Quarterly*, 34 (135), 1984.

Watson, I., *Towards a Third Theatre: Eugenio Barba and the Odin Teatret*, London and New York: Routledge, 2003 [1993].

Whitehead, A.N., *Aims of Education*, New York: The Free Press, 1929.

Whyman, R., *Stanislavski: The Basics*, London and New York: Routledge, 2015.

Witts, J., *The Science of the Tour De France*, London: Bloomsbury, 2016.

Wolford, L. and Schechner, R. (eds), *The Grotowski Sourcebook*, London and New York: Routledge, 1997.

Woodwood, W.H., *Vittorino da Feltre and Other Humanist Educators*, Toronto, Buffalo and London: University of Toronto Press, 1996.

INDEX

acting 4, 9, 15–21, 25–7, 39–45,
    50–3, 55–63, 67, 70–4,
    81–5, 91, 94–6, 101, 109–14,
    121–5, 131, 134–7, 149, 154
Agamben, G. 49–52
animal laborans 25–6, 103, 153
anxiety 112, 133–4, 154
appearance (state of) 23, 27–9, 35,
    51, 65, 77, 91–2, 94, 97–8,
    101, 105, 121–2, 127, 136,
    138–40, 145, 151, 155–6,
    158–60
apprentice (and apprenticeship) 42,
    91, 152
Aquinas, T. 42, 73, 107–8, 156–7
Arendt, H. 5–6, 9–12, 18–35, 37–8,
    41, 47–9, 57, 65–9, 73–5,
    77–9, 86–99, 102–10, 116–
    17, 131–2, 138–40, 145–61
Aristotle 16–18, 26, 30–3, 37, 40–1,
    49–52, 56–9, 87, 107–10,
    127–8, 131–6, 148–9, 157
art (artworks) 60, 65–6, 87, 97,
    101–2, 107–8, 156–60

being (metaphysics) 5, 10, 21–35,
    65–6, 74, 91–2, 138–9,
    143–8, 151–9
betterment (ideology of) 153–4
bodybuilding 35, 104, 105, 111, 153

conservatoire 4, 8, 53, 58, 61, 64,
    81, 111–16, 129, 132, 152

contingency 11, 19, 35, 108–10,
    117–18, 145, 148, 152–5,
    159, 161–2
cycling 8, 34, 93

Decroux, E. 111
diving 8, 128

embodiment 6, 15, 32, 47, 61, 122,
    133–4, 138, 146, 151
epiphany 28, 37–8, 44, 47–8, 63,
    117, 148
epistemology 5, 30, 122, 136,
    145–6, 162
exercise (and exercising) 33, 62–9, 72,
    82, 86, 95–9, 114–18, 123–7,
    133, 136, 144–7, 152, 157
extinction 3, 20, 101, 103, 106, 117

feelings 69, 71–2, 81
futurology 35, 79, 92, 96, 99, 110,
    118, 153

Gambon, M. 40–52
Grotowski, J. 72, 95, 111–13, 135
gym (and gym-going) 28, 82, 123–7,
    153

Heidegger, M. 21, 26–7, 86–9, 98
history (of thought; of philosophy) 5,
    16–19, 24–5, 30–4, 49, 57,
    65, 77–81, 88–90, 130–2,
    140, 143–54, 161–2
homo faber 25–6, 103, 153

ideology 22, 67, 73, 90–3, 97, 99, 123, 150–4, 158
imitation 56, 84, 123–4, 127–9, 132, 133, 135–40
improvisation 33, 62–74, 94–5

Kant, I. 17, 18, 60, 63, 73, 97, 138, 156–7, 161
Kleist, H. von 1–3, 12, 39
knowledge 11, 16–18, 20, 24–30, 55–6, 77–81, 88–98, 116, 122–3, 132, 139–40, 143–61

Lecoq, J. 61, 111
logic (in the history of thought) 89–91, 94–5

method of physical actions 62–70, 97
mimesis 135–9

National Theatre 42–3

Olympics 93
ontic 3, 6–7, 12, 35, 143, 155–61
ontology 26–7, 35, 65, 73, 143–5, 155–60
O'Toole, P. 40–4
overload (and overloading) 103–4, 111–17

perrenism 154
potentiality (and of potential) 32–5, 37–53, 69, 74, 92, 109–10, 117–18, 132, 148–56
progress (and ideology of) 35, 37, 77–80, 92–3, 97–9, 101–10, 116–17, 148, 152–3

Read, A. 4, 20

Saint-Denis, M. 111
sameness 17, 31–2, 147–9
self-display 28, 138, 140
skill (and skill acquisition) 16, 40, 49–53, 62, 83, 96, 112, 115, 127, 130–2, 144, 152
somatics (and dance) 8, 35, 116, 129

sport 7–10, 28, 33–4, 45–52, 58–63, 73, 80–2, 93, 99, 101–5, 111–18, 124–8, 167
stage fright 8, 154
Stanislavski, K. 15–18, 33, 56–60, 62–74, 83–97, 111–14, 135, 153–4
survival 56, 64, 88, 101–3, 149
Suzuki, T. 111, 115
swimming 8–9, 34, 81–2, 104, 109, 114–17, 123, 128

talent 33, 37–53, 72, 109, 112, 148–55
tapering 114–16
techne 16, 30, 47, 90, 103
technique 24–33, 72, 82, 91, 95, 118, 124, 132, 144–52
temporality 3, 11, 18, 23–33, 38–41, 47–9, 59, 66–7, 71–5, 77–81, 101, 116, 132, 143–51, 160–2
terminological façade (the) 38, 40
Theatre Royal Plymouth 4–9
thinking (of thought) 5–6, 10, 15–35, 57, 66–75, 77–82, 86–99, 110, 131–2, 143–51, 160–2
thoughtlessness 18–24, 86
time 5–12, 15–35, 37–41, 56–9, 65–75, 77–89, 98–9, 108–10, 117–18, 121, 139–40, 143–55, 159–62
   and cyclical metaphor 34, 65–74, 116, 146, 149–50
   and concept of the future 18–35, 37, 45–7, 53, 59, 64–75, 77–80, 99, 109, 110, 116–18, 121, 131, 140, 143–50, 160–2
   and concept of the past 15, 23–9, 32–5, 37, 47, 53, 63–9, 73–5, 77–9, 116–18, 121, 140, 143–50, 160–2
   and concept of the present 15–19, 24–5, 29–35, 50–3,

55–75, 77–8, 110, 116–17, 121, 138–40, 143–62
and rectilinear metaphor 34, 65–74, 149

vocation (and vocational) 2–4, 10–11, 16, 31, 40, 81, 90, 113

yoga 8–9, 35, 116, 128–32